LONG

the odyssey of a lesbian mother

WAY

and her children

HOME

jeanne jullion

CLEIS PRESS
A WOMEN'S PUBLISHING COMPANY
SAN FRANCISCO, PITTSBURGH

Published in the United States by Cleis Press, P.O. Box 14684, San Francisco, California, 94114 and P.O. Box 8933, Pittsburgh, Pennsylvania 15221.

First edition. First printing.

Cover design: Pam Wilson.
Typesetting: Coming Up! Graphics, 867 Valencia St, SF 94110.

ISBN: 0-939416-05-0
Library of Congress Catalogue Card Number: 84-73040

Printed in the United States.

Grateful acknowledgement is made to the *San Francisco Chronicle* for permission to excerpt articles published in that newspaper, and to Randy Shilts and St. Martin's Press for permission to reprint portions of *The Mayor of Castro Street*.

Some court transcripts have been edited for grammar and readability. Other court proceedings have been reconstructed from memory. Cleis Press accepts the authenticity of this story, but cannot assume responsibility for any factual inaccuracies found in these pages.

To my sons

Contents
BOOK ONE

BOOK TWO

BOOK THREE

You might as well sit back because it's a long story. It will take you to Italy and back again many times. It goes through some of the headiest times of the gay rights movement.

I was a lesbian and didn't know I was one. I married a man I thought was my friend. I had my first child in Italy and my second years later in Rochester, New York. These children would then be the price exacted from me for being a lesbian.

But let's back up and let me step aside. As you will see, the story will, piece by piece, tell itself.

BOOK ONE

CHAPTER ONE

La Geemie

Jeanne met her husband's parents for the first time in the marble lobby of the Jesuit dormitory in Viale Don Minzoni. Having learned that their only son was once again doing little at the University of Florence and that he was also seeing an American *studentessa* regularly, his mother and father came to Florence one Sunday morning in April to see for themselves.

"*Dio buono,*" exclaimed his father when the elevator doors opened and out stepped Jeanne. "I'm going to need a chair to stand on to kiss her on the cheeks!"

Jeanne laughed at the agitated reaction of this short, round man and stole a look at the unamused face of his wife behind him. Jeanne was tall, nineteen and in the middle of her junior year of college in Florence. Beside her stood Franco, twenty-one, handsome, smooth-faced and pale. The morning razor had left white tracks across his cheeks.

"Geemie?" Nuncio stepped forward smiling, extending his hand. There was a swarthy handsomeness to his dark face.

"No, papà, Jeannie," corrected Franco.

"Geemie?" his father tried again as his wife, Anna, stood by in icy silence. Both parents were shorter than Franco, and she shorter than he. Anna was bundled in an attractive camel coat with a lush fur collar that her gloved hand held closed at the neck. In the crook of her elbow hung an elegant alligator handbag. While surprisingly young and blond, there was a tired look to her face that seemed to have been there for a long time. The disapproving and bitter bend to her woman's mouth made Jeanne look away.

"No, *mamma e papà,*" Franco was explaining, "her name is Jeannie. With an 'n', like Gina."

"Ah, Gina, Geemie, G-geemie. *Beh!*" Nuncio threw his hands up in the air, "let's go have a good meal, *va bene?*" he boomed gregariously, taking in Jeanne's long, slender figure with a smile.

Nuncio benignly held the steering wheel in the palms of his hands and careened down the narrow road through the olive countryside outside Florence.

Seated at a table soft with four layers of linen cloths, Jeanne glanced again at Anna's face. Life had pulled the corners of her mouth down and her blond skin gathered in slight pools at the corners of her mouth. At nineteen she had had a wartime marriage, and gave difficult birth to their only child. In the worst days of World War II, she stayed awake nights to chase hungry rats from the baby's crib, and by day dashed into strangers' houses as she heard the shriek of bombs falling. She strung coverings over the open hole where the ceiling and upper floor of the apartment house used to be.

At war's end, Nuncio returned to Ravenna, brusquely renamed the two year-old child as Franco and then wasted no time in demonstrating to his young wife that he intended to maintain his village reputation as a virile man amongst a townful of boastfully virile men. Ambition and tyrannical tactics pulled him up in the administration of the regional transit system and Anna bore down with ambition of her own. A fine seamstress, she began taking in clients of her own. At its peak, her shop employed eighteen girls from the countryside and some of the finest ladies of the town passed through her fitting room.

Tormented by the violent anger and escapades of her husband, Anna doted on her unhappy and growing son. Finally, the spoiled and slightly overweight child had been bought, bribed and cajoled through Classical High School and, at his mother's insistence, was the first in either family to attend the University. Franco insisted on a Political Science major, insuring his attendance at the University of Florence and his long-awaited move away from the manic atmosphere of home.

Franco revelled in the freedom of his first year. At year's end he had not attended any clases nor taken one exam. The second year he was obliged to live with a respectable family and eat his meals at the Jesuit dormitory at Viale Don Minzoni 25. For twenty years his mother had planned his future wedding, designed and re-designed the bride's dress and dreamed of the companionship of her future daughter-in-law. As could be seen by her face on that spring morning outside of Florence, a tall, gangly, shy American girl was despicably out of the question.

1

At the close of the school year, Jeanne's love for Italy and Franco ran inextricably together. She agreed to spend the summer at Franco's home in Ravenna. Once there in the hot, seaside town, Nuncio alternated between friendliness and verbal hysteria. Anna's jealous harassment was unrelenting. Jeanne lay on the beach and inwardly counted the days until summer's end.

In August, Franco and Jeanne left to return to Florence. They headed his father's van out of Ravenna and at Bologna spontaneously decided to take the old mountain highway to Florence. Franco sang. A fine drizzle began. They talked of a cheap apartment and student jobs for the new year. Then, dreamlike, the van hit an oil slick on the moistened road and slid into the opposite lane. Franco cramped the wheel to no avail. They slid forward towards a break in the ancient retaining wall. Jeanne looked out and could see only the tips of trees. As if on a cloud, they floated over the edge.

The ambulance never came. Passing English tourists curled them into their small rented Fiat and took them to the local town hospital. Jeanne was given morphine for the pain and remembered only moments of the next five days. With injuries to her back and knee, she was transferred to a well-known clinic outside of Bologna, and then—to Anna's relief—flown home two weeks later.

2

Two years passed before Jeanne and Franco saw each other again. Then Franco came to study at the Jesuit university in Spokane on a Fulbright scholarship. Seeing Franco again, Jeanne pulled back her bedcovers as if it were the thousandth rather than the first time. Her legs creaked open, spreading muscles that modesty had taught to clamp tight. She felt as if bats and other dark, winged creatures flew out from that long-sealed crevice. She felt air and the daytime sun on a part of her body that had always been kept dark and covered. And she felt like something was over, that she had been caught in the corner of a maze from which others had long since found their way out.

She really felt nothing more. Absent was the passion of their misty nights in Florence. Lacking was the complete and exquisite agony of those first and all-expressive kisses. A few months later, Franco phoned his mother with the news:

—*Mama.*

—*Franco, Franco, how are you?*

—*Fine, mamma, fine. Listen, mamma I have something to tell you. I'm getting married.*

—*WHAT? To whom?*

—*To Jeannie.*

—*Come home immediately!*

—*But mama, I can't. I'm not over in Florence, I'm in America.*

—*Come home immediately!*

—*Mama, I'm getting married, the 31st of December.*

—*You're disowned.*

It was raining outside St. Charles Parish Church the morning of New Year's Eve 1966. Jeanne's father and mother sat stiffly in the first pew. Further back sat a young, green-eyed nun in black garb, sobbing.

3

SPOKANE, WASHINGTON,
MAY 1967

On Sunday, heavy steps came down the hallway and then there was a knock on the wooden door of the apartment.

"That must be Judy," Jeanne said over her shoulder. "Or rather Sister—oh god, what's her name again? Oh well," Jeanne muttered to herself, "she's Judy to me."

Franco grumpily answered the door.

Judy stood in the hall, smiling at him in her black, floor-length Franciscan habit. He coughed and reluctantly invited her in.

Jeanne blushed at the pleasure of seeing her old friend again while Franco, a fierce anti-cleric, could not surmount his alarm at having a nun in his living room—a room which, at the drop of the Murphy bed, was also his bedroom.

"Well," he announced with a false and fawning smile, "I guess I'll go visit Giulio."

As the door closed behind him, Jeanne stepped forward and reached out with both hands.

"I guess I scared off your husband," Judy observed, squeezing her hand and expelling a loud laugh.

"Oh, he's just skittish about clergy, almost superstitious, you might say. For men to be against the Catholic Church is a tradition in the province he comes from. Romagna," Jeanne's arm inadvertently flew in the air like an Italian. She laughed. "He thinks priest and clergy should all be burned—no offense."

"Oh no," Judy chuckled, adjusting her veil.

"So, J—, er, Sister—"

"—Judy Ann."

"Oh, yes. So how long has it been since you went back East to the convent? Five years?"

"Yep."

" 'Yep'—now is that a very nunly thing to say, 'yep'?"

Laughter and talking came easy. In five years, Jeanne had not gotten over missing Judy. The two had been inseparable since the age of seven. In high school, friends dubbed them Pete and Repeat. Their relationship stayed with Jeanne, unslacking in spite of the recent years of separation.

As the afternoon lengthened, an amber light took over the room. Jeanne looked outside through the branches of the maple trees and then back at the striking green eyes of her closest friend.

"You know, our friendship has spoiled me," she confessed, "being able to talk like this. I try with Franco. I beat him over the head," Jeanne whacked the air and laughed, "with ideas, speculation, philosophy, theology—"

"And?"

"And he'll listen and say something..."

Sister Judy Ann slowly folded back the edge of her black gauze sleeve and looked at her watch.

"Well, I have to go," she said in a low voice. The beads of her long, brown rosary crackled as she stood up. "You can tell Franco he can come back now," she shot over her shoulder as she stepped into the hall. "Tell him the big black bug is gone."

4

Franco glanced up from the table, the thick lines of his dark eyebrows drawn together in a frown. His hand brushed a few silken strands of hair off his smooth high forehead, revealing the sharp indentations of his hairline and accentuating his large, doe-brown eyes. His broad and sensuous lips pursed slightly, a reflex to cover the tops of his poorly crafted front caps and stained lower teeth.

Jeanne sidled in the door from her job as a welfare caseworker, a bag of groceries in each arm, her glasses inching down the bridge of her nose. Her naturally curly hair steadfastly resisted her attempts to straighten it and had parted on waves of its own in the heat of the early summer day. A minor headache coincided with the sight of the half-drawn curtains, the unmade bed, and the dishes still in the sink.

Franco scraped his chair back and stood up almost before the door closed. His Italian slacks puckered under his slight belly. He threw the Italian cards he was playing with down on the kitchen table.

"Father Steward has cancelled my scholarship. Because we got married."

Groceries still in her arms, Jeanne tilted her head back and looked at her husband. "What? Say that again?"

"It's true. Cancelled because I am no longer a 'cultural asset to the University.' "

"I beg your pardon?" she blinked. "What changed you by being married to me?"

Franco stepped forward and took the groceries out of her arms. "I no longer live in the dorm and expose these little American boys to my European culture," he spewed sarcastically. "But sit down," he motioned, lighting them both a cigarette, "there's more. I have to leave the United States after graduation and I can't come back on any other visa for two years." The fine print of his Fulbright Scholarship. Jeanne lowered herself slowly to the kitchen chair.

"Well, I tell you," he pointed at Jeanne with the cigarette glowing between his fingertips, "I'm *not* going back to Italy. I'm not going back to working for my father. I think we should go to Vancouver for two years and then come back."

"But what about Italy?"

Well," he conceded, "if I don't go back by the time I'm 26—which is next year—and do my military service, then I can't go back."

She looked at him with alarm. "Never?"

"They can arrest you and put you in prison for six years if you go abroad to avoid military service..."

The young couple sat in the gathering dusk of the early summer evening, not speaking. Then Jeanne rose slowly, "Two years... We have to go back."

5

Three months later, waves of anxiety gripped her as they drove down the Autostrada. RAVENNA — 37 km. The sign slipped by on her right. A little voice was trying to chant reassuring mantras in her head — *you're a signora now, not just a studentessa his mother can torment.*

Nervous himself, Franco broke the tangible silence.

"It's alright," he said, taking her hand on the seat of the car. Jeanne's long fingers recoiled from his touch.

"*You* wanted to come back!" he snapped in the dark. "I wanted us to go to Vancouver," he reminded her with bitterness.

"I don't want to go back to your house," Jeanne qualified with sullen fear. "The summer I spent there was hell."

"But, Jeanne, we don't have the money for an apartment. This isn't like America. You don't just find a $100 apartment to rent and some second hand furniture. It doesn't exist. Besides my family has a certain standing. We will have our own apartment — behind my parents' house, over the garage. They will buy us beautiful furniture."

"Yeh, and you have to walk right by your mother's workroom window any time you want to get out the gate," Jeanne hissed.

"Now, Jeanne, all you do is come in and give her a kiss and talk a little. Just be friendly and you'll see — it will be fine. They're so excited we're coming back. And you know my father likes you. I know my parents — they'll cover us in gold."

Shivers skittered up her spine in the warm summer night. She stared out the window into the blackness and wondered at what price.

In Ravenna, for the first time Jeanne tasted what it is like to be a wife. At first she taught long hours of English classes at the Interpreters School on the narrow main street of town. But gradually she accomplished less and less. The winter's cold and the provincial town held her spirit. The piercing fog curled and sought her under dim porticoes as she walked home late from classes.

She was chided to dress properly to simply walk to the baker or the butcher. With still Catholic subservience, she allowed her mother-in-law's ideas to mold her and her hands to dress her. 'You're a Benelli now,' the whole family chorused. Hairdresser's hands pulled and ironed the curls and waves out of her hair and then streaked it blond. Her eyes looked out from large, designer glasses. Her feet were beautifully bound with delicate alligator boots from Florence and, in her seamstress shop downstairs, Anna pushed the girls hard to sew Chanel originals for 'la Geemie'.

CHAPTER TWO

Contractions

RAVENNA, ITALY
OCTOBER 1968

Signora Baldassari stood with her hand in Jeanne's vagina at the foot of the bed. "Why, Signora, you have a womb like a bank vault! With contractions like this and you still haven't dilated more than three fingers!"

This the midwife announced at the top of her voice while lowering the stiff, white sheet down over her legs. The contractions came back to back, without pause, one barely subsiding before the next would begin. Pain twisted Jeanne's long back in its grip, breaking open a fear inside her that something was wrong.

The absence of doctors and the nodding, vigilant eyes of the other women in the room compounded her fears. With an air of ancient resignation, the women sat waiting for nature's next elaboration of itself, whispering a litany of sad and tragic stories.

"There in that bed, Signora Manfredi almost died last month. Finally they pulled the baby out with a plunger, but he isn't quite right. The umbilical cord was around his neck for too long."

"And Signora Zanucci," another began, "they transferred her to the hospital but there two doctors pushed so hard on her belly with their elbows that her spleen ruptured."

"I know, one of them was all the way up on the table pushing on her stomach..."

The next contraction locked Jeanne's hands around the cold iron bar that ran the length of the bed. Jeanne cried for help in two languages.

"Breathe, Signora, breathe," Signora Baldassari coached. "Like in class. I'll count — *uno, due...*"

Directly opposite Jeanne a woman in black, no taller than four and a half feet, walked up and down beside her daughter's bed. Her wizened face peered out from under a tight bandana. In her arms, she vigorously rocked a cleft-lipped newborn, insistently humming an ancient, nasal *ninna-nanna*.

"Franco, Franco? Where is Franco?" Jeanne called.

"She wants her Franco. But, Signora, your husband's gone out a bit, to buy a newspaper. It's 4:00 and he's been here all day," her midwife reasoned sympathetically. "Now you just breathe."

It had been dark outside for hours when Signora Baldassari snapped off her rubber glove and announced, "Ah, at last! Now we're on our way. Into the delivery room we go and one big push, *uno grande spintone,* and this baby will be born. *Coraggio,* Signora, you're almost through."

Tears of relief dampened on Jeanne's cheeks. She felt a wet spreading as they lifted and pushed her on to the delivery table and into the stirrups. *One big push, uno grande spintone,* Jeanne chanted to herself.

Not just once but again and again she pushed.

"Now *push,* Signora," they coached. Frightened, Franco stood behind her head, sweating and pale. He tried to help roll her shoulders forward. Then she felt his trembling hands let her shoulders go. Whispering that he couldn't do it and was sorry, he retreated from the delivery room through the swinging oak doors.

A cluster of flies honed circles above the delivery table. Two dormant incubators were parked idle and unready in the corner. The obstetrician who had been called in to humor this young American stood passively beside the delivery table. His grey face watched the work of the two midwives who sat beyond Jeanne's vision below the edge of the white sheet stretched between her spread and stirruped legs.

"*Push*, Signora! The head can be seen."

But Jeanne lay limp with exhaustion. Suddenly, a man's elbow dug hard into her mountainous belly. She was rolled forward. She felt herself spread incredibly and then a slippery oozing and slithering out of a wet form.

The room was silent. The silence lengthened.

"*Che cos' è?*" she had to ask.

"It's a boy, Signora."

"*Sta bene?*"

"*Si, si, un bel maschio.* You've done fine, Singora, *brava.* Now you just rest."

Numb, Jeanne sank back against the hard metal table. Her body began to quake. A rough, olive-green blanket was put over her. She felt the umbilical along the curve of her ass. In cold relief that they had both survived, she submissively waited for their ancient washing to be done. At last, packaged in white bindings to his chin, the small infant was lifted up for her to see.

His composure shocked her. His face was flushed as if delicately tanned. Eyes closed and sleeping, his face was relaxed in a smooth peacefulness. Strawberry blond hairs lay with uncanny perfection around his forehead and ears.

"Now you rest, mamma," cautioned Signora Baldassari. She reached around and simply laid the infant on the top of a marble table in the center of the room.

The oak doors swooshed forward and in came Nuncio with Anna and Franco behind him. He stood behind his daughter-in-law, his dark face and prominent nose leaning upside-down into her field of vision. Stroking her damp forehead and hair, he inquired as to her condition. Then, in his short, Napoleonesque way, he strode over to his new grandson.

Jeanne stared numbly. It appeared as though he was partially unwrapping her son, looking down at his legs. He poked the covers back around the boy infant and walked away, snorting unimpressed—"This one takes after his mother's side."

A weak vein of shock and revulsion washed up over Jeanne. But while her head hung softly to the side, her eyes did not blink or move from the distant, softly moving bundle. They named him Paul.

1

ROCHESTER, NEW YORK
JUNE 1973

After two years, a scholarship for study at the University of Rochester was Franco's ticket out of the Italian army and Jeanne's release from the provincial town of Ravenna. They returned to the States, this time to the hard winters and humid summers of upstate New York.

Paul grew plump and gorgeous, molting from an angelic infant into a furious two year-old. Playing contentedly one minute, he would be banging his head full force on the hardwood floor the next. "The two's," their neighbor assured them.

Just as Paul's speech was progressing beyond the level of 'car-car' and moving on to full sentences, a ride on the airplane took him back to Italy where suddenly 'car-cars' were '*macchine*', the table a '*tavola*', and mommie '*mamma*'. The city was Rome and it was the best year of Jeanne's marriage. The joys of Italy minus a mother-in-law, the richness of Rome, its long history layered on its streets like an Italian pastry.

In addition, there were four hours a day that Jeanne had all to herself. Each morning when Franco left to do research in the National Archives on the far side of Rome, Jeanne placed Paul in the Montessori school's van, threw kisses at it until it rounded the corner, and then lept on the nearest city bus, bearing with heady lightness for all the Roman art and history she could absorb.

In the afternoons and evenings, she read and studied what she had seen in the mornings. Arm and arm, she and Franco entered bookstores, emerging with art books he insisted she buy. One evening Franco walked into the steamy kitchen of their top-floor apartment, "Jeanne, I really think you should go to graduate school in Art History when we get back."

She looked up through brown curls and hazy glasses, slapped the tin lid on the pot of water and smiled at him in astonishment at the perfect fittingness of the idea.

Back in Rochester after more than a year abroad, Paul faced another task of re-culturalization. In the maze of university apartments, his best friend Stevie sat on his Big Wheel, pleased at his return, but without English they couldn't talk. At a quick lunch at MacDonald's, Jeanne and Franco placed a straw in a tall cup of thick substance and told Paul in Italian that it was good and to suck. Unfortunately, it came more naturally to blow. Great globs of strawberry shake lifted up in the air and then sank to the table with a splat. As Jeanne and Franco blotted the table with napkins, people turned and looked curiously at a four year-old who apparently did not know how to drink a milkshake. Gradually, however, '*tavola*' reverted to table, '*aqua*' to water and '*letto*' to bed.

The University of Rochester formally cancelled its Masters in Art History the year they got back, a small act in the growing attrition of Humanities programs in the early seventies. For Jeanne, a miscarriage was followed by another pregnancy. With a growing belly, she attended one upper level course at a time and at home translated Franco's dissertation into English. By the second semester, her belly became like a basketball sitting in her lap between herself and the desks. She felt peaceful inside but lost patience with the unpleasant range of looks she continually received as a pregnant woman on campus.

When Paul was four and a half, his brother was born. The event did not seem of great consequence in his life. Paul found his infant brother, Jesse, amusing and he seemed to relish his expanded freedom and new status as big brother. As he lept onto his Big Wheel and sped down the sidewalk, his mother waved goodbye whereas before she may have followed.

Jeanne rolled over on the lawn and pulled back the yellow blanket in the bassinet. Tiny fists and toes were flailing the air with mounting agitation. She smiled lazily, drunk on the early summer sunshine and relief that this birth, too, had gone well. She lifted the infant boy up in the June air. Her nipples prickled with milk.

Inside the sparsely furnished student apartment, she carefully toppled onto the patch of sun on her bed. In a minute his suckling pulled the lids of her eyes peacefully closed. His curled fists gently scratched at the roundness of her breast. The back of her head buzzed and lightened. Eyes closed, she drifted back in time to the room at the Clinica di San Francisco.

"Alright," she could hear Signora Baldassari's loud voice the day after Paul was born, "let's see if Signora is ready to give some milk to this hungry little *bambino*. Unbutton your gown."

Jeanne could feel the attention of both family and strangers in the room coalescing in her direction. Three generations of her husband's family stood watching beside her bed, including the infant's great-grandparents. Still weak and shaken from the long labor, Jeanne felt her stomach clutch with embarrassment. Signora Baldassari reached forward and was helping her slow, chilly fingers with the buttons on her gown.

The unprecedented size of her own breast startled her. Signora took it in her hand and gently washed her right breast with a damp cloth, noting aloud—"Yes, there will be lots of milk for this little *Jesù bambino*. Now we have to start the milk, Signora." She took the purplish nipple between her thumb and forefinger and began a regular squeezing motion. It hurt. Jeanne squirmed slightly.

"*Pazienza, Signora*. You have to start the milk. Why don't you try."

She placed Jeanne's left hand on her right breast. Clumsily she squeezed but it was tender and hard to hold. And nothing happened.

Anna, a serious new grandmother, stood directly behind Signora Baldassari, brusquely rocking Paul in his laced port-enfant. *She's rocking him too hard,* Jeanne thought nervously. Besides, she resented her taking him out of his crib and holding him before she had.

"Here, Signora, let me try again," offered Signora Baldassari. Pain bit through her breast as her midwife administered a few more healthy squeezes. She wiped away a small amount of brownish liquid and concluded, "Well, we'll let this baby do this." Seemingly on queue, she turned and Anna ritually consigned the infant to her midwife.

Then it was Jeanne's turn. For the first time, she held Paul in her arms. He laid peacefully inside the richly embroidered port-enfant as if slid inside an ornate envelope. The small, curved mattress was bulbous and in the way. *I can't feel him at all,* Jeanne thought with frustration.

Pressed on by the business at hand, she tilted him, port-enfant and all, face forward towards her exposed and taut breast. Head first, his face finally touched her skin and his cheek lay askew against her breast. *You don't seem to know what to do any more than I do,* she confided silently. Signora Baldassari, directress of operations, reached around and again with her thumb and forefinger, took ahold of his blond cheeks and puckered his mouth into an oval opening. She then realigned his head, fitting his mouth over the soft nipple.

The nipple immediately slipped limply out of the corner of his mouth. *Jesus,* she thought. Cold and clammy, she felt all eyes trained upon her. Her hand shook as she reached over to catch her wayward nipple and tried to match it to his mouth again.

"Ow!" she cried inadvertently as he got it. He sucked hard. Jeanne's right shoulder rolled forward as she felt he was going to pull it right off. It felt like many needles were being drawn through the length of her nipple, the fine channels of milk being forced open for the first time.

Suddenly, he jerked his head away and started to cry for the first time. Jeanne felt tears sting the corners of her own eyes. Fumbling and desperate, she glanced up at Signora Baldassari. She steadfastly tried to ignore the ring of observing eyes behind her.

"Now, now, the milk hasn't started coming yet," she consoled her. Again, she reached over and massaged the soft brown nipple. A few beads of bluish liquid appeared at different spots on her nipple.

"He will get this *bella titta* to milk. Here, let's let him do it," she repeated, aligning his mouth with the full breast.

"Ow," she repeated in spite of herself. Tears bit at her eyelids. It hurt. She felt like he was either going to draw milk or have her nipple. Luckily, some amount of milk forged through. In fact, she could actually feel it being pulled through the tiny tubes in the narrow canals of her nipple. It continued to be painful but she bore down on her jaw with stubborn composure.

"*Brava,* Jeanne, *brava mamma,*" she heard Nuncio announce. The ritual was over. People began to move and talk. Jeanne reached out with her left hand to savor her first real touch of her first-born child.

The next morning, Nuncio waited downstairs to take her home. "Cover him! Cover him!" a stranger shrilly scolded her as she stepped shakily out of the Clinica and into the crisp, winter sunshine.

"No," she remembered saying, reopening a tunnel through the blankets that had been draped over his face. Nuncio smiled and opened the door of the white sedan. In her years in Italy Jeanne was to never become accustomed to the totally unsolicited and obsessively doting interventions of passers-by as to the care of children. However, having absolutely no idea of how to begin to take care of a small child and being a continent away from her own mother and culture, she was often paradoxically dependent on their suffocating reasoning.

"The air and sun are good for him," she insisted under her breath and bent carefully into the car with her son.

Alerted by Jesse's arms flailing gently against her skin, Jeanne stirred on the bed and the past slipped away. Carefully, she shifted him from her deflated right breast to her tautly stretched left. His suckling syphened off the pressure of the milk as he drank his fill in her arms. *Ah, yes,* she thought to herself, *a world of difference.*

2

MARCH 1974

Snow fell in sheets through the streetlamp's light at the corner. Inside the sparse university apartment the children were asleep and the 11 p.m. news flickered on the screen. Franco pushed himself up and out of the dark green armchair and moved to adjust the TV, reiterating adamantly — "I won't allow it."

Jeanne's hands suspended their automatic folding of the kids' laundry. "But what is this — you won't allow it."

"That's exactly what I mean. That program isn't worth anything. What you need is to get your Ph.D." His voice ended with a nasal tone of academic superiority.

"Thanks alot," Jeanne rejoined dryly. She picked up a crumpled pair of tiny jeans and snapped them hard in the air. "Now where am I going to do that? And what program's going to accept me? My undergraduate work is not in Art History and what I know is what I've learned on my own in Italy."

"Don't worry. You'll get in," he waved his hand. He sank back into the chair and reached for his cigarettes on the corner of the stereo.

"Franco," Jeanne exploded in frustration. "Syracuse University *has* accepted me and is offering me a complete fellowship as well! It's a quick one year Masters in Renaissance Studies with good teachers. I can commute to Syracuse until December for my classes and then I can take Jesse with me to Florence. I'll be able to study with Ugo Procacci, Director of the Uffizi Gallery," she went on excitedly. "And Luisa Becherucci—you know what giants they are in Art History…"

"Oh, you'll probably never even see them. You know how Italian professors are. It's not like here."

"I'd have free access to the Uffizi and there are so many American students in Florence, you know I could find childcare for Jesse. And your parents are dying to be close to their grandchildren." The words were tumbling fast and urgent now. "The program ends in May and you and Paul come as soon as school is over. You know your parents would pay the ticket and we could all spend the summer in Ravenna at the beach. Now you know you'd like that. You and Paul could do fine for a couple of months. It'd be good for you…"

"No, Jeanne, I won't let you. I won't let you separate the family."

"But it's only for a few months."

"No, the program isn't worth it—"

"It is, too!"

" — and besides I won't let you. You need to get into a good Ph.D. program." The persistent tone of academic superiority annoyed her. For months she had been translating his dissertation into English.

"When? How? I've already taken all the credits I can transfer from here."

"I don't care… You'll have to wait. Maybe I'll get a teaching job somewhere that will have a program," he said skittishly, twisting his cigarette out in the round green ashtray.

"Wait," Jeanne said weakly. She felt a great tiredness sweep over her. The Nightly News was coming to an end. An aching sat like a puddle at the back of her head. She persisted, "Franco, it's been seven years. You got your doctorate from the University of Florence and in a couple of months you'll have your American Ph.D. — "

"For all the good — " he threw in cynically.

"Please, Franco, I want to accept this fellowship. Please."

"No," he said with finality, shaking his head. "I won't let you separate the family."

Silence followed on the heels of this edict and sat like a stranger in the room. Great swirls of snow beat off the roof, bumping into the still falling sheets outside. Jeanne looked across the room and tried with her eyes to call him back, to make him reconsider his oddly patriarchal stance, but he shielded her gaze with his cheek, keeping his eyes clearly averted and out of contact. The matter was closed.

"It's past 11:30," he said in a life-goes-on voice, pushing himself up out of the green brocade chair. "I'm going to bed. Are you coming?"

"No," the word came out hoarsely.

He glanced obliquely at his wife and then shrugged. "Well, *buona notte.*" He paused an instant for a reply that didn't come and then walked into the bedroom.

Jeanne leaned back among the little piles of laundry on the green vinyl couch and cradled the headache at the back of her skull. He had never talked to her like that before but she wasn't sure that mattered. She sensed that he had let slip something she'd never been aware of up until then. Something that had been there for eight, nine years had just crystallized in the last half hour.

How stupid! How could I have not recognized it before? Blood flushed to her face. Humored. All of a sudden she knew she had been humored, humored and cajoled by his proverbial sunny Italian nature, humored for years, humored to Ravenna and his parents, humored to housekeep, humored to cook Italian feasts for his friends, humored to secretary his slightly slipping academic career.

She stood in the bathroom with her back towards the mirror. She popped the white lid off a brown plastic bottle, then turned and carefully put it back out of a child's reach on the highest shelf of the medicine cabinet.

Now, Mrs. Benelli, she silently mimicked her gynecologist's voice, *I'll give you some codeine for your headaches and some Valiums. They'll help... bring you out of your shell.* She mocked his chuckle in her throat.

The smaller bottle of Valium sat untouched on the glass shelf beside the codeine. She closed the door to the medicine cabinet and her face flipped into view. "Ugh," she remarked out loud to her tired reflection and went into the kitchen. Her ears wiggled and reached out to drink in the midnight quiet of the house. She got a drink of water and went to bed.

3

Several months later, while Jesse was napping and Paul was sprawled on the braided rug with his friends watching Sesame Street, Jeanne dialed a long distance number. Gingerly she pulled the phone cord as far as it would go into the hall and closed her other ear with two fingers.

"Judy? How are you! Listen, I'm so glad you're in San Francisco now. I'm coming out there to visit my family. Did you get my last letter? Yeah, then you know about my sister's husband dying... Well, it's pretty hard. Mom and Dad moved to California to help her with the kids.

"Yeah, I'm going to come visit. Actually I'm on my way to Italy. Very funny, I know it's the wrong direction. But I'm taking the kids to Italy for the summer to see their grandparents. Franco will come after his classes end in August. No, still no teaching position. Hm? Well, I'm not sure how I feel about being at the Benellis by myself for two months. But I'll have the kids. So listen, I'll be at my sister's, just south of San Francisco the first week of June and I want to see you. Hm? Oh yes, I'm doing fine. Well, a lot of headaches. What? Oh, almost every day. They are kind of incapacitating. Anyway... What? That's the kids, they're watching TV. You were a teacher, you can relate, right? Wrong, oh well. Listen, Judy, I can't afford this. I want to see you, okay? I need to talk to you. I'll call you from Carol's. June 4th."

4

SAN FRANCISCO, CALIFORNIA
JUNE 1974

Jeanne wasn't at all sure. Nor could she have articulated any of it. But she wanted the whole evening with Judy, and the night as well. She settled the kids at her sister's and drove to San Francisco. The door opened and she sank into the soft fullness of Judy's generous hug and felt an old-time contentedness.

Except for the visit after Jeanne's marriage, they had not seen each other since they separated after high school.

"We're best friends, no matter what," they had sworn on the train platform in 1962, as the Northern Pacific creaked forward out of Spokane, taking Judy back East to the Franciscan novitiate. "I love you," Judy called boldly as the porter urged her inside.

Unavoidable change. It was the end of high school and a time of their lives. The end of Saturday nights sneaking girlfriends into the drive-in movies in the trunk of the Buick and dropping off Judy last. Of sitting parked, and talking until late, at the curb in front of her house. One time their hands crawled towards each other across the blue vinyl seat. In the dark, they looked at each other in silence for a long time, then said, "I love you." It seemed so serious that time that a twinge stayed with Jeanne, a small cold sense that they had done something wrong.

Now, twelve years later, Jeanne stepped back from the long welcoming hug at her door. Dressed in jeans, Frye boots and a loose Indian shirt, out of the convent three years, Judy had become a powerful, critical and soon cynical woman, deep in the electoral politics of the San Francisco chapter of N.O.W. She loosely identified herself as gay, something she had mentioned to Jeanne on the phone.

Sinking into a round arm chair in the living room, Judy lit a long cigarette with a slim, silver lighter and snapped it closed. She shot her friend a rich smile. Jeanne's smile grew proportionately and her face felt very warm. Although Jeanne hadn't smoked for years, cigarettes on the glass coffee table beckoned her. As they visited eagerly and late into the night, Jeanne plucked cigarette after cigarette from the crystal holder.

One o'clock, two. The issue of their long-standing love for each other grew more and more palpable in the room. Three o'clock. With the clarity of a Flemish painting, the door to Judy's bedroom stood ajar to her left.

"I love you," they said.

Four o'clock. "I'll sleep right here," Jeanne said with an artifical lilt to her voice, patting the couch firmly and trying to summon some moral certainty. Five o'clock. Judy shook her dark head of curls and took in Jeanne with her emerald eyes. Then she said slowly, "Alright, okay, but you sleep in my bed... I'm going to smoke another cigarette."

Jeanne entered the room on her left and closed the door. Her clothes quickly slipped from her to the floor. She spread the covers back and slid diagonally across the sheets. Tossed by the invisible hands of an energy she couldn't name, she rolled from side to side of the bed. She drew her legs up against her aching belly.

Suddenly afraid that Judy would go to bed and the evening would truly be over, Jeanne sprang soundlessly to the door. Her head thumped from the nicotine. The San Francisco cold that hung in the high ceiling, Victorian room quickly chilled her. She pulled the door open and crossed the hall into the bathroom. When she heard the rustle of Judy leaving the living room, she stepped out and mumbled, "Uh, Judy, uh I suppose it's okay if we just... sleep together."

Naked, cold and taut, Jeanne walked back into the gathering morning light in the room. She heard her friend stand fixed for a moment and then come to bed.

Jeanne rolled in a ball with her back staunchly turned toward her friend, but in an instant waves of years-old passion rolled her up over Judy's large body. She felt the velvet rush of their bodies coming together for the first time. Her mouth gulped in great draughts of her, her hands scared and startled at her own kind. Judy's breasts were everywhere. With a childlike moan, she slipped down on her, startled at the absence of penis, rolling on the soft of her belly. Gently her hand slid the silky black hairs open and her mouth followed. The wetness, strange smell, alky taste didn't matter. Her fingers searched and followed the opening, so different, damp and close. Feelings took her and shook her like a rag doll. It all happened very fast.

Jeanne yanked herself back and groaned with embarrassment. She crawled back on her side, but too late. Judy's arm circled her and drew her close. Jeanne did not shrink from the contact of the full breast resting in the middle of her back nor from the smooth mound touching silken against her ass. But no, no more.

Morning light was seeping into the room. As she lay in Judy's arms, Jeanne felt a presence growing in the corner of the room. It condensed into forms and lingered. She rolled her arm up over her face and sunk back against Judy. It remained and she muttered into the pillow, "Judy, maybe this sounds silly but I can see God and my parents...up in the corner of the ceiling."

Silence.

"You know," she continued, raising her arm across her face as if to ward off a blow, "at a diagonal, like a Baroque painting... about to strike."

Dressed and dazed, Jeanne could not compose herself or mask her stunned wonder at what had just happened. She sat on a stool in the windowless, Victorian kitchen. Her mouth hung open, drying with the weight of what had occurred. Jeanne tumbled scrambled eggs over a curled strip of bacon on the yellow plate that Judy had passed her but could only manage a mouthful.

"I have a few errands," Judy cleared her throat, ending the conspicuous silence. "Then I can drive you back to your sister's."

"Okay," Jeanne answered vaguely. "I should call Carol and see how the kids are doing."

Life resumed, altered. Uncanny calmness settled in over that early morning's experience and generally coated Jeanne throughout her summer stay in Ravenna. At the end of July, her parents-in-law left on a camping trip with Paul and Jesse. The house was stuffed with mid-summer's heat and Jeanne found herself stalking the empty house like a ten foot cat. She paced and called Judy's name, wanting her more and still and since such a long time.

These feelings seeped back underground by summer's end and Franco's arrival by train via Bologna. That night, they made love from one end of his room to the other, their bodies runny and soaked in the humid heat. The next morning Nuncio danced around, tittering about love-birds and giving Anna schoolboy kisses on the neck.

They gathered the children, took two cars and a basket of food and left for the beach. Together they sipped espresso at the bar. Franco flipped open the newspaper on the counter and they were stunned by the headline: MASSACRE AT BOLOGNA. In the long tunnel outside of Bologna, neofascists had firebombed the train following the one Franco had arrived on two hours earlier.

A couple of months later, at home, Jeanne told him. She told him as she was serving him dinner. Cheese hamburgers sizzled in the frypan in her hands. She began talking about something that had some remote and minuscule relation to Judy—horrified, she realized what she was doing. She wound round and round, circling the point and, like a plane that spins and spins and finally dives irreparably to the earth, she bumblingly blurted out what had happened in June.

Shocked by her own admission, she stood motionless, wrists aching from the weight of the cast iron pan, looking at Franco's startled face. Jesse banged on the tray of his high chair. Paul, thank God, was over at Stevie's for dinner. Finally....

"I—I feel torn," he said slowly, his brown hands resting at either side of his still empty plate. "Do...do you...love her?"

"Y-yes," she replied tensely, "I've always loved Judy. You've known that. But... it doesn't mean anything."

"I—I feel torn," he said again. "My right hand wants to hit you... and my left hand understands."

It was let go at that.

CHAPTER THREE

Fly East, Fly West

ROCHESTER, NEW YORK
MAY 1975

Their new apartment on Lilac Drive looked out on the steep side of an expansive park. When Jeanne hiked there with the kids, it almost felt like wilderness. The vestiges of six months of snow lay in mushy patches under the trees and in the corners of the lawn below. Paul, now six, ran in circles with a new friend and kicked at the slush that was turning red in the sunset.

Upstairs Jesse, now almost two, toddled past the TV in grinning pursuit of the cat. Paunchy and worried, Franco sat in the living room, a bluish airmail envelope on his knee.

He leaned back against the inhospitable green vinyl couch that he and friends had dragged cursing up the stairs to the new apartment six months ago. A move off campus, the purchase of a new red Fiat and a color TV, a concerted reaching out to the components of the American dream. Still his depression had not lifted. Teaching jobs had evaporated like water beads in a frypan. No sector of the country seemed to escape the sudden economic drought. Jeanne had watched Franco grow increasingly despondent.

Cold and hungry, Paul clammered in from outside. Kneeling over stuck, wet laces, he glanced around.

"Mom, Jesse's got the cat again. Jesse, let 'em go," he warned his little brother. "Mom!"

"Wash up," Jeanne ordered as she struggled tensely with the cascading details of getting the family fed. *Oh these drilling headaches.* She squinted through the pain and the light steam in the small, red and white kitchen. All present, she plopped the curled pasta into the rolling mushroom of grey boiling water.

As she closed the door on the children's bedroom that evening, Jeanne looked into the living room and watched Franco fold the thin, airmail letter from his mother after yet another reading. In the bathroom she broke off half a codeine. The powder nipped like bitter needles at her tongue. As she came into the living room, Franco spoke up without looking at her.

"Jeanne, I think I'll call home. I just want to ask my mother about these teaching jobs in Ravenna she's talking about."

Jeanne lit a cigarette in silence and watched him cross the room and phone Anna in Italy. Her heart seemed to stop as she heard him say, "*Si, mamma, si. Benissimo, mamma.*"

She shook her head in disbelief that he had just told her he would move the family back to Italy without even talking to her. She told him flatly that she could not go back to living in Ravenna.

"I can't believe you told her you're coming back. You know what that means to them. I can't go back, I can barely manage now."

She looked at his face and realized that it had been no slip of the tongue.

"Is this permanent, for good?"

"Yes, Jeanne, it is," he shot defensively. "Jeanne, there's nothing here. At least in Italy we can have a quality of life, good food, cinema, opera, and maybe I can teach. And for *you,* you can go to the University of Bologna, have a maid, become a *dottoressa,* too."

Jeanne laid her glasses down on the table and closed her eyes on the gilded cage of his promises. She coaxed the codeine through her veins, waiting for it to get to its target, the base of her skull. Tilting her head gingerly forward to her hand, dark cobblestoned streets immediately closed around her like labyrinths. The memory of an evening years ago swam in and around her like dark water. It was Siena. She was sitting on the bed inside a hotel. Franco, dressed in his army uniform, stood by the head of the bed.

"*O mio dio, o mio dio,*" he kept repeating into the receiver. He hung up the phone.

"What, what is it?" Jeanne asked shakily.

"O god. Remember when we met Giulio's brother and his wife? She's English, a nurse?"

Yes, yes, such a story. Handsome, fast-living Italian crashes his sportscar in England, falls in love with and marries his English nurse. Ten years the English woman had spent married in an apartment in Livorno, eyed by the neighbors and still with no one she felt she could talk to. Jeanne had also met their high-strung, six year-old daugher — sharp eyes and black hair, speaking so loud, so fast, frantically grabbing candies and spinning out of her mother's reach.

Franco looked stunned and brushed back thinning wisps of his black hair.

"*Mio dio,* in the apartment in Livorno, she put a pillow over their daughter's face and suffocated her, and then put her head in the oven and turned on the gas. They're both dead."

Jeanne recoiled from Franco as he sank down on the hotel bed. Cold, she went on alert inside. This can kill.

In May, giant, transatlantic cardboard crates took over the living room and in went their belongings, much of which had crossed the Atlantic more than once before. Franco left precipitously, to apply for teaching positions his mother said existed there.

He took Paul with him to begin learning Italian for school in the fall. He returned to his parents' house in Via Redipuglia. He returned to the provincial life of that foggy Italian town, dreams washed down with espresso in the central piazza, hoping inside that his wife would indeed come.

Jeanne did not know what to do. The thought of choosing or separating or losing either of the children was unthinkable. Her deepest thoughts were still with Judy; once that winter she had almost left to visit her. Sitting on the sofa, shaking her hed, she had told Franco, "I can't take this anymore. I just have to see her."

But she didn't. Now it was understandable that she would go spend time with her family in California before moving back to Italy for good. She would go to her sister's and decide.

Thus as Franco and Paul boarded a plane East to Italy, Jeanne and Jesse boarded a plane West to San Francisco.

1

LOS ALTOS, CALIFORNIA
JUNE 1975

Days, then weeks passed in the peaceful cul-de-sac in Los Altos where Jeanne and Jesse stayed with Carol and her children. Judy, less than an hour away in San Francisco, was unreachable. Deeply involved in a new, turbulent relationship, she made one nervous visit to see Jeanne, entreating a friend to come with her as a buffer. She then disappeared back into her life in the City.

Left hanging by her absence, Jeanne longed not only for her but for the entire quality of her relationships with women. For the first time, there at her sister's, the word 'gay' surfaced in her mind as possibly having something to do with her own life. There it was, a word floating inside of her, sobering and secret, as she fixed sandwiches and played catch.

The vinyl covering of the kitchen nook bench grabbed at her bare thighs as she slid in next to the kitchen table. Children outside, Jeanne stared at the freshly-cleaned and well-ordered kitchen. Glasses, plants, fruit sat in the California light with the existential sharpness of a Dutch painting.

She leaned back against the coffee grinders, potted plants and wooden pepper mills of the nook's oilskin wallpaper and exhaled deeply but couldn't release the clutch in her stomach. She reached over and took a pencil and orange notepad out of the redwood holder on the counter. Alone in the house, she picked up the phone and dialed nearby Stanford University. She asked hoarsely if they had a gay student union group. Or ''meetings for women''. She felt like she was making an obscene phone call. A layer of blood surged up her face to her hairline, burning her face red.

''Well, it's summertime and not much is happening. But there are meetings every Tuesday night at 7:00—you're welcome to come.''

That evening, Carol sat on the black naugahyde couch, sewing. The orange and yellow zigzags of Mother's afghan covered her lap and legs. Across from her, Jeanne squeezed the arms of the brown recliner and pushed her weight back until it yielded. Evenings found her tired and restless. She laid her head back a few minutes and then resumed the unfinished letter to Franco in her lap.

June 19, 1975

...It's later and I'm too tired to remember what I was going to say. Believe me, three kids are exhausting. They are 'good' but their demands on your time and attention are so absolute.

Anyway, what I really want to say, Franco, is how uncertain I continue to be. I've lost 10 lbs., headaches, etc. and still the situation refuses to resolve itself. It is terrible being faced with such a decision. Anyway I'm tired of thinking (rationalizing) about it and somehow I feel confident that I will make the right decision when the time comes, i.e., the beginning of August. If I come I will do so after my birthday and before yours.

In the meantime I'm realistically looking at what staying in this area with Jesse would really mean in terms of work, daycare, school, people, but there is such at atmosphere of freedom and possibility that I think I could really be myself again. That's what makes it so hard, having to decide between that gut feeling vs. my dismal track record in Ravenna. Anyway it's obvious I cannot continue or return to anywhere near the state I've been in. Yet the thought of severing this tie to you or loosing Paul—it goes literally beyond words.

Jeanne laid the letter next to the lamp and snapped the recliner into an upright position.

"Carol, would you mind if I go to Stanford Tuesday night? There's a concert... Starts at 7:00. I'd need the car..."

"Sure," she said with a tinge of weariness, "go ahead."

"Thanks."

After dinner on Tuesday, Jeanne slipped the orange notepad with its thinly penciled directions into her purse and drove Sarah's bronze sportscar to Stanford. She parked and stood up beside the car. A bleached, surrealistic light seemed to bathe herself and everything around her.

Purse under her arm, she leaned into the heavy door on the second floor of a low Moorish building. She stepped into the large conference room bare except for six or seven young women gathered at the far end.

"Oh no," she whispered to herself. One glance told her that she was out of place, that she was ten years older than anyone else there and that the appearance of these 'gays' scared her. She found herself walking forward as if in an unsettling dream.

"Hello," she said, nodding.

Her eyes sought out their hiking boots as theirs sought out her pumps. A young woman sank down on the couch and casually put her arm around the other girl sitting there. Jeanne averted her eyes and didn't know what in the hell to do with her purse. Inwardly, a voice was berating her ferociously, *how could you have done this? what were you thinking of? what are you doing here anyway? are you queer? they are!*

Soon, she picked up her purse from the floor, and smiling apologetically, said she thought she should be going. Her heels clacked loudly across the yellow room until her hand and shoulder at last reached the cold metal of the heavy door. Shaking and clammy, she clomped down the stairs. Her head ran riot. *What's happening to me? who am I? what am I doing? what am I going to do? I can't go home, what time is it—7:45, too upset, where's a phone?*

"Hello, Judy? Look, I'm really sorry to bother you. I'm… having a hard time. I just need to talk to someone."

Judy referred her on to two friends of hers in Palo Alto whom Jeanne had briefly met. She dug out another dime and called.

"Hi, come on in," Diane greeted her at the door. Jeanne stepped into their house, trembling with an acute awareness that these two women were lovers. She sat down on the sofa, expecting on some level to be bit or attacked or tainted. Nothing looked threatening, she had to admit—books, stuffed chairs, the TV. Sue joined them and sat on the sofa as well, covering her knees with an orange and brown afghan curiously like her sister's.

"So, what's happening?" Sue began with a low, warm voice.

"Oh, I don't know," Jeanne sighed. "I don't know what's happening with me. Judy won't have much to do with me…" How strange that sounded out loud, a new and embarrassing admission. "She's so involved with Sandy… And I don't see how I can go back to Italy. I'm sure I'd go crazy there but my son's there and they are expecting me to come. And my family is getting increasingly nervous that I might not go back to my husband. I think I've decided to start going up to Berkeley or San Francisco and look for a place

for Jesse and me to rent, if only for a month or two, until I decide...
And I have very little money. And then," Jeanne added, raising
her gaze from the rug and looking at their faces with a small laugh,
"I don't know. Tonight I went to a meeting at the Stanford Gay
Student Union and — it was awful!" she exploded.

They chuckled, looking at each other and asked, "What was it
like?"

"Oh god, I don't know what came over me to go there. They were
all just kids! Why didn't I think of that. And..." Jeanne flashed
on their hiking boots, the ease of their arms around each other, the
unfeminine solidity of their dress, manner, jobs. "I don't know,"
she continued wearily, her gaze returning to the rug. "They sort
of — scared me." She glanced up quickly, afraid she had offended
them. They smiled unperturbed and they talked on.

"Well," Sue began, "if and when you do move up to the City,
there are some groups. In fact, Diane, isn't there a Lesbian Mother
group in the City or is that no longer happening?"

LESBIAN. Lesbian? It was the first time she had ever heard that
word said. *Lesbian, wait a minute, this is all going too fast, I've simply
had this intense friendship with Judy, lesbian — they are assuming that I
am a lesbian, wo-oh, wait a minute...*

*and lesbian mother? what an odd concept, how strange to hear those two
words together—lesbian and mother. An organization? Oh god no. I want
to go back, go back home, go back to my sister's home, the kids in bed, the
TV going, me married, me normal.*

"Well," she cleared her throat, reaching down on the floor once
again for her purse, "I said I was going to a concert and should
be getting back. I just need some time... to figure things out."

At last, she headed the tapered nose of the sportscar back to the
Expressway and drove in silence. She eased the purring car into
the darkened double garage and went into the house.

"How was the concert?" Carol called from the family room.
Jeanne stood in the unlit kitchen, rolling her neck stiffly from side
to side.

"Oh, a little heavy," she answered wryly. "Mostly Wagner."

2

By Jeanne's birthday in August, her welcome had worn thin. Impatience grew with her reluctance to return to Italy and the seriousness with which she was considering staying. Her life was tilting, righting itself in one long, major seismic shift.

With a hundred dollars left, she applied for welfare and got ready to move to Berkeley. Through notices in community centers she found in Berkeley parlance, 'a shared living situation'. She decided on a flat with a talkative nurse named Sheila and her sprightly three year-old daughter. Judy came to give them a ride on the evening they moved.

"I really appreciate being able to stay here," Jeanne told her sister on the front porch of her house.

"You're welcome," came the cool reply.

"Give your aunt a hug, Jesse."

Closing the car door, Jeanne murmured to Judy. "Let's go."

Judy slipped the silver Datsun into reverse. Sarah stood wooden and unmoving on on her porch. Jeanne waved goodbye to her two nephews as they streamed by on their bicycles.

Jeanne adjusted two year-old Jesse in her lap. She spread his favorite blue and yellow checked blanket over them both, and tucked her arm close around his belly. The car pulled up onto the 280 North on-ramp, past a green sign with shiny rivets spelling SAN FRANCISCO. They rode on in silence, the casual elegance of the California countryside sliding past the windows.

Ahead of them and to the left, the setting sun was squeezing out increasingly intense streaks of orange and violent magentas between masses of storm clouds. The orange increased to liquid fire against the halloween black of the clouds. For miles and miles the entire sky was afire, blazoned with long broad simmerings of orange. The browns and greens of the earth cowed to purple beneath the fierce sky. Finally, the pulsating color eased and merged slowly into the blackness of the clouds. Scared, Jeanne held Jesse's small hand in hers, stroking its softness. Headlights on, they continued northward.

"You should go back to your husband, Jeanne," her mother

warned her ominously before leaving. "And what about Paul? You're on welfare, living with strangers — why, the courts will just take Jesse away from you, too."

"Mother! Don't even say such a thing!" Jeanne gasped, quaking inside. "And I don't know what to do about Paul."

"Well, the court will give them to Franco and they're right. You should go back with your husband."

But Jesse grew and blossomed into his second year and Jeanne into her thirty-first. She sucked in the California winter sunshine, so free of the haunting mistiness of northern Italian winters and the soggy length of the six-month winters in Rochester. In Berkeley she could breathe.

The sun reflected off the glaring Bay and heated her face as she walked down the sloping streets from the bus. She walked into the marbled quiet of the Bank of America office on Shattuck Avenue and opened a checking account in her own name. She then stopped at the optician's and left sporting thin lavender frames.

Meanwhile her eyes sought out every child of Paul's age or appearance and a particular taste gathered in her mouth with the longing to see him there, moving in the same warmth and mobility. Her stomach closed on the thought of him embedded in the cold of a Ravenna winter, his father working in nearby Bologna, gone until late six days a week, his mother not coming, an ocean and continent apart.

In the spring, Jeanne and Jesse moved by the same process into a brown shingle house with another single mother and her daughter. In back was a large garden, six chickens and a stubborn goat named Sam.

The mild winter had passed and May quickly arrived. Somehow an entire year had passed since they had boarded planes in opposite directions in Rochester. Then she received a letter from Franco — he was returning to the States to see her and Jesse. She panicked inside.

"Com'on, Mom," Jesse urged, pushing her shoulder with both hands, sending rocking waves knocking back and forth under the letter that lay beside her on the waterbed.

"It's time to milk Sam," he insisted. His blond hair tumbled around his tanned cheeks. Now a veteran of daycare and pushing three, he stood looking at her in his overalls and curls and with a farmer's concern with the gathering dusk.

"Hm? Yeah, okay. You're right." Jeanne rose slowly and elephant-like off the sloshing waterbed that had come with the room. She looked west out the window over the garden at the sliver of shimmering bay in the distance. Jesse persistently pulled on her arm.

"Okay, okay, Jesse. Let's go," she said with a lingering heaviness. "Here," she grabbed a coffee tin as they went through the dim kitchen. "Take this to gather the eggs."

His hand still in hers, they wound down the back stairs. At the gate, she balanced the steaming pan of disinfectant in her left hand and pushed the metal clasp down on the lock, yanking the chain away. Jesse dragged the cyclone gate open and strode immediately into the chicken pen. Six hens squawked and scattered in bedlam to top rungs.

"Look out!" Jesse boomed. "Gotta get the eggs."

"Jesse, you crack me up," his mother chuckled, relatching the gate. "Okay, Sam, you look like you're about to burst. Jesse was right. We are a bit late tonight." The bony Nubian stood stiff-legged in the long shadows, unimpressed with her excuses. "Come here," she coaxed, looping the short yellow rope down over her long, silken floppy ears and around her braced and stubborn neck. "Com'on Sam. Move over."

Pushing into the goat's bony black hip with her shoulder, she bent down and reached in the pan of steaming water for the sterile rag. Keeping her weight into her, she eased down on one knee and swathed her two bulging grey udders. She stomped.

"Com'on, Sam," she talked to her, aligning the bucket and beginning the rhythmic squeezing of her hot udders. *Tzit, tzit,* the milk hit the bucket in a hard, narrow jet. She stomped again. "Com'on, Sam, be good."

Jeanne loved sitting on the fine brown ground each night, bound to this evening chore. The warm rhythm of the milking was soothing after a day of housekeeping jobs or daycare, soothing like meditation.

Seated and settled into the milking rhythm, Franco flushed into her head again. Her ears could hear his voice on the phone, the difficult phone calls to Italy the first months after they moved to Berkeley.

"Jeanne! When are you coming?" his voice cracked through the ocean cable.

"I don't know, Franco. I don't know. Listen, I'm in Berkeley. I can't come to Italy. Not right now."

"What do you mean, you're in Berkeley! Did you leave your sister's?"

"Didn't you get my letter?" she realized with exasperation.

"No!"

"Damn *la posta,*" she swore. "I wrote you, two weeks ago. I just couldn't come back right now and I found a place—for a month or two."

Silence. "I told you in Rochester, I can't go back to that life. I'll go crazy. You know that. But listen, how's Paul?" her voice cracked.

"What the devil am I supposed to tell him?" he shot back in an undertone. "Here, he's right here—you talk to him."

"Mamma?" came a young child's voice across the line.

"Paul, Paul, Paul," her body wracked, "how are you?"

"*Bene,*" he responded politely in Italian. "Mamma, when are you coming?" he asked quietly. Her stomach contracted.

"I don't know, Paul, I don't know. I'm going to stay here a little while longer. It's so hard to explain. I just can't come back right now. I—I wouldn't be happy." How thin the words sounded. At a loss, she continued. "But I love you, remember that. I miss you. Are you still going to the beach?"

"*Sì, con papà.*"

"Good," she replied softly. "Listen, Paul, this costs so much and I don't have much money. Let me talk to your father again. Would you write me?" *He's only six years old.* She struggled on. "Please, let me talk to your father. I love you."

And subsequent calls.

"Why, why won't you come back?"

She shook her head no.

"My headaches are gone, Franco."

"But you can have a maid. You can go to the University of Bologna in Art History."

"Franco, I hate Paul being there. And you're not teaching and not happy either. Come back, bring Paul back. We could have our

separate places and the kids could go back and forth, in the same
neighborhood..."

"But WHY?"

"Franco, I'm... gay."

The wire buzzed silent in her ear. "I'm... lesbian," she announced weakly.

"Well," he said slowly, his voice flattened to a lower register and
now without resistance, "if that's so, there is nothing I can say."

"I think it's true," she said softly, as if to an old friend. "It wasn't
just Judy — I don't even see Judy," she added wryly. "I think it's
who I am, who I've always been."

Sam kicked the side of the bucket.

"Look out!" she snapped at Jesse, jolted back to earth.

"Walk real slow around Sam, Jesse," she warned grumpily.
Jesse edged in behind her in the dusk and leaned against her back.
He drummed his stubby fingers gently on her shoulder as she
milked.

"Did you get the eggs?"

"Yep."

"Good boy," she turned her face and kissed his dusty hand.
"You are a good farmer, a natural farmer, that's what you are."

A pleased humpf came in reply. Her spirit regathered into her
body.

"Well, that's about it," she decided, running her fingers down
the flat grey udders. "Good girl, Sam," she coached, deftly grabbing the foaming pail out of the way of her impatient hooves. "Jesse,
you put out some straw for her and I'll check their water."

The sunset had dried to black by the time they climbed to his
upstairs room for his bedtime ritual. A time to lay down side by
side, to joke and scramble words and read fables — in short, the
closest time of the day.

"Jesse," she began with some weariness as she closed the cover
on yet another reading of *The Hungry Caterpillar*. "Do you remember
your daddy?"

"Daddy?"

"Yeah, your dad, your father."

"I don't know," Jesse answered vaguely.

"Well," she continued, "You *do* have a father *and* a big brother,

Paul. You know, we've talked about Paul..." she urged, glancing over to his head beside hers on the pillow. *Well, not very often, I guess,* she had to admit. *God, this is awful.* "Well, anyway we got a letter from your father and he's going to come here. He wants to visit you and me." She looked over at his face beside her.

"Yeah?" he offered quizzically. His eyes darted over to read his mother's face. Neither of them had much of anything to say.

"Jesse?"

"What?"

"You know something?"

"What?"

"I love you!" she growled into his neck. The un-understood heaviness dispelled. He gurgled and tossed his yellow pajama-ed arms around her neck and squeezed her with startling strength. "I love you too, Mommie."

"Thanks, Jessie. I love you."

"I love you," they reiterated lazily.

Worried, she soaked up the warmth of the yellow pajama hug.

"Let's turn off the lights and see if we can see any stars out your window. You need to get to sleep," she recommended, pressing the tip of his tanned, upturned nose. "You know, tomorrow is (click) another day."

3

In June, Franco came for a visit, leaving Paul with his parents in Italy. He stayed with Jeanne, in her room. They made love deftly, quickly, in a way that was wiser, somehow more worldly, and accomplished than their eight years of marital love-making. She feared his arrival. She feared the years of love she had with him. She feared the power of desire for reconciliation. She feared the power of the loss, guilt and remorse she felt about Paul. She feared walking back into a cage she'd left. She braced herself for his visit with steel bindings around her heart and a resolve to stay free.

On the third night of his return she noted the seeping warmth of his arms, the familiarity of the silken black hairs curling high on his chest. She felt her fatigue. She felt how hard it was to struggle alone, independent, among constantly challenged values and lifestyles, second-hand clothes and cleaning people's houses, slow buses and incompatible roommates, her family's silent condemnation of her struggle. She feared this intimacy, his easy answers, his boredom, his laziness, his subtle guilt-tripping, his laying on the couch, his having lied to Paul that he'd only be gone from Italy—had sworn he'd only be gone—"eleven days, papà, eleven days, promise?"

The next afternoon she made love with a forlorn woman she had spoken to and helped a few weeks before. That evening she made love with Natalie, her lover since September. She made love on purpose and with a certain desperation, to block out that intimacy with him, to cling to her own, hoping that the tides of nostalgia she was feeling would not tear her away from the moorings of her hard-won self.

In a few days Franco left to visit Jeanne's family in Los Altos. His reception there was warm and sympathetic, particularly on the part of Jeanne's father. He secured a part-time teaching position at a Catholic seminary in Mountain View. In August, friends were travelling to Italy. They would bring Paul back with them.

BOOK TWO

CHAPTER FOUR

Now Entering Oakland

OAKLAND, CALIFORNIA
NOVEMBER 1976

Only a sign separates Berkeley from North Oakland. The streets of pastel wood frame houses continue on either side of the line without much difference. The differences are in the neighborhoods and Jeanne had moved to a predominantly black one.

Jeanne cast her eye up and down the North Oakland street. A half block east was San Pablo, a busy street paralleling the Bay, a six-lane artery of storefronts, second hand shops and liquor stores. Yet it did not disrupt the almost sleepy residential quiet of 55th Street where she now lived with her lover, Shana, and Shana's four children. The houses were well painted and maintained but you rarely saw who lived there or maintained them.

Jeanne turned and looked up at the tall wood frame house behind her. Her exchange with Franco in front of the house was still reverberating in her ears.

"I'm going to see my lawyer!" he had bellowed at her over the roof of his car.

"What?! Franco!" Jeanne shouted. "Jesse, go in the house," she ordered.

"If you are going to live... with THAT woman... in THIS neighborhood..." He dropped down into the seat of his car and slammed the door without finishing. He scraped the ignition on and screeched out of sight around the corner. Momentarily torn, the quiet of the neighborhood closed back in.

A lawyer...that woman...this neighborhood. Jeanne looked up at the affordable old two-story behind her. She tried to imagine what it looked like to her husband, her parents, potentially in court. The old house seemed to bulge out over its cement foundation like a stuffed bag. Parched remnants of marigolds drooped in the wooden flower boxes on the front porch. Except for the bay windows on the far left, the front of the house was all siding and oddly windowless. Only one small rectangular stained glass window had been placed high under the eaves of the first floor.

Jeanne's eye scanned to the large windows in the peak of the second story. Four tow-headed children between the ages of one and six — Jesse included — had spotted her on the lawn below. They rushed to the window, boisterously beckoning her. A bit stiffly, she waved back at them.

A blond haired girl and a tall, sturdy woman with short brown hair sat on the porch with their arms around each other, watching Jeanne closely.

Shana, a young mother of four, tapped her blond square-toed boot impatiently. She hugged the cotton shirt that covered long breasts that had fed a steady succession of four children. Although her own divorce was not yet finalized, her concerns about custody were behind her. Her husband, also gay, was a frequent and welcomed visitor at the house. Since their separation, Shana, now twenty-eight, had managed to keep a step ahead of the demands of raising four young children alone. Her style of parenting was emotional, direct and authoritarian. She was at times totally harrassed, at times totally ingenious. The kids had to depend on themselves a lot, and on Hannah, the eldest, in particular. The laundry generated by four children was at times left until it reached staggering proportions. And there was frequently a feast or famine swing to their fortunes.

But the kids did not seem to mind because life with mom was life with mom. And life with mom, while crazy at times, also abounded with laughs, adventure, and great Jewish warmth and tradition. Generous hugs and loud kisses were regularly showered on the heads of all.

Jeanne met them and within weeks had fallen in love with mother and children alike. They merged their households and rented the five-bedroom house on 55th Street for $350 a month. The result was a new concoction of five children and two rather recent lesbians. It was chaotic. And it was exciting.

The word feminism was never really used. But once learned, the words sexist, racist and ageist cropped up a lot. There was genuine excitement in the household as both mothers expanded and re-thought who they were as women plus considered how to build a family headed by two lesbian mothers. Family pictures from three generations on both sides went up in the hallway and, laughing, Shana framed them with a banner from the women's bookstore that proclaimed THE REVOLUTION BEGINS AT HOME. For Hannah, the only girl, it meant sharing directly in this new burst of vision of themselves as women, complete, whole and free. For the boys, it meant having two mothers shielding and redefining the onslaught of conditioning directed at them as boys.

Shana's brood unanimously loved and welcomed Jeanne and Jesse into their midst. Then on weekends, they met Paul. Hand-some, slightly stiff, a few months Hannah's junior, Paul caused some controversy. While loved as well, he brought a burst of Bruce Lee and aggression into the household. While Hannah and Aaron, age six, played and bluntly confronted him, the forty-eight hours of a weekend visit were never enough for him to find another pace.

On the outside, what did their life look like? Jeanne had seen in a flash that it didn't look good. It looked unorthodox (possibly radical), poor and low class. She herself struggled violently with her own values through it all. When they went into second-hand stores of children's clothes, the elegance of Italian lace port-enfants and tailored Italian clothes haunted her. Nuncio and Anna regularly mailed Franco supplies of fine new clothes and hundred dollar bills but to Jeanne and Jesse came nothing. Jeanne knew the rate at which five children broke in, wore out and outgrew pants, shirts, socks and shoes. She knew that, for a dollar or two, the clothes in the second hand store were clean, sanitary and often practically new.

But still it was hard. Shana often had little patience for the wrack-ing battles that erupted inside Jeanne. Nonetheless, regardless of the direction of their arguments, with five children, simple finan-cial reality always settled the matter in favor of thrift.

All this was too much for Franco. And for Jeanne's family as well. For the latter, it was alarm at seeing their daughter clearly leave the beaten track. For Franco, it was still also a question of love and his own dislocation, and it hurt. The openness of her lesbian life and his instant dislike of Shana snapped the last threads of understanding between them.

1

The woman behind the broad desk in the simple law office look-ed at her two new clients. Shana sucked on a cigarette, green cor-duroy slacks pulling tight around her thighs and calves. Jeanne sat thin and serious in the chair beside her, also smoking. A tiny, oval pin with the word ''dyke'' was clipped to the lapel of her faded jean waistcoat. Equally faded jeans hung loosely around her long legs.

Jeanne had frozen behind the wheel of the car before coming in.

''I can't, I just can't,'' she 'd whispered hoarsely to Shana.

''Jeanne, get ahold of yourself. You heard what he said. He's going to a lawyer.''

The woman lawyer placed a fresh yellow legal pad in front of her and began.

''You have two children?''

''Yes,'' Jeanne replied, clearing her throat. *I want you to come back and live with me,* she remembered telling Paul on his last weekend visit. The last year of separation seemed to melt away in one burst of light from his face at her words. He fell forward into her arms.

''You and I just got separated,'' she apologized with long held-in feeling. Her words spread like a salve of reassurance and equi-ty. ''Your dad and I just can't seem to work it out,'' she continued regrettably, speaking into the mass of his thick hair against her cheek. ''It looks like we're going to have to talk to a judge. I'd love for you to live with me and you could live with your dad during the summers...''

His little body jolted slightly realizing the choice with which he would be confronted.

· ''I—I'm lesbian,'' Jeanne explained with some difficulty to the feminist lawyer seated in front of her. The lawyer smiled slightly and nodded towards Jeanne's lapel.

''Oh, yes,'' Jeanne conceded. ''Well, what is it like in court as a lesbian? What are my chances?''

''Will your husband use that?''

''I'm afraid so.''

''Well, this is the Bay Area. I'd say a judge — depending on which judge we get — probably would not change custody of... Jesse, is it? He's always been with you, right? And you'll probably have a 50-50 chance of getting your oldest son back. Judges like to keep kids together.''

She counselled Jeanne and Shana to keep Paul on his next weekend visit, file for divorce and custody of both boys, and, when the time came, ''dress for court''.

Children ran along the cement walkway outside of sprawling two-story apartment complexes in Mountain View. Inside No. 207, dishes, an espresso pot and demi-tasses sat unwashed in the sink. A soprano soared into an aria on the small Sony TV set at full volume. Franco reached into the pile of Sunday laundry on the couch. Distractedly folding, he thought, *Jeanne is always late bringing Paul back, but then she was never on time when we were married either.*

The doorbell chimed. He twisted out his cigarette in the green glass ashtray, a wedding present. Jeanne came in with Shana a few steps behind. Franco bristled. Shana laid some papers on the kitchen table. Franco turned his back and asked over his shoulder, ''Where's Paul? Did he stop to play outside?'' He lowered the volume on the opera.

''No, Franco. Listen, I want Paul to come back and live with me. I don't know if your lawyer has filed papers yet but I have. Paul's staying with me — until the preliminary hearing...''

The blood drained suddenly from his face at her words. Jeanne clutched her keys and her eyes grew large, not leaving his face. Paul's absence in the small apartment seemed to roar around his ears. He stood ashen and shaking.

''You bloody cunt!'' he screamed and shoved them both out the front door.

Monday morning Franco stood in his good Italian suit in front of Judge Minder in a courtroom in Oakland. Mr. Armin Horowitz, his counsel, shrilly informed the judge that the mother is a lesbian, living with her lover and her lover's four children in a black neighborhood. The sympathies of Judge Minder, a conservative Republican, appointed to the bench by then-Governor Ronald Reagan, changed decisively. The temporary change in custody of Paul to his mother was reversed.

Within an hour, Franco and Mr. Horowitz were standing on the front porch of Jeanne's house, papers in hand. Seeing Franco, Paul bounded down the steps, two at a time, and fell forward into his father's arms as he had tumbled into the arms of his mother the week before.

2

On the day of the preliminary hearing, two friends arrived at the house on 55th Street to stay with the children. Inside, hopes were high amongst the children that Paul would come live with them. Jeanne cooked two fried eggs and managed to keep them down. She studied herself in the antique beveled mirror in the living room. *These clothes look out-of-date*, she worried and glanced over at Shana. Seated on the arm of the green brocade couch in a black pants suit, Shana was drawing in great draughts of her menthol cigarette and exhaling last minute instructions to the two oldest children.

"Aaron, pay attention." The six year-old's cheeks twitched uncontrollably with the urge to laugh.

"Aa-ron," Hannah elbowed him sisterly, "this is serious. They're going to court." She turned a wayward strand of long, blond hair behind her ear.

"I-ee know, Hannah," Aaron sing-songed. He crossed his slim arms and then slipped two fingers of his left hand into his mouth to plug the giggle.

"Now, we won't be gone more than an hour, two at the most. We're going to talk to the judge about maybe Paul coming back to live with his mother, to live with all of us."

"Yippie!" Aaron slurred softly through his fingers.

"Yeah, you'd like that, wouldn't you, Aaron," nodded Shana to Paul's devoted friend. "Well," she ended, slapping her knees and rising to her feet, "we've got to..."

"Mommie! Jeanne!" Long-haired Dov clammered down the stairs and into the living room.

"Mommie! Mommie!" mimicked three year-old Jesse right behind him, tumbling on tip-toe towards Jeanne. Dov threw himself dishevelled around Shana's leg.

"Dov!" she scolded, "Look out, you'll get my one court outfit dirty."

"But, Mommie," Dov pleaded, slowly peeling himself off her leg, "can Jesse and I have some yoguht?" Dov rarely pronounced an 'r'.

"Yes, yes," she agreed impatiently. "But com'on, Jeanne. It's almost 1:30. Can't keep the boys waiting."

"Yeah," Jeanne concurred nervously. She reached down and squeezed Jesse's plump, corduroyed thighs in the palms of her hands. She planted a loud kiss on the top of his curly head and straightened up.

Her lawyer told her it should take about twenty minutes.

3

ALAMEDA COUNTY COURTHOUSE
FEBRUARY 4, 1977

DEPARTMENT 15, THIRD FLOOR, Jeanne read, setting foot inside a courthouse for the first time ever. Memories in black and white, Perry Mason on late Fifties TV.

When the elevator doors parted on the third floor, Jeanne immediately saw her father down the cool marble hallway. *Dad?* The tactile familiarity of his fine camel sportscoat lurched across the distance between them. Shana nudged Jeanne forward out of the elevator. The doors swooshed shut behind them.

Men lawyers in three-piece suits and briefcases walked in and out of Department 15, a tall, cavernous room. One woman lawyer came and went. The judge's chair sat empty behind a high, paneled desk. The bailiff looked bored and not too intelligent, the judge's clerk vaguely curious.

"REMAIN SEATED. COURT IS NOW IN SESSION. Judge Gordon Minder presiding."

Out from the chambers came a short man in pleated black robes. His smooth white face was framed with neatly trimmed grey hair.

With only brief glances out into the courtroom, he sat and quickly dispensed with two or three cases. Then Jeanne's lawyer motioned her to join her at the long table. The red-haired clerk handed the judge the folder for the case:

"CASE OF BENELLI," Judge Minder announced.

"Excuse me, Your Honor," Jeanne's lawyer began politely. "I believe that Ms. Jullion is the Petitioner in this matter and therefore the case would be called by her name — JULLION."

"She's still married, isn't she?" the judge asked, cooly.

"Yes, but she has taken back her maiden name for some time now."

"Well, the case will be called by Mr. Benelli." The judge nodded towards her husband's end of the bench. "CASE OF BENELLI," he reiterated. "Call your first witness, counsel," Judge Minder motioned to Jeanne's lawyer.

"I call the Petitioner—Ms. Jeanne Jullion."

Oh god. As Jeanne stepped forward and turned to be sworn in, her father's face came into view towards the back of the courtroom. In the hall outside, he had said hello, then turned to whisper with Franco. She wished she could draw comfort from the fact that he was there, but a static of confused emotions rippled through her instead. She shut it out.

"Do you swear to tell the truth, the whole truth and nothing but the truth, so help you god?"

My god, do they really say this? A giddiness swept through that reminded her of Aaron. "I do."

"State and spell your name and take a seat next to His Honor."

Jeanne's lawyer, a large-boned, articulate woman in a herringbone tweed jacket, commenced.

LAWYER: Now, Ms. Jullion, please tell the court — how many children do you have?

JULLION: Two — Paul who is eight and Jesse will be four in June.

LAWYER: Do you love your children?

JULLION: Yes, very much.

Warmth coated her at the thought of them, melting the pale rigidity of her face. She felt a little better. Step by step, her lawyer led her through a synopsis of the situation, her separation from Paul and her parenting of Jesse.

·LAWYER: I have no further questions, your Honor.

JUDGE: Mr. Horowitz?

Jeanne instinctively hated Mr. Horowitz from the beginning. He looked like he'd stepped out of a cartoon to meddle tirelessly in her life. Jeanne's lawyer shook her head with a slow, wry smile when she told her who her husband had retained. She explained that he was intelligent and unscrupulous, dressed unswervingly in drooping suits and bow ties and aimed mainly at unnerving the witness. He was known as a master of the needle.

Adjusting his horn-rimmed glasses with two fingers, Mr. Horowitz appeared to savor the initiation of his new case. With a loud, aggressive voice, he began.

HOROWITZ: Where do you currently reside, Miss Jullion?

JULLION: At 1153-55th Street in Oakland.

HOROWITZ: And who else resides at that address?

JULLION: I live there with my son, Jesse.

HOROWITZ: And who else lives there?

JULLION: Shana Ascher and her four children — Hannah, ten; Aaron, five; Dov, four; and Reuben who is one-and-a-half.

Judge Minder slowly turned towards the witness in his high-backed swivel chair. Mr. Horowitz raised his voice dramatically and virtually shot the next question at the witness.

HOROWITZ: Is it true you're a lesbian?

JULLION: Yes.

HOROWITZ: I see. Are you currently in a sexual relationship with Miss Ascher?

JULLION: Yes, I am.

HOROWITZ: And where do you sleep?

JULLION: Pardon me?

HOROWITZ: Where do you sleep in your residence on 55th Street?

JULLION: I sleep in the bedroom downstairs. The children all sleep in the three bedrooms upstairs.

HOROWTIZ: And where does Miss Ascher sleep?

Jeanne glanced over at the judge. Her eyes bounced off his thinly drawn lips and she turned towards her lawyer, bracing at this line of questioning.

LAWYER: Your Honor, I don't see what this has to do with the custody of the children.

JUDGE: State your objection, counsel.

LAWYER: Irrelevancy, Your Honor.

JUDGE: Objection overruled. You may answer.

Must answer, you mean. Mr. Horowitz was gathering something from his bulging briefcase on the table as Jeanne answered.

HOROWITZ: Now, Miss Jullion — oh, by the way, Miss Jullion, you are still married, aren't you?

JULLION: Yes, legally I'm still married.

HOROWITZ: And what name is 'Jullion'?

JULLION: It's my maiden name.

HOROWITZ: Did you just *decide* to change your name?

JULLION: Yes, I did. When my son and I moved to Berkeley and I knew that I was not going back with my husband, I took my maiden name back.

HOROWITZ: Did you tell your husband you were changing your name?

JULLION: I don't remember. I may have written him. He was in Italy...

HOROWITZ: Did you *ask* your husband if you could change your name?

A muscle contracted in her stomach. She replied measuredly, "No, I did not ask him."

"I see," Mr. Horowitz stepped towards her. She could see that he had photographs in his hand.

"Excuse me, counsel," he remarked, stopping behind Jeanne's lawyer. "Perhaps you'd like to see these before I question your client."

As the photographs passed from one hand to another, Jeanne sought out Shana's eyes in the back row of the courtroom. Their lawyer had strongly objected to her being present in court. She feared that seeing them together would concretize the label of lesbian in the judge's mind, fuel fantasies, possibly threaten. Yet Shana insisted she could be present inobtrusively and Jeanne had agreed.

Mr. Horowitz strode toward her, arm outstretched and demanded. "Do you recognize the house in these pictures?"

Stunned, Jeanne took the photographs being held towards her and murmured after a glance, "Yes, I do."

There were about ten snapshots, several out of focus as if taken hurriedly, perhaps from a car. Blurred pictures of Shana, Jeanne and the children leaving the large, bulging white house, a torrent of children coming down the front wooden steps, a shot of the North Oakland neighborhood highlighting the House of Joy Club around the corner from San Pablo Avenue. Jeanne shot Franco a full look in the face for the first time in the preceedings. She then glanced up at the round, bold-faced clock on the wall. *I thought this was supposed to last twenty minutes...*

Mr. Horowitz lingered over the pictures before entering them into evidence.

"And what is this one — your front door?" he resumed.

"Yes," Jeanne mumbled. A life-sized red, white and blue poster of Wonder Woman covered the beveled front door window. *This is ridiculous,* Jeanne thought to herself, *yet the stakes are so high — Paul.*

HOROWITZ: And what is on the front door?

JULLION: It's a poster of Wonder Woman.

JUDGE: Can I see that, please?

HOROWITZ: And what does this say above the door?

JULLION: Uppity woman unite.

Jeanne's lawyer shook her head slightly and slowly clipped the lid back on her pen. She had come to the house to discuss the preliminary hearing earlier that week. She was accompanied by their witness, Dr. Wroblewski, a child psychologist. She had stood wide-legged and perused the hall wall, covered by three generations of Jeanne and Shana's family pictures, framed on top by a sign reading, THE REVOLUTION BEGINS AT HOME. She then said that while *she* understood, no judge would like children being exposed to such strong, feminist ideology.

"You really should consider taking your posters down. They could be damaging in court..."

After the February hearing, Shana did roll up and retire Wonder Woman. She covered the front door with paintings from all the children and a sign lettered: Welcome To The Home of Shana, Jeanne, Hannah, Aaron, Dov, Jesse and Reuben. Inside the hall, Jeanne reluctantly moistened and removed the banner over the family pictures.

A crackling of angry looks rippled between Jeanne and Franco at Mr. Horowitz's next, indefatigable line of questioning. Judge Minder stirred and made a note: welfare recipient. All the stigma that that entails hung in the room like sulfur. *No use even looking towards my father.* Jeanne permitted herself another quick glance towards Shana in the back row, like a sip of water.

"And is Miss Ascher also on welfare?"

"Yes, she is. However, we are trying to get the money together to start a small business." Curious, half-amused looks spontaneously sprung to the faces of the men in the room. "My... Shana used to have a janitorial service and an antique shop named the Wizard of Odds in New Jersey. We are trying to start a janitorial service here of the same name. We have the business license."

"The Wizard of Odds?" Mr. Horowitz sneered.

"Yes," Jeanne rejoined coldly.

"And who could work at these jobs — you and Miss Ascher?"

"That's correct."

"And who would stay with the children?"

"We would take turns."

"Tell me, Miss Jullion," Mr. Horowitz's voice rose ominously, "do you ever leave your children without a babysitter?"

"No," Jeanne lied, her heart skipping. Unable to afford babysitters, they had advertised for a live-in sitter for the small bedroom off the dining room. Neither of two live-in sitters had lasted more than two weeks, each retreating with mumbled excuses, overwhelmed by the demands of five children. In case of need, Hannah had sometimes been left in charge.

"Is it true that on the evening of February 1st you and Miss Ascher left the home at 5:10 p.m.?" Horowitz bore down as if to close a trap.

"I don't know," Jeanne replied incredulously. "Perhaps..." Her memory scrambled to catch up. February 1st, three days ago, Friday evening, Dr. Wroblewski's office, the psychological evaluations of Jesse and Paul. As co-parents of all the children, Jeanne and Shana had been scheduled to be interviewed together for court.

"Who stayed with the children?" Mr. Horowitz demanded.

"A babysitter," Jeanne lied again. *You're the world's worst liar,* her head taunted her but the urgency of the situation smothered that voice. But on its heels was another voice — *Why aren't we talking about Paul, wasn't it a change in custody for Paul that was in question?* It hadn't even come to the fore as an issue. With a warm gush the realization swam in around her that her husband and his laywer were out to prove her and her circumstances generally unfit. *That means Jesse!* A cold wave of fear washed through her long body, bolting it upright in the blue, swivel chair. She quickly looked at the three men, now aware of the scope of what was happening.

HOROWITZ: And if I were to tell you that a private investigator saw you and Miss Ascher leave and no one enter the house, would you still tell the court that the children, including Jesse Benelli, were left in the care of a babysitter?

JULLION: Yes, he must have missed her.

HOROWITZ: The investigator knocked at the door and no one answered. Could you explain that, please?

JULLION: We often tell the sitter not to answer the door when we leave.

It was a stand-off. He moved on.
From there, Mr. Horowitz had her name one by one the places

where they had lived since leaving Rochester, New York. He began with Jeanne's sister, Carol — the only roommate he did not question as to whether she was lesbian and insinuate that they were having a sexual relationship.

HOROWITZ: By the way, you share the same bed with Miss Ascher, is that correct?

LAWYER: Your Honor, I object to this line of questioning on the grounds that it is irrelevant to the welfare of the children.

JUDGE: Oh, I think the witness may answer. Objection overruled. You may proceed.

HOROWITZ: Tell me, do the children ever come into the bedroom when you and Miss Ascher are in bed?

What I should say, she thought, *of course, they come into our bedroom just like your kids come into yours, they come in and do weird unnatural things like jump on the bed, beg to be tickled or kissed, cuddle when they're upset, hurt or sick.* Jeanne answered the question slowly. Her head felt as if underwater, compressed by the necessity to lie.

JULLION: No, they generally do not come into our room. They are all told to knock and can come in only by permission.

HOROWITZ: Do you ever have sexual activity in front of the children?

In anger, Jeanne jammed the swivel chair to the left. Her lawyer scraped her chair back and quickly intervened.

LAWYER: Your Honor, I object on the grounds of irrelevancy and invasion of privacy.

JUDGE: I think she may answer — objection overruled. Answer the question.

JULLION: No, I do not.

HOROWITZ: Do you ever express physical affection in front of the children?

JULLION: Only hugging, maybe a kiss — on the cheek.

HOROWITZ: By the way, Miss Jullion, who takes care of the

business in your — 'family'?

JULLION: We share the work and chores just like we share the raising of the children.

HOROWITZ: Uh. I see...

Mr. Horowitz criss-crossed back and forth over the past two years of Jeanne's life, snagging whatever he could. Gradually Jeanne was worn down. Scared and shaken, she was numbly, mechanically answering questions when Horowitz at last said he had no further questions.

Jeanne straightened her legs stiffly and looked over to the judge for permission to get down. He startled her by beginning to question her directly.

"Tell me, Miss— Jullion, what is more important to you — your relationship with Mrs. Ascher or your children?"

The question stunned her. And she knew exactly what he was talking about: conditional custody — you can have your children if you do not live in a relationship. Shana and Jeanne had discussed it at length with their lawyer and between themselves.

JULLION: Excuse me?

JUDGE: What is more important to you — your relationship with Mrs. Ascher or your children? Which would you choose?

JULLION: I don't think I should have to choose between my children and my home.

JUDGE: Answer the question. Which is more important to you?

JULLION: Nothing is as important to me as my children.

JUDGE: You may step down.

Judge Minder swung away from the witness in his high-backed chair and called a recess after two hours of testimony.

When the proceedings resumed, the psychologist, Dr. Wroblewski took the stand as an expert witness. Due to the fact that he was employed less than full time, Mr. Horowitz succeeded in having him disqualified as an expert witness. He was thus not allowed to give any professional conclusions or recommendations. Despite Mr. Horowitz's harassment and protestations that everything Dr. Wroblewski was about to say was a professional conclusion which he was not qualified to give, the thin, kindly psychologist did manage to summarize his testing of the two boys.

Paul: intelligent, showed love of both mother and father, when asked to tell what was happening in cloudy pictures, he told stories marked by fear and considerable violence; he systematically changed figures usually identified as female to male, he appeared to overidentify with the male role and had an exaggerated loyalty towards his father.

Jesse: highly intelligent and well co-ordinated; at age three he tested consistently at five and six year-old levels; strong bond to his mother yet very independent and without anxiety when interviewed alone.

HOROWITZ: Are you gay, Dr. Wroblewski?

DOCTOR: No, I'm not.

HOROWITZ: Do you have gay friends?

DOCTOR: Uh, well, yes, I know some people who are gay...

Mr. Horowitz seemed to smile slightly as he reached into the bulging labyrinth of his briefcase. Jeanne's attention had wandered and she started as she realized he was standing behind her at the table.

"Perhaps your client would like to read this first," he said to Jeanne's lawyer, dropping two pages on the table between them.

Jeanne picked up the affidavit, and began sorting through the 'legalese'. Her mother and father's names jumped off the page at her: recommend that the care and custody of the minor children, Jesse Benelli and Paul Benelli be given to the father...

She turned the page, skipping through the last sentences. She saw their signatures, their handwriting, the shapes of the letters of their names, familiar to her since childhood. Her eyes stared stock still at her mother's name — *there must be some mistake, no mistake, unmistakable script...*

Mr. Horowitz reached over Jeanne's shoulder and took the document out of her hand with an almost slight embarrassment. Jeanne no longer edited out her father's presence in the courtroom. She slowly turned all the way around in her chair and looked straight into the face of her father in the back row and he squirmed in his chair. *What? Look me in the face, Dad, what are you doing, Dad, and why did you and Mom do this?* She wanted to scream but turned measuredly back around, barely breathing, eyes staring through objects in front of her.

Dr. Wroblewski was soon excused. Mr. Horowitz opened and closed his case by briefly calling Jeanne's husband to the stand. Then it was over.

That is, direct testimony was over. Judge Minder continued to question Jeanne from the bench. She sat in a silence he took to mean admission of guilt, guilt primarily to being on welfare. He ordered her to be off welfare by the next hearing which he set for three months hence — Friday the 13th of May.

Reiterating for a second time that what these kids need is a "normal" home, he appeared frighteningly close to changing custody on the spot. Instead he ordered a home evaluation and custody recommendation by an officer of the Probation Department, a routine procedure, and proceeded to set up a weekend and Easter vistitation schedule. Jeanne and Franco disagreed about who got which weekend and the judge lost his temper, warning her that if he wanted to he could order that Jeanne's lover not be in her own home when Paul visited. *Okay, I see your power, judge, set up the visitation any way you want.*

THE NEXT HEARING IS SET FOR MAY 13th. COURT IS ADJOURNED.

Shana, Jeanne, Dr. Wroblewski and their lawyer moved wordlessly into the vacant elevator from the third floor. Jeanne's father clustered with her husband and his lawyer in the hall. When the doors swooshed closed, Jeanne's chest began to heave. Tears streamed down her face. She stood tense and brittle, feeling like she would break if she moved. A painful silence enveloped the closed space. Dr. Wroblewski said he was sorry…

Outside, Shana and Jeanne spoke for a few minutes with their lawyer. Across the plaza, Jeanne watched her father come out of the glass courthouse doors, cross the street huddled close in step with Mr. Horowitz and Franco, his head bent, intent on catching every word.

It was almost 6:00 when they reached home. The children were hungry. The two women staying with the children took one look at their faces and didn't ask why they were so late.

CHAPTER FIVE

Courting Favor

The four poster bed consumed most of the space in Jeanne and Shana's downstairs bedroom. The stained glass window, sole adornment on the front of the house, spread the purple hues of its floral design high on the wall at the top of the bed. Shana stood at the foot of the bed, hand resting on the redwood post, watching in dismay at the toll the day's events in court were taking on her lover. She scooped her short brown hair across the side of her head in exasperation. Jeanne would not let Shana come near her or hold her. She raged across the broad, four-postered bed in fury and a fear, now real, of losing Jesse.

Finally, Shana exploded.

"Why don't you call and tell your parents what this means to you, what's happening, let them see—"

"You kidding?" Jeanne spat. "I feel hysterical," she croaked hoarsely. "One doesn't even raise one's voice in my family and there's no way—"

"Then scream! Maybe your mother will understand. At worse they'll stay where they are which is against you but at least you might feel better." With that she scooped up the phone and plopped it down in front of Jeanne.

Jeanne quieted some, taking long, heavy breaths in slowly. She stared at the blue phone on the crumpled quilt. Finally, in a low voice she asked Shana to get her address book for the number.

Jeanne dialed the white stucco and shingle condominium in Los Altos where her parents lived. Her mother answered and she heard her father lift the extension in the study.

"I just wanted to call you and talk to you both a minute." Jeanne began carefully. "I was in court all afternoon. I read what you wrote and I just don't understand how you could do that."

"Well, Jeanne," her mother answered sternly, "I told you when you moved to Berkeley that the courts would take away your kids."

The words that filled the car as they sat at the train station in August came back to Jeanne.

"They will, too, Jeanne. You being on welfare, living with strangers. Franco won't stand for that and he'll get both kids."

Silence hummed on the phone. Then Jeanne's voice started climbing as she spoke.

"It's bad enough, Mom and Dad. It's hard enough. How could you do this?" she pleaded into the receiver.

Her father jumped in, righteously. "Now, Jeanne, I don't think those kids *should* live with you, the way you're living — living with that woman, on welfare. I think he should have the kids!"

"STOP!" Jeanne screamed. "They are my *kids!* I love them! It was horrible, today, horrible. You can't take my kids away from me! I've lost Paul — you can't take Jesse, too!"

"Now, Jeanne, stop yelling at us." Her mother's familiar voice flooded and filled her head. "We didn't do anything. You've done it to yourself."

"Mom, you *did* do something today. You signed that affidavit. I *saw* your signatures."

"Come on, dear," Jeanne's father beckoned his wife through the extension with a pained voice, "we don't have to listen to this."

"Please, Mom and Dad, *please,* they're trying to take my kids away! Please," she begged.

Click.

That sound froze her for a second. Then a roar raked out of her throat as she slammed the dead receiver down. She beat the patchwork quilt with an arm and fist that felt like iron rather than bone and skin. The blue phone jumped. The receiver bounced off like a rag doll. Shana cursed. Suddenly Jeanne buried her face in the quilt, remembering the children upstairs, not wanting them to know what was going on — not yet, not today, not this way.

In the next few weeks, Jeanne tried to talk with her mother on several occasions without success. Jeanne had first told her parents that she was a lesbian in October when she and Shana decided to rent a house together. Jeanne decided to do so by inviting her mother up for lunch.

Nervously, she waited with Shana in the living room of the house in which she and Jesse were living. Hearing the Buick pull up outside, Jeanne looked through the long, beveled glass panels that bordered the door and nearly had a cardiac arrest — her father had spontaneously decided to accompany his wife.

Jeanne began babbling out loud to herself.

"I can't go through with this, I can't go through with this," pushing Shana backwards into the living room and clutching her arm. "I can't do this!"

"Calm down!"

The doorbell rang, twice. Jeanne returned to the entryway and opened the door. Heart in her mouth, she invited them in and introduced her parents to the unexpected second person standing behind her in the living room. Suddenly, it felt stiflingly warm in the sun-filled room.

She sat her parents down on the beige couch across from the oak fireplace. Looks indicated her parents were clearly beginning to wonder. Jeanne's father smoothed the soft down of his white hair back over his ear with his freckled hand and pulled the corner of his dark blue sports coat out from under the edge of his leg, waiting. An ever so slight smirk gathered on his face as he eyed the sturdy, smoking woman sitting beside his tall, curly-headed daughter on the sofa. His wife sat waiting beside him, her black purse still caught in the crook of her elbow.

"Well," Jeanne leaned forward on the couch, eyes darting over to Shana as she began, "uh, Mom and Dad, I — uh, I want to tell you something. I know I've moved several times this year but I'm going to move again. You see, uh—" a childlike giddiness made her feel lightheaded. "I — you see, I'm gay. A lesbian," she added in the back of her throat. "Guess I always have been, really. And — well, Shana and I love each other and we're going to get a house together. Shana has four children…"

Jeanne's voice trailed off at the sight of the blood leaving her father's face. He went pale as if he'd been run through with a sword. Her mother didn't blink an eye. She said flatly, "Well, I've known that for a long time, Jeanne."

"You have?" Jeanne gasped incredulously, flashing on the long process it had taken her to come to that realization herself.

"Yes, I knew that was going on with you and Judy back in high school."

"What?" Jeanne laughed in spite of herself and glanced over at Shana. "You're right that I loved Judy and always have but I didn't know that I was gay."

"Oh, Jeanne, and then there was Deenie... and that other girl, Mary Lou, in college."

"Mother!" Jeanne burst out laughing again. "I wish it were true!"

"Well, it is," her mother stated with Irish stubbornness.

"Mom! Look, it really doesn't matter, but I asked you up here today to be honest with you and I've told you about Shana and who I am. There's no reason for me to lie now if it really did happen. But I tell you — well, unfortunately, it never did!"

"Well, I know better," she replied, entrenched.

Jeanne ventured a look at her father — he and the couch looked like Mt. Rushmore.

"Hm. Well, maybe we should go to lunch."

The four of them stiffly ducked into the Buick and left for a seafood lunch at Spengler's, during which Jeanne's mother chatted openly with Shana and Jeanne's father sat rigid and silent. He broke his silence briefly to ask Shana what her education and family background were as if she were a prospective in-law and then again to order a second Manhattan although it was only noon.

Once done, Jeanne was not excessively dismayed by her parents' reaction. She had never expected open-armed jubilation. On the basis of the 'coming out' stories she had heard, and knowing her staunch, Catholic family, she had estimated in her own mind that it would probably take two years before they would begin to realize that she was still the same person, only happier. Unfortunately, within three short months the legal proceedings had begun and her parents not only took sides but took part.

1

Jeanne did not see her lawyer for over a month after the first hearing. Days came and went and at times she wondered if it had happened at all. She'd lie in bed with the day's first glow, listening to Jesse's voice upstairs, toys scraping across the floor. Then, remembering, her stomach would tense and she would roll into Shana's arms, bury her face in her long breasts and think gratefully that May and the next hearing still seemed far off.

Then one morning her lawyer called. She said the Probation Officer assigned to the case, Fred Spence, had contacted her. She understood he was new and she didn't know much about him. She added that in eight years of dealing with the Probation Department on home evaluations, it was the first time she had a man assigned to a case. Chance, perhaps... They had spoken on the phone and he seemed nice. She offered to send him some literature. He said fine. Jeanne was to call him to make an appointment to see him in his office. She gave Jeanne the number.

The critical importance of the Probation Officer's report had been clearly conveyed to Jeanne and Shana. The officer would meet with both parents and the children, make one visit to each home and interview other related parties — grandparents, teachers, etc. The Probation Officer then would write an evaluation and make recommendations as to where the children should be placed. The disfavored parties could ask that it not be entered into testimony and not be considered by the judge in his deliberation. However, the judges usually rely heavily on the Probation Officer's recommendations — the "eyes and ears of the court" and perhaps the single most influential external factor in the proceedings.

It was obviously crucial that Jeanne and Shana do everything within their power to insure the most favorable evaluation possible and, if at all possible, secure a recommendation in favor of placing the boys with them or at least not removing Jesse.

Fred Spence — sounds like a character out of Dick Tracy, Jeanne thought to herself. *The Probation Department, hm. Why the Probation Department? Sounds ominous.* Jeanne avoided calling.

In about five days she received a card in the mail with a tentative appointment time, asking that she call to confirm. She did. She couldn't tell much from the man's voice on the other end. The appointment was for Thursday of the following week.

A short, dark-haired man in a nondescript brown suit came down the institutional green hall and into the waiting room on the 6th Floor of the County Building.

"Miss Jullion?" he extended a slightly moist hand. "This way."

He and Jeanne sat face to face in a tiny room over a metal desk. He was a bit nervous and a bit hard to read. An hour later Jeanne left the building, feeling uncertain as to how it had gone. Disbelief and a smoldering anger rankled inside her as she walked to the corner and waited for the light to change. *Franco's really waging an all-out campaign,* she muttered to herself. He had already met with the Probation Officer and, as it ultimately would appear in the report, sworn that Jeanne

> ...had permanently dedicated herself to a lifestyle which rejects almost all normal and conventional standards present in American life... that she has an openly lesbian relationship with Ms. Shana Ascher in an exaggerated feminist environment which takes great pains to promote despisal of the male role... and that this is extremely damaging to the boy's normal personality identification.

I told Mr. Spence I'm not a separatist, Jeanne muttered to herself as she stepped off the curb. *How could I be with two sons and three other boy children I'm helping to raise! I told him I'm trying to arrange a mediation for my parents with two Catholic priests.* Her long stride swallowed up whole lengths of the asphalt as she headed into the parking lot in the shade of the overpass. *I told him about Paul's tension and hyperactivity, the confusion of his psychological testing by Dr. Wroblewski. I'm sure it would be good for Paul to live with me during the school year, he could spend the summer with his Dad, go to Italy even... I told him how much a stranger Franco is to Jesse, that he's doing so well now, it's preposterous to think of removing him...*

Eh! she sputtered, swinging open the door to the ageing white Comet, *I don't know, I don't know.* She plopped down on the black vinyl seat and then just slammed the door on her attempts to figure it all out.

2

Some of the happiest times Jeanne and Shana shared had been working on the old North Oakland house. A veritable challenge. Despite negligible resources, the old house gradually changed.

Jeanne remembered the day Shana threw on her oldest jeans, her K-Mart tennis shoes and an oversized shirt and marched upstairs to begin a Peanuts mural on the wall of the newly painted boys' room. Jeanne chuckled, wondering if she could really do it, and climbed back up the ladder in the living room to work on restoring the coffered ceiling.

After about an hour she heard commotion and giggling in the hallway upstairs.

"Jeanne," the kids chorused, "com'ere, com'ere."

Jeanne backed down the ladder. Four little legs dangled through the bannister above her as she sprang up the stairs two at a time.

"Look, look," they squealed, pointing to the hall wall.

I LOVE YOU, JEANNE was boldly painted on the wall beside Shana.

"Shana—"

"Don't worry, don't worry," Shana effused. "The hall's next to be painted."

Jeanne wrapped her long arms around her, burying her face in her neck. As if to a magnet, the kids joined in until a seven-person cluster teetered precariously at the top of the stairs.

"Okay, okay," the two women laughed, "com'on. Get these rooms picked up, you guys. Tomorrow's Saturday and we're going to the Alameda Flea Market to look for bunk beds."

"Alright!" exclaimed Aaron.

"To work!" commanded Shana, sidestepping a wobbly Reuben who was balancing against her legs. Palette in her right hand, acrylic brush in her left, like some matronly Rembrandt, she strode back into the little boys' bedroom and the Peanuts mural in progress on the wall.

Now once again they poured energy into the old frame house but this time with a hard sense of urgency. The old house now seemed to balk at their efforts to somehow magically transform it into what the "eyes of the court" would prefer seeing. Jeanne painted trim across the broad, unadorned front of the house, trying to revive her.

Inside, the house was purged of anything that smacked of feminism. A great amount of paranoia was felt about the upcoming inspection and often Jeanne would slip into tense, frightened arguments with Shana, at odds as to what was important to do.

Beyond the basics, there was now little time and energy for the children.

The morning of Mr. Spence's visit Shana was hurriedly uprooting the dried marigolds from the freshly painted planter box on the front porch and brusquely inserting fresh chrysanthemums. A blue Datsun stopped at the curb. Franco got out and brought Paul up to the house. He made a smug slur at their last minute efforts at beautification. Jeanne told Paul to come on in and shut the door without speaking to him.

The visit lasted barely an hour. Mr. Spence seemed extremely ill-at-ease. All six children milled around the living room as introductions were made. Jeanne could see that Mr. Spence lost track of who was who halfway through — except for Paul who said, "Oh hi, Mr. Spence," which sort of surprised her. Jesse leaned up against his mother's legs; Jeanne sought to get Mr. Spence's attention twice.

"This is Jesse... This is my son, Jesse..." She couldn't tell if it registered. Shana suggested the children play outside while they talked. Mr. Spence readily agreed, looking relieved.

After a tour of the house Mr. Spence, perspiring slightly, declined coffee or tea and sat down on the couch next to the piano. It looked as if his hips were barely back far enough to keep him from falling on the floor. A warmed-over version of the office interview ensued. Twice Jeanne suggested that the children come in and both times he said no, that they seemed to be doing fine outside. Then, after having seen the children and mothers interact for less than five minutes in all, the visit ended and he left.

"Yikes!" Jeanne exclaimed, collapsing on the couch. Shana reached for her cigarette on the mantle, looking very tired. *Next hearing is May 13th,* Jeanne's mind wandered ahead to his report. *The lawyer said we could see it ten days before...*

The back door flung open, dispersing her thoughts. In clammered six hungry, arguing children.

"Aaron, it was Jesse's turn," protested Dov.

"Uh-huh. Paul had the ball."

"Okay, okay," Jeanne waved at them to stop. "Shana, let's splurge and go the Smorgasbord tonight, what do you say?"

"Yeah, let's. We all deserve it," she sighed. "Except you

guys..." she teased.

"Mom!" they chorused as she disappeared into the bedroom for the keys.

3

Along with courting the Probation Officer's favor, the two women wrestled with the problem of a strategy for a case that would be heard before a hostile judge. First of all, a new psychologist had to be located as an expert witness. Jeanne's lawyer made an excellent contact in securing the services of Dr. Byron Nestor, a prominent child psychologist in Berkeley and a frequent appointee by the Court itself on other cases.

Once again, Jeanne began the process of having complete psychological work-ups done on all concerned. Franco refused to co-operate or participate and his lawyer prevented Dr. Nestor from ever meeting Paul. He did, however, see Jesse on several occasions and was genuinely impressed. This was to become the mainstay of the case at the May hearing.

While this was a more hopeful development, Jeanne and Shana did not see light in two other areas of concern: money and a persistent lack of consensus with their lawyer.

The eyes of the half dozen people in the laundrymat on San Pablo Avenue widened with each new bundle of laundry the two women brought through the glass doors. Two blond children, one with curls, and the other with straight and long hair, clammered around the bundles, chasing each other. A third child, Reuben, sat patiently in his car seat in the now emptied white car at the curb. The two women quickly began sorting and stuffing a long line of waiting washing machines. The laundry began, they kissed each other lightly on the cheek. Shana then gathered up the children and departed on errands.

As the car pulled away, Jeanne pretended to ignore the vaguely curious stares of a few people seated on red plastic chairs, patiently monitoring the progress of their own wash. She got a drink of

water and sat down on an unmatched chair that looked like it had
come from a school. Worried about money, Jeanne counted the
washers churning with their loads. One dryer for two washers. She
divided by two and multiplied by a minimum of 50 cents per dryer.
She pulled her zippered leather wallet out of her pocket and counted
the one dollar bills. *Should be okay if the dryers work right,* she thought.

Lulled by the clicking, churning and spinning of the surrounding machines, Jeanne stared patiently at the rolling cylinders of
the dryers in front of her. Her lawyer's voice rose in her head as
clear as a bell.

"It might be easier in court if you were living alone, not... in
a relationship. If you and Jesse had your own apartment..."

Jeanne squirmed in the small wooden chair and unfolded her long
legs in front of her in a long, nervous stretch. *Oh boy,* she shuddered,
the specter of headaches, isolation and doing it all alone rising over
her right shoulder. She wrapped her arms around herself and yawned
tensely, her jaw joints popping. Blood rushed warmly to her slightly
puffed eyelids and she rubbed them wearily.

Damn, she swore to herself. *Move out? How can I move out? I love
these people. Do you know how much money ahead it'd take to get an apartment by myself? Conditional custody, that's what she's going for, I've heard
of that. You can have conditional custody of your children if you do not have
a homosexual, god how I hate that word, relationship that is visible to your
children or the Court. Great, that leaves you with a life of sneaking, abstinence
or being totally in the closet, even to your children. Ugh,* she shook her head
and her curls flopped. *I've just come OUT of the closet,* she thought
with exasperation. *Now what am I supposed to do, go back in and have
the Court close the door behind me? Live alone for how long — until Jesse
turns 18? That's 15 years. And if I ever did start a relationship, would I
then run the risk of having to go through this all over again?*

Jeanne shook her head. *What a transparent ruse it'd be — who'd believe
me at this point? Everyone knows I feel damn good about being a lesbian and
that's really the issue. No one's questioning my parenting or how Jesse's doing — which happens to be great — she nodded, only my 'lifestyle'. Would
scurrying off into some straight stage setting allay their fears? I just don't think
so,* she thought to herself, *I just don't think so. It has to be dealt with.*

*But with this lawyer? It's April and the hearing is May 13th and we aren't
doing anything. We have no strategy except to hide. Hey, we're going to lose*

the kids like this. Minder will simply do whatever he wants.

Jeanne stood up, feeling a little faint. The ten washers shuddered to a stop like a chorus line. When Shana returned a half hour later, Jeanne stepped out from behind the mountains of fresh linen she was folding and announced, "Shana, I'm not moving out and we need a new lawyer."

A brilliantly blue April sky stretched out over the Bay Area the last day of that week. Large tankers sat still on the smooth Bay. The white Comet powered heftily into the tunnel of Treasure Island, holding its own in the Friday afternoon traffic on the upper deck of the Bay Bridge. The grey skyscrapers of the Financial District glinted in the sun as the Comet came out the other side. The old car barrelled over the second span of the bridge and down onto the Fifth Street off-ramp. With luck, a stretch limousine with darkened windows glided away from the curb near their destination, Ninth and Market. Jeanne and Shana slipped into the parking space and went into the lobby of a tall, granite building. WOMEN'S LITIGATION UNIT, the directory said, FOURTH FLOOR.

In the fourth floor office, Jeanne and Shana explained to the dark haired woman behind the desk that they were in the midst of a custody litigation and asked for names of feminist attorneys in the Bay Area. Then Jeanne asked, "Our present lawyer gave our Probation Officer some material from a Lesbian Mothers Resource Manual she said you were putting together. Would we be able to look at it?"

"Sure. It's on the shelf in the last office."

"Thanks."

Jeanne and Shana poured over two large binders, frowning at the legal jargon. Shana returned to the front desk and asked if they could xerox sections to take home and read.

"Sure. Go down to the Third Floor. You can use the machine there. If anyone asks, say it's from this office," she smiled.

"Thanks again."

At home the articles and transcripts were put into a box in the study and were read and discussed long into many nights.

Money was another factor that served to pull Jeanne and Shana out of their isolation as parents and relatively 'new' lesbians and into the women's community. Already they faced bills of over a thousand dollars and preparation for the second hearing had not even really begun. They began thinking of doing some kind of benefit.

Up to this point neither Jeanne or Shana had been politically active or really connected to the amorphous yet strong, lesbian-dominated women's community of the Bay Area. On occasion they had attended a women's concert advertised in the calendar section of the local women's newspaper, *Plexus*. They had also begun to do some work on the Feminist School for Girls project, wanting to see the school open so that Hannah, age nine, would have an alternative to the sexism and racism of the neighborhood public school. Yet they knew enough about how the struggles of the women's community were financed — by benefits and fundraisers.

"What about a dance?" Shana suggested.

"Yeah!" exclaimed Aaron, intent on finding a way to have Paul come and live with them on a full-time basis.

"Yeah, Mom," Hannah agreed, looking up from the envelopes she was stuffing. Jeanne sat beside her, addressing their newly arrived Wizard of Odds business reply cards. They had one job to bid on thus far.

"I think so, too. Damn good idea," Shana congratulated herself, laughing. "With a woman's band. And we'll get it on the calendar in *Plexus*."

"*Plexus*?" queried Aaron.

"You know, Aaron," Hannah replied with big sisterly patience. " The women's newspaper."

"Oh, I knew that. You don't have to tell me everything, Hannah. Gol-ly…"

And thus out came the acrylic brushes and paints again as things began perking in a more positive vein around the old wooden house for the first time in almost three months. Posters were lettered and flyers readied for the dance.

The next day Shana parked the car on Channing Way and, flyers underarm, climbed the broad, redwood steps to the Berkeley Women's Center. As she searched for space on the crowded bulletin board inside, she noticed a flyer for an event in Golden Gate Park on Sunday, A Day For Women's Rights. *Hm*, she thought to herself, *it'd be fun to take the kids to Golden Gate Park. Maybe we could make an announcement about our dance, explain the situation...*

However, Jeanne felt her voice run out of her just looking at the enormity of the speakers' platform when Sunday arrived. The green knoll and sloping valley deep in Golden Gate Park were covered with several hundred women and lined with tables and displays. A women's rock band was playing on stage as a few short-haired women danced with and without partners below.

Jeanne and Shana wound through the crowd with their cluster of small children and spread a blanket to the side. The children tore off to play frisbee. Jeanne stood chain-smoking several cigarettes, rolling Reuben's stroller back and forth with her foot, before setting out for backstage.

In back of the high platform Jeanne stiffly tried to explain what she wanted to a monitor. The woman replied that there were already too many speakers but she could fill out a 3 × 5 card with the information and it might get in the announcements. Jeanne did so without much sense that it would do any good.

As she walked away, she recognized Margaret Sloan, a well-known feminist and originator of the idea for a Feminist School for Girls. Jeanne said hi and briefly explained the situation.

"Could you please make an announcement?"

"Jeanne, you're the *fifth* person to ask me. I only have *three* minutes!" she exclaimed with a resounding laugh. "I'll be mentioning the Women Library Workers and I'm afraid that's the best I can do. Sorry..."

Jeanne moved on through the crowd, past more tables. Women in Sports. Women Police Officers. Reproductive Rights. Yvonne Wanrow Defense Committee. Berkeley Women's Health Collective. San Francisco Women Against Rape. Disabled Women's Coalition. Inez Garcia Defense Committee. Olivia Records. She found Shana. Reuben's stroller clogged sluggishly in the spring mud as they again circled around the back of the huge platform. Again no luck with the monitor. However, she pointed to the woman speaking at the microphone.

"She's a lawyer and she's talking about lesbian child custody cases. Maybe you can talk to her."

The short, red-haired woman finished speaking and came carefully down the wobbly metal stairs at the back of the platform. Shana and Jeanne waited as she talked with someone else. Then they stepped forward. "Excuse me, this is my lover," Jeanne explained. "We're in court over my children, our current legal advice says I should move out, hide, be ashamed — what do you say?"

"You're living with a lover?... Have you heard of conditional custody?" she asked, shaking her head slowly.

Jeanne and Shana's eyes met. It was sobering to hear the term out loud. "Yes, we've heard of it."

"That's about the most judges will give a lesbian mother if she does get custody. They don't want children around homosexuals, you know. I'm sorry. I wish I could tell you differently. It's a hard decision whether to move out or not, and the hearing's in a few weeks...? Things are rough in court and the stakes are so high... Good luck."

Jeanne felt cold. A bad dream... *if only I could wake up. Jesse and Paul caught her eye in the distance. The court, the judge, lesbian, what's happening to people's heads? I'm the same person! Conditional custody — move out, three weeks before the hearing? Ridiculous.*

Hannah stood beside the blanket, watching their slow return.

"Hannah," Jeanne sighed, looking at her serious and wise young face, "call the boys, will you? It's time to go home."

4

There was only one lawyer who Jeanne and Shana had not been able to reach, a feminist lawyer who had handled the conclusion of another lesbian mother's case. Her name was Jill Lippitt and the two women she had defended, Cynthia and Faith, swore by her.

"Talk to Jill! Talk to Jill! Bullshit, you should move out," Cynthia swore. "That's what they tried to tell us. That's what they all say. They don't understand. You aren't doing anything wrong! Talk to Jill. Jillie's good people, good people. Her father's dying of cancer in L.A. and she may be down there but you have her number? Keep trying, keep trying."

Sitting on the bed one night, Jeanne picked up the blue phone and dialed the home number for Jill Lippitt once again. It rang. Someone answered, "Hello?"

"Hello. Is this Jill Lippitt?"

"Speaking."

Jeanne reached over and pulled Shana's sleeve, covering the receiver — "Jill Lippitt," she whispered. Shana bounded upstairs to the other phone.

Jeanne briefly explained the situation. Jill asked who the judge was. "Judge Gordon Minder."

"Oh no. That's not good..."

A time was set for the following day. She was to meet with her legal partner-to-be, Sheila Goldmacher, at MacArthur Mall in Oakland and Jeanne and Shana would join them there.

In the Mall, Jill walked towards Jeanne and Shana with a broad grin and outstretched hand. Her left hand with its large turquoise stone held a chocolate brown briefcase bulging with legal folders. She appeared to be in her early thirties. Her long auburn hair was parted in the middle and from there seemed to leave on wavy paths of its own. It hung over the front of her shoulders as if waiting to be braided. A long skirt wrapped around broad hips and fell to the tops of puckered Russian boots that were well worn. Round, doe brown eyes, lit with a mixture of intelligence and mischief, looked straight out lightly tinted glasses. But it was her wide smile that dominated her appearance.

Sheila Goldmacher walked out of the MacArthur Mall Bookstore towards them, smiling with some satisfaction.

"Well, that's that," she exclaimed, pushing her black and grey streaked hair off her forehead with relief. "My last day at that job! Now on to Law School and working with Jill Lippitt, Esquire. How are you doing, partner?" she laughed raspily, extending her arms.

"Fine." Jill threaded her arm through Sheila's. "Sheila, I want you to meet Jeanne and Shana. They're in court over custody and we need to talk."

"I see," said Sheila, quickly focusing in on them intently. "Glad to meet you."

"I'm hungry," Jill mentioned with slight nasal twang. "Anybody mind us talking over something to eat?"

Red plastic baskets of hamburgers and fries sat in front of each of them as they began. Jill and Sheila alternately queried Jeanne and Shana about the situation and chattered vibrantly about the Law Office on Valencia Street they were about to open. Jeanne and Shana ate, listened and eyed the two talkative women carefully, absorbing the difference between them and the other lawyers they had consulted. They sensed no professional chasm between them. No meter ticking off the minutes at $50 an hour. But were these two women 'professional' enough? Did they have the knowledge and skills necessary to counteract the legal machinery already drastically set in motion?

Jeanne and Shana left after an hour, feeling at once excited and uncertain. They walked arm in arm down the echoing mall towards the parking lot.

"I wish Jill had taken notes," Shana stroked Jeanne's hand and shook her head. "A lawyer *has* to have a yellow legal pad and take notes." They called Jill the next day and asked for another meeting.

"Good," Jill agreed. "Why don't you come to my home about 8 p.m., okay?"

The white Comet rumbled around the block in the Mission District for the third time, vying with slick low riders for non-existent parking places. Jeanne and Shana peered out the windshield in the darkness. Finally, following suit, they pulled up onto the sidewalk in front of the address Jill had given them.

Their hearts pumped as they climbed the narrow, three-story flight of stairs that stretched upwards in a straight line from Jill's front door. At the top, the stairs veered right into the long, white hallway of Jill's apartment. The lights of Potrero Hill glittered out the bay windows in her high, modest living room.

Jill strode into the living room, yellow legal pad and pen in hand. Jeanne and Shana looked at each other and smiled. Jill bent over the curled, sleeping form of a small dog on the paisley seat of the rattan chair.

"Move, Munchkins," Jill announced, cupping her hand around the reddish rump of the small, sleeping animal. Two enormous, soft brown eyes popped open.

"Com'on," Jill coaxed, tilting the chair forward. Munchkins extended her very short front legs toward the floor at the last possible instant. Glaring inhospitably at the guests, she pranced out of the room with an air of great inconvenience.

Jill took her place on the warm cushion, lit a cigarette and began in earnest. It was a relief to Jeanne and Shana to hear Jill's concerns about the judge. It was a relief to hear Jill talking about presenting their relationship and their home non-apologetically, as the positive environment for the children that they felt it to be. Jeanne and Shana's sense that they had at last found compatible counsel grew as they worked on into the clear April evening.

It was midnight when Jill folded up the curled, yellow sheets of her legal pad.

"Well, how are you feeling?" she asked the two women across from her.

"Good," they both agreed.

"I have to get some rest because tomorrow I will be in court on your side of the Bay. Why don't I stop by when I'm through and meet this family and these children we've been talking about?"

The next day, the enchantment of the children spread to her as well and the agreement was sealed. Jeanne phoned their first lawyer and formally gave notice of their change of counsel. She agreed that they saw the case differently and wished them luck. The bill was $1,758.

Jill travelled to the North Oakland house over the next three days due to the expense and difficulties of childcare for Shana and Jeanne. She disembarked from her yellow Vega with cigarettes, briefcase and dog Munchkins, grinning and ready to work.

Inside, Munchkins eyed the children closely and snapped at the cat.

"Munchkins! This is not your house — you're the guest," Jill scolded.

Dov climbed into Jill's lap on the couch. He leaned his blond head wistfully on her shoulder. The children milled around and Aaron began telling Jill why Paul should live with them.

"He's so sex-ist!" Aaron wailed, laughing. "He thinks Hannah should just play with dolls and take care of Reuben. You know, if there's a diaper to be thrown away or something. And he's so rough — he's kind of hard to play with..."

"Yeah," Hannah continued, "he can't stand to lose. You know, his dad gives him all that sugar and TV and violent movies. He always wants to fight."

Jesse stood plumply on one leg in his brushed cotton overalls, listening to the children talking intently to Jill about his brother, his father.

"Yeah, but—" Aaron started to rise to Paul's defense.

"I know, I know, Aaron," Hannah skipped ahead of him. "He's really neat when he settles down. But he just starts to change and it's time to go back."

"Jill?" Dov asked spacily. "You know what?"

"What, Dov?" she asked softly, moving a wisp of long, silky hair to the side.

"I can play the guitah."

"Dov!" Hannah chastised him for the non sequitur.

"Oh Dov," Aaron concurred, "we're not talking about mu-sic. We're talking about Paul. Jill's Mom and Jeanne's lawyer. She's going to talk to the judge."

"Yeah, but I want to play a song for Jill," Dov persisted softly with a whine.

"Okay, okay" Jeanne stepped in. "Let us get some work done. Then we'll get the instruments and play for Jill later, okay? Now let's go. We've got a lot of work to do."

In those three days, Jill was filled in on the history of Jeanne's marriage, Franco, Jesse and Paul, her parents, psychological testimony and the legal proceedings to date. On the third day she gathered her papers, called her dog, Munchkins, and left, saying she needed to distance herself, digest the material and regain her objectivity as lawyer in the situation. However, to the house on 55th Street that waved goodbye to her she had become family as well as friend.

Jill checked with the Courthouse daily to see if the Probation Officer's report had been filed yet for it was now indeed ten days before the hearing. Finally, she received an affirmative.

"Jeanne, I'll come by and pick up Shana. We'll go the courthouse and get a copy. We'll call you, though, as soon as we have it in hand."

The afternoon was summery and quiet. Jesse, Dov and Reuben were out in the backyard playing in shorts and no shirts. Hannah and Aaron weren't home from school yet. Jeanne got out the lawn mower and decided to mow the tall dryness that was the front lawn. She pushed hard into the rusty mower, dragging it reluctantly back and pushing it grindingly forward. Jeanne had put the phone on the front porch so she could get their call. She continued her path around the small front yard, her head empty, waiting.

Time passed. All of a sudden she stopped. It hit her. She knew they had lost. She knew that Fred Spence had, in fact, capitulated. She knew too much time had passed. She sensed Jill and Shana had already picked up the report *but, of course,* she realized, *they would never call and tell me over the phone that I was probably going to lose both my children. They're on their way back to the house...*

She let go of the mower where it was. *Oh god no, this can't be happening, god no.*

She turned and walked up the front steps, her hand scooping up the phone as she went by. She walked into the cool living room, setting the phone down on the arm of the sofa. *Perhaps they would call...?* She sat down on the green sofa, the May afternoon hanging quiet in the air in the plant-filled room. Jesse and Dov's voices drifted in through the open kitchen window. She sat. After a while she heard Shana's heavy steps taking the porch steps two at a time, then rush in the open front door. She came in the living room, her eyes looking scared and slid in next to Jeanne on the couch, putting her arms around her, pulling Jeanne's rigid body towards her.

"Oh Jeanne, we lost. He recommends both boys go to the father."

"I know. I knew it."

"Oh Jesse," she said, sobbing into Jeanne's shoulder. Jeanne held her woodenly, patting her shoulder, numb, feeling no tears come yet, looking up to see Jill's serious face looking at her.

Shana recovered with anger.

"But you should hear what he says, Jeanne. It's such bullshit, such bullshit!" she swore. "He doesn't say anything against you as a mother. But the *stigma,* the stigma the kids would have with you as a lesbian and that they'd have more access to *your* family if the kids were with him. Do you believe it? Your family makes me sick. They're in it, your sister, too. You should read what she has to say! Your sister's worse than your parents. She doesn't want *her* children to associate with 'homosexuals'," she mocked.

"Stop. I don't want to hear."

"Here, you can read it."

"No," Jeanne said, pushing the papers away from her. "The bottom line's all that counts. He recommended against us... Jesse, too?" she asked helplessly, eyes filling, looking searchingly into Jill's eyes, then Shana's, back to Jill, wanting them to lie, *tell me it isn't so.* Silence.

Jeanne got up. Shana talked on, outraged at paragraph after paragraph of the report. Tears pressed painfully at Jeanne's eyes. She braced against them. To cry was to let this new reality in, to feel it, to accept that this threat was real, to realize that she was not going to be given any consideration for custody of Paul and it was going to take everything they could muster to prevent Jesse from being removed.

Paul. It was like losing Paul all over again, this time officially and for good. She felt him recede, fade. She knew in her rational mind that he was, according to man-time, an hour's drive away, no longer an ocean and continent apart, but she saw him clearly and she saw him as if at a great distance, a distance that just that day had increased drastically.

And Jesse? She went crazy inside, pain erupting in muffled explosions inside her chest. She kept trying to sever her contact with these feelings that were too strong, too preposterous. *Why? Why should even Jesse be taken away from me? What have I done? He's never been away from me a day in his life.* But she knew the basic reason why it was happening was prejudice, and prejudice is not reasonable and that stunned and scared her. How do you fight what people have carried around in their heads and had reinforced through decades of conditioning — starting with childhood jokes, taunts, teasing, through school, at work, at parties...

She shook her head trying to clear it, still trying to contain the panic, the desperate explosions breaking loose inside her. She moved about, jamming her fists into the pockets of her thinly worn jeans, turning this way and that, trying to get out of the way of the pain, look at it differently, perhaps it didn't mean what it seemed. She looked at Jill's face, her eyes, as she was to do at so many points along the way, searching her friend and lawyer's face for what all those documents and procedures and mystifying legal double-talk meant. She saw in her face the truth of the situation, a friend's honesty mixed with a great measure of compassion and I wish I could tell you differently...

Jeanne turned on her heels and went into the bedroom, shutting the door. The room felt cool. The tears started to come, though still blocked, choked back. She lay down on the bed. *No, no this didn't mean that. There's still the second hearing —* Memories of the first interminable hearing before Judge Minder flooded back over her. *No, I won't go through that again. You HAVE to go through that again.* Jill had already told her that this hearing would probably go two if not three days... *Alright, alright, I'll go through it but not to lose both my kids. Walking into court now, before that conservative man, with a Probation Officer's report to back him up, that's like lambs being led to the slaughter and I'm not going into that.*

She lay there, incredulous, blinking, swallowing, rolling, anything to change the reality, to make it come together differently. Thoughts, feelings slid over her and over each other. *I hadn't known, why hadn't somebody told me it'd be like this, I should have known, but I came out here, in the San Francisco Bay Area, the gay center of the world, where gay men and lesbians can walk openly on at least some of the streets and at least have some trace of economic and political power.* But Oakland is not San Francisco, she was to be told too late, and things weren't even that much different in San Francisco except for one benevolent judge at that time on the bench.

Shana opened the door gently. Jill stood a few feet behind. Shana laid her body over Jeanne's, kissing and stroking her wet cheeks. Jeanne's eyes were locked wide open, still holding on inside, her shoulders stiff and set like poured cement. Shana's warmth and weight felt good.

"Jeanne," Shana began gently, "we'd better talk, talk about we're going to do."

"Huh? Sure. Come on in, Jill."

Shana sat up and so did Jeanne slowly, her head spinning. She reached through the momentary blindness towards Jill coming into the room. As she felt her take her hand and wrap her other hand over it, more tears escaped. Swallowing, Jeanne reached on the nightstand for a cigarette.

"Jeanne," Jill began, still holding one hand, "I know you're feeling terrible but there's not much time. Today's Wednesday and the hearing's a week from Friday. Now, I've read the Probation Officer's report and it's a piece of shit. Your parents and sister are in there, doing their damage. He doesn't say anything against you as a mother. The whole thing is bias and prejudice but Minder got just what he wanted. Judges don't very often go against Probation Officers' recommendations..."

She paused. Jeanne sucked on her cigarette, looking at her lawyer out of the corner of her eye, thinking *is this supposed to make me feel better?*

"So what are we goin' to do?" Jeanne articulated the obvious.

"Well," Jill continued carefully, "I think we need to organize. I think we need help. I think we need to form some sort of defense committee." She paused again. "I know some good women in the City who'd probably work and there's probably some more here in the East Bay. Anyway, I think you should think about whether or not you want to do that."

Defense Committee. A Defense Committee? Jeanne had only heard about the Defense Committee for Inez Garcia, the women who killed the man who held her down while his friend raped her. She was convicted of murder but finally was acquitted — $60,000 in debt.

A Defense Committee. The two words reached through the fog of her pain. Maybe that makes sense. She wasn't quite sure how it worked but she knew it meant organizing resistance. It also sounded frightening. *A Defense Committee. Would that hurt or help my chances in court,* she wondered. *Chances? There's little chance for the case in court before this judge, with this P.O. report and with my family's opposition.*

Jeanne looked at Shana and Jill and saw it was a consensus. It was agreed. They would call a meeting — for tonight.

CHAPTER SIX

Resistance

Bedtime was an early 7:00 that evening for all the children but Hannah. From the bedroom, Jeanne listened to the children retreating upstairs amidst protests that it was still light outside. She waited a few minutes before opening the door. She crossed the kitchen to the bathroom, avoiding Hannah's look. Bending over, she ran cold water into her hands and held it against her reddened face. She slipped her lavender glasses over her puffy eyes, sunk a pick into her matted curls, slapped her cheeks twice, tried to shrug off the weakness she felt inside and returned to the kitchen.

"Okay, you guys, that's enough complaining," Jeanne heard Shana managing bedtime from the bottom of the hall stairs. The upstairs was their domain, a community of children — with five and sometimes six, it was a group process. Hannah was the eldest, the boys' own Wendy from Peter Pan, calm, loving and responsible, playing house with real children. "Take a book to bed and quiet down up there. Now, good night."

Bang! Something hit the floor followed by a shriek from Reuben.

"Mom? The milk in Reuben's bottle's sow-war," sing-songed Aaron. "He keeps throwing it on the floor and screaming."

"Aiee," exclaimed Shana. "Okay, okay, Aaron. Drop it down to me — carefully! — over the bannister." *Aiee,* Shana repeated to herself, looking at her watch. The meeting was called for 7:30.

R — ing!

"Hold on, Aaron. Don't drop it! Take it down to Hannah in the kitchen to wash and fix a new one." *R — ing!* "I'm getting the phone."

"She swung the door open into the dimming light of the study and minutes later, emerged grinning and slapping her thigh. Noting that all was now quiet upstairs, she strode through the living room

with a long gait and, rounding the corner into the kitchen, exclaimed, "Jeanne! Hannah, Aaron! Guess what?!" Jeanne and Hannah turned around from the sink where they were finishing the
dishes. "That was Dennis."

Blank stares.

"You know, Dennis. He lives with Cynthia and Faith and the
kids. Anyway, he knows we've been trying to find a live-in sitter
and he wants to know — get this! — wants to know if he could stay
here awhile in exchange for helping with the house and the kids!
What a godsend!"

"Wow," exclaimed Hannah.

"He's on his way over."

Gr-r, ground the front doorbell.

"Oh no," they chorused.

"I'll make a fire," Jeanne motioned. Hannah was drying her
hands. "Hurry, Aaron, here's the bottle. Hannah, quick, turn on
the lights in the living room."

As Hannah started for the living room, Jeanne impulsively reached out and caught her with one arm.

"Thanks for all your help, Hannah," she said with a hug.

"It's okay. That Mr. Spence did us in, didn't he," she said, right
on target. Jeanne nodded her head on top of Hannah's, tears immediately stinging the corners of her eyes like needles. Hannah sensed a dam about to break above her, pulled on the arm that was wrapped around her.

"The fire, Jeanne, start the fire," Hannah prodded, hearing the
sound of voices in the hallway.

Lights went on, flames rose in the blue fireplace and down jackets
quickly piled up in the study as women arrived. A young boy clung
closely to his mother — Marya Grambs. She sat down on the old
loveseat and pulled her son close to her. Her large brown eyes took
in the situation at hand. In a minute she was joined by an old friend,
an efficient, frizzy-haired woman with a spiral notebook and pencil already in hand — Pam Miller. A short woman with a low, rich
voice was greeting Jill in the hall — Shoshana Rosenberg. Lean,
tanned, with the look of a rugged Capricorn, one of only two women

from the East Bay stepped into the living room — Connie Janssens. The second was Bobbi LaNoue, a slim woman with a time-worn face who stood quietly to the side, drawing on a long, thin brown cigarette.

Loud talking and stomping marked the arrival on the porch of the last two women — Sheila Goldmacher, the only woman Jeanne and Shana had already met, and her younger, taller, equally vibrant sister — Suzi Goldmacher. The piano bench, sofa and what chairs there were soon were pulled in around the fire and Jill opened the meeting.

"First, I'd like to thank everyone for coming, especially on such short notice. Jeanne and Shana have been in court before Judge Gordon Minder — conservative, white man —" Jill noted with finger in the air, "for custody of Jeanne's two boys, Paul and Jesse. Jesse's three and upstairs and Paul's with his father in Mountain View. Excuse my English but this piece of shit —" she reached forward and picked up a document from the coffee table, "is the Probation Officer's report, which, sadly, we got today..."

Jill let it drop back onto the white wicker table with a slap. Massaging her left hand with her right, she proceeded to explain how the threads of lesbianism, welfare and external family opposition wove through the report and were ultimately relied upon to justify his recommendation: both minor children to the father.

"Now, we have a very solid psychological testimony on Jesse and Jeanne from a well-respected doctor the court itself uses frequently, Dr. Byron Nestor. He will testify adamantly that it'd be a grave mistake to remove Jesse who's doing wonderfully with his mother."

The women looked over at Jeanne and Shana with slight nods. Marya wrapped her arms around her son.

"But that's the scary thing," Jill exclaimed. "Nobody's looking at Jeanne as a mother! All they can see is that she's changed, she's come out, she's a lesbian, a dyke. Jeanne's been on welfare. Well," she amended, "you're off now as of the first of the month, right?"

"Right," Jeanne nodded.

"The judge warned her to be off welfare by the time she came back to court. Of course, he can't do that, but he did." Laughter rippled through the room.

"There are five children upstairs — Shana is a mother of four. Now that's obviously full-time work, wouldn't you say?"

"Oh, woman's work is seldom recognized as such, we all know that," Suzi scoffed. "The kids are supposed to raise themselves, right?" she laughed.

"Really," Jill continued. "So we've got trouble — no leverage in court and this subtle and not-so-subtle report." Jill picked it up again and waved it in the air. "I really wish I could read you some passages but it's against the law to disclose it. So unfortunately, I can't." Again she dropped the stapled copy back down on the wicker table with a whap. "So, what do you think? They don't want to lose the kids. I think we need outside help..."

The woman gathered in the living room of the house on 55th Street were clearly not new to these situations. In fact, the ensuing discussion moved with a swiftness of analysis and directedness of action that startled Jeanne and Shana. Clearly support was needed. Public support. The public is reached through the press. A press conference. Where. When. Who should speak. Who should be notified. Press releases...

Jill suddenly caught sight of Jeanne and Shana's intimidated faces.

"Wait a minute," she signalled, calling the discussion to a halt.

The women instantly realized how fast they were going. *A press conference,* Jeanne thought preposterously. *Send out press releases?* It was almost beyond belief. And it was frightening.

"Would I be at the press conference?" Jeanne asked, the words seeming strange in her mouth.

"Only if you feel okay about it," Connie clearly spoke the mind of the group.

"None of this will happen if you don't want it, Jeanne," Pam Miller hastened to add, "if you don't think it'll help."

"We're going too fast," Suzi proclaimed, sinking back into the couch.

"Yeah," Bobbi concurred in a soft, clear voice. "This might make things worse. Judge — what's-his-face?"

"— Minder."

"Yeah, this Judge Minder will be real mad seeing this in the papers. Would it make it on the news, on TV, do you think?"

"I don't know."

"Yes."

"I bet so."

"There's so many gay people here," Sheila spoke up raspily. "The media will be there!" she assured them. "It's an important issue, especially here."

The fire flickered low and Jeanne reached over with a stick to spur it.

"Who would be there?" she asked slowly.

Shana and Jeanne listened carefully to the proposed plan. It would be held in Glide Memorial Church in San Francisco, site of many civil rights activities. Reverend Williams would be asked to be there, as well as a Board Supervisor of San Francisco.

Shana and Jeanne looked at each other. They knew these decisions were entirely their own as would be the repercussions. The boxful of material they had poured over at night had confirmed their feeling that what they were experiencing was not an isolated incident but almost matter of course for lesbian mothers or gay fathers in court over their children. They knew that children were regularly removed from their gay parent and placed with the other parent, relatives or even in foster homes. In Jill's previous case, Cynthia had been accused of molesting her own daugher and was kept from seeing her until she was finally returned to her from a wealthy, Orange County foster home. One statistic from that boxful of reading lodged in Jeanne's mind — there are approximately one and a half million lesbian mothers in the United States. How many children does that affect, she wondered, two, three million?

Shana and Jeanne looked at each other again and then took each other's hand in the space between their chairs.

"Well," Shana spoke up smiling, "I guess in our own way that's what the two of us have already been doing, you know?"

Jeanne nodded.

"We've been reading cases, we've done a flyer, we're doing a benefit dance. Then this stupid, lousy report by that stupid, scared little man came," her anger boiled to the surface. "And now we've got to face it — we know we don't really have a chance."

Jeanne felt incredibly tired. It was hard to sit on the straight back chair much longer.

"Yes, yes," she motioned to the woman, "we just had to catch our breath. It's all happening so fast now. But I really am not feeling well…"

"Jeanne, go lie down." Suzi, a nurse, quickly interjected. "That report had to be a shock to your system."

Jeanne nodded, tears welling up again. She realized she was still holding the poker stick in her left hand. She let it fall to the blue, painted stone hearth and, nodding to the group, rose and left the room. Behind her, she felt a slight hesitation and then heard the meeting resume.

Instead of opening the study door and going into the bedroom, Jeanne's hand reached out to the darkwood banister and she began climbing the stairs.

It was quiet and the last light of the day hung reluctantly in the little boys' bedroom. The yard-high figures of Shana's mural stood smiling in flat, primary colors in the twilight. Peanuts and The Gang each holding a balloon with one of the kids' names on it. Except, that is, for Dov. His name was on a balloon held by Pigpen on the adjacent wall, Dov's place of honor as the most disorderly of them all.

"Jeanne?"

"What, Dov?"

"Com'ere." Two small arms stuck out from the top bunk. On the bunk below Jesse's eyelids drooped half shut and then caught themselves.

"Mommie!" he called.

"Hi, Jesse," Jeanne responded, "I wanted to snuggle with you a bit and say goodnight."

"Snuggle with me! Snuggle with me!" Dov protested.

Jeanne took Dov's small extended hand in her left and with her right pulled the purple chenille spread up under his chin.

"I'll tuck you in," she said to Dov.

"No, snuggle with me, like with Jesse," he persisted.

"No, Dov, I'm just too tired." *Thank heavens, Dennis is coming,* Jeanne thought to herself. "Here, let me hold you a minute and give you a big kiss goodnight."

Ignoring his last no's, she put her head next to his fine, blond

hair and held him close. She could feel that in the increasing tur-
bulence of their lives it was a drop in the bucket. But, drained, she
could resist no longer. In spite of his whines, Jeanne disengaged
and collapsed in one movement on the iron bed below. She let her
heavy arm fall across Jesse's smooth back. He was now asleep.

"Jeanne! Jeanne!" Dov continued above.

"Be quiet, Dov!" Jeanne snapped sharply out of the corner of
her mouth. Guilt immediately washed in *but I feel needy myself,* she
retorted inwardly.

In the dimness, tears seeped onto the pillow. The warmth of
Jesse's round body, half the length of her own, felt good. She lay
there as the darkness grew, feeling scared and childlike herself, wish-
ing she could wish it all away — Franco, Judge Minder, Spence's
report, yes, and the press conference and the second hearing, now
only a matter of days away... Feeling nurtured in the darkness of
this children's room, soothed by the rhythmic sound of the three
children's breathing, she let go and fell asleep, drifting down soft
tunnels in pursuit of her sleeping child.

1

The dry spring persisted and the next morning's dawn broke
clearly over the Bay Area with more crystalline, dry air. It was as
if prisms were on the verge of appearing randomly in the air. The
house jarred as Aaron and Hannah slammed the door and bounded down the front steps, only slightly dishevelled and only slightly
late for school.

At 10:00 Suzi, Sheila and Shoshana came boisterously up the
wooden steps and rang.

"Hello-hello!" Suzi greeted Jeanne and Shana cheerily, stepping into the hall with a single long stride. "You get some rest?"
she peered closely at Jeanne.

"Ah, my sister, the nurse," lamented Sheila, "never off duty.
Hi, kids," she hugged each of them, "how are you doing this
morning?"

"Okay. Com'on in, Shoshana." In stepped Shoshana in a handsome leather jacket, typewriter in hand.

Suzi was already in the study. "Well? Com'on, you guys," she called in an exaggerated Brooklyn accent, "we ain't got all day. Let's set up in here and get this press release *out!*"

"Yes, Ma'am," mocked Shoshana, swinging the typewriter up on the desk.

The doorbell growled again. Shana swung the beveled glass door open and there stood two women whom Jeanne and Shana had not met before.

"Hello," one of the women quickly began in a rather high-pitched voice, "I'm Elizabeth Hirshfeld from U.N.A., United Neighbors in Action. We are a grassroots community group doing neighborhood canvassing, especially for nursing homes. And this is Ruth Hughes." A woman with closely cut hair and a good-humored smile nodded beside her.

"We were notified of what's happening and I'm very sorry. I have three kids of my own. I brought over our press list," she indicated a bulging business envelope in her hand.

"The press list — good!" came a voice from the study.

"Thank you. Come on in."

Jeanne and Shana stole a look at each other as Elizabeth and Ruth stepped into the study. Elizabeth looked like a middle class woman who would have been calling on either of their mothers rather than them. Jeanne perused the olive-skinned woman being introduced in the study in her two-piece peach pantsuit. Her eyes travelled down to Elizabeth's shiny, narrow-heeled shoes, half-buried in the blue shag rug. *She holds her billfold and keys much the way mom does when she's about to go out shopping,* Jeanne thought to herself.

Elizabeth remained standing and in a rather high, childlike voice quickly began discussing how the press releases should be sent to get the maximum attention and assure a worthwhile attendance at Thursday's press conference. Shoshana checked the wording of the press release again and began typing the final copy. Ruth sat down on the window bench that lined the bay windows and divided U.N.A.'s press list with Sheila and Suzi. They began addressing envelopes to all the local newspapers, TV and radio stations, clearly marking them to the attention of potentially sympathetic or key newsroom personnel. Some were stamped for mailing but the most important were marked for hand-delivery — *The San Francisco Chronicle, The San Francisco Examiner, The Oakland Tribune,* major TV stations.

A schedule was then set up to do two sets of follow-up phone calls to make sure they had received and read the release and, secondly, to secure a commitment to attend the press conference. The thoroughness of this instant media operation amazed Jeanne and Shana. The phone began ringing, more and more often, from that day on, increasing to the level of near insanity within the next two weeks.

The following night a second meeting of the Defense Committee was held with two new women in attendance: a frizzy-haired radical nurse with sharply defined leftist politics, Barbara Maggiani, and a quick-witted, blue-eyed therapist and shop owner from Menlo Park, Joann Gardner-Loulan.

At this meeting it was decided to go one step further. It was suggested that a list of demands — stating basically that lesbianism be removed as an issue — be drawn up and endorsements sought from prominent individuals and organizations in the community — this would then be sent directly to Judge Minder.

The word *demands* smacked of insurrection to Jeanne's ears. Her one, first-hand experience with the American judicial system in February had done nothing to evoke feelings of respect towards the judge or the judicial process in general but it had impressed her, in all seriousness, with the scope of its power. *How can some man sitting up there in a black coat tell me I can or can't have my children?* she mulled.

And a second lesson seemed clear to Jeanne after the first hearing: the judicial procedure is like a play, enacted and performed for the benefit of the judge, governed by itemized rules and strict protocol. It is hierarchical with the judge definitely on top.

Therefore, how brazen to make *demands* on His Honor! It scared her to defy the total atmosphere and tradition of deference towards his seemingly absolute power, particularly in cases of Family Law.

But then it was clearly no time for timidity. The point of the press conference, which had already been called, was to get a clear and vocal message to the judge.

"What if he doesn't read the paper that morning," Pam pressed on.

"Yeah," Bobbi agreed. "he has to be stopped. He has to get back in bounds and be kept there."

"Judges think they're gods. It must feel sometimes like they are," Marya mused wryly.

Bobbi bore on, "The message has to get right to him — and with some clout — or this is just going to make things worse."

Connie bent forward on the couch, lean and controlled, and speculated, "I *know* we could get powerful endorsements for a statement that says custody should be determined on parenting and not on the sexual preference of the parent. I mean Willie Brown, Ron Dellums..."

"Pete Stark..."

"Senator Cranston..."

"I can contact two unions," Suzi threw in.

"Art Agnos, the man who was elected to the California Assembly," Shoshana suggested.

"—and, of course, all the women's groups and gay organizations in the area," Joann added. "But most importantly, the political big guns, the straight ones, the ones who will make a judge stop and think — politically."

A list of demands sprang quickly from the end of Jeanne's pen that night:

1. that custody be determined on the basis of parenting;
2. that lesbianism be proven to be of some actual harm to the children or be removed as an issue;
3. that questioning into sexual activities not be permitted far beyond what would be tolerated if directed to a heterosexual parent;
4. that the punitive anti-gay practice of awarding custody contingent upon the parent not living with a lover, which was alluded to at the first hearing, not be considered as a disposition in this or in any other case;
5. that the court recognize Jeanne and Shana's home as a viable family unit equivalent to a married, heterosexual household and not to be discounted solely because the heads of the household are gay.

Endorsements came in and were mounted like sandbags in the line of defense. California Assemblyman Willie Brown gave his name and the offices of U.S. Congressmen Ron Dellums and Pete Stark not only endorsed the demands but sent personal letters of support. Doctors, professionals and agencies added their names to the list which was soon more than fifty. The Service Employees International Union Local 616 endorsed the guidelines as well as the pastors of three churches, two of whom sent accompanying letters of endorsement as well. Word spread, flowing efficiently through the expanding communications network of the women's and gay communities. In the ensuing months, these communities would become saturated with word of the case.

Names continued to come in up to the last minute when the packet was xeroxed and mailed to Judge Minder, Department 15, Alameda County Courthouse.

2

Thursday had arrived and the press conference was set for 10 a.m. Suzi and her lover, Kay, Jill, Shana and Jeanne squeezed into Suzi's metallic brown Datsun. The car sped past the wooden slat sculptures in the mudflats along the Bay. Traffic was only moderate. At the bridge Jeanne glanced out the window at the neon-lined hands of the toll clock — 9:05.

Suzi piloted the car up onto the Bay Bridge, through the Treasure Island tunnel and off the other end into the morning traffic of downtown San Francisco.

"That's Glide," she announced as she cut left into a parking lot and came to an abrupt halt. Jeanne's insides lurched. The side doors snapped open and the five women spilled out. They crossed Ellis Street and entered the glass doors of the well-known, urban church.

The long, basement room was as bland as any meeting room in any school or church. Coffee perked in a large urn and Connie and

Ruth were setting out long rows of donuts — an important detail for reporters at their 10:00 assignment. A press list for them to sign was placed near the door so the committee would know who had attended.

Soon loud voices and laughing were reverberating down the hall and crews started to arrive. Technicians adjusted microphones clustered on the long formica-top table that faced five rows of folding chairs. Jeanne made sure Jill's chair was close to hers behind the long table. Her mouth felt like it was filled with ajax and her heart thumped erratically when all was finally set and Jill began.

"We've called this press conference today regarding the child custody case involving Jeanne Jullion before Judge Gordon Minder in Alameda County Superior Court. Jeanne is seeking custody of her two children — Paul, age eight, who currently resides with his father, and Jesse, age three..."

Pens wiggled quickly across small notepads. Strong lights flicked on and off and TV cameras purred. Jill's voice was strong and steady.

"Jeanne is a lesbian and the anti-gay bias of the court was very apparent at the first hearing. Last week Jeanne received a copy of the Probation Officer's report which recommends both children be awarded to the temporary custody of the father, again citing Jeanne's lesbianism as the deciding factor. We are here to seek public support that custody be determined on the basis of parenting and not the sexual preference of the parent."

As she paused, several reporters began speaking at once until one prevailed. His question was directed at Jeanne. The TV flood lamps clicked back on. A cameraman stepped in closer, adjusting the focus of the long lens pointed at Jeanne.

Jeanne began answering questions in a low but determined voice. The word 'lesbian' came out of her mouth reluctantly. *How strange,* she thought, *to be saying this word so rarely heard not only to a roomful of strangers but into that black, purring box on those two men's shoulders, a plastic box that could and would reproduce my words, my face, my name on the Nightly News.* Jeanne flashed on her father sitting in his green recliner, watching the 6:00 News, *seeing me, his daughter, saying to everyone that I am that despicable word — lesbian.*

Her voice faltered momentarily. But she drew strength from the half-circle of supporters standing behind her — Margaret Sloan's large figure behind her, Maggie Rubenstein's strong voice booming in to set the record straight, with a sense of authority Jeanne could not have, the smooth, mellow speech of Rev. Cecil Williams, pastor of Glide. Jeanne smiled slightly when an *Oakland Tribune* reporter, whom she instinctively disliked, was interrupted by Jill and Maggie. "We are here due to a specific instance of discrimination in court which is likely to cost Jeanne Jullion her children and not to discuss her personal history," Jill levelled.

Soon it was over. The TV cameras and microphones were gathered up and the crews left for their next assignment. Members of the more alternative press remained longer, gradually abandoning formalities altogether.

Jill motioned Jeanne and Shana to come to the side of the room.

"I don't know how you feel about this," she began in an undertone, "but Channel 5 would like to do a follow-up story and come out to the house this afternoon. They're interested in interviewing you and Shana and getting some shots of the kids. I don't know — how do you feel about that?"

Shana and Jeanne looked at each other, surprised.

"I don't know," Jeanne replied hesitantly. "What do you think, Jill?"

"I'm not sure. In a way, it'd be good. It's a good sign. They're interested in the story. There are lots of gay people in this city. We wanted coverage and that's what they're offering us. It depends on how you feel about them coming into your home and filming the kids. It's certainly true that people can relate to that better than a press conference."

Again Shana and Jeanne looked at each other. They talked it over and then nodded affirmatively. It seemed that the strategy thus far was taking hold.

Suzi, Kay, Jill, Shana and Jeanne left the church and tucked themselves back into Suzi's small car. The press conference over — and seemingly successful — they headed for 55th Street to ready it for the press.

The telephone was ringing off the hook. Holding Reuben in one arm and perspiring slightly, Dennis reported that Channels 2 and

7 had called wanting to come and film. Maura Nolan from *The San Francisco Examiner* had also asked to come and do a story. Sparks seemed to jump from the women's eyes.

The other children tumbled down the stairs at their mothers' return. They squealed with excitement as they were told that TV camera crews would be coming within a matter of hours and that they were going to be on TV. Everyone pitched in to finish cleaning the house. Suzi and Kay went outside to finish mowing the front lawn, left unfinished ten days earlier.

The reality of being back in front of Judge Minder in court the next morning lay deep inside Jeanne like a murky pool. She was grateful for the gathering momentum, knowing they'd probably need every bit of it. *I wonder if he's received our demands and endorsements yet,* she thought as she dug three oversized Lego blocks out of the couch, *I wonder what his reaction to the publicity will be. Hopefully to tread more lightly,* she prayed. She caught Jesse running across the living room and scooped him into her arms — *oh yes,* she squeezed him, Lego blocks clattering to the floor, *certainly worth fighting for.*

The children were dressed and groomed by many hands upstairs. Then everyone assembled in the plant-filled living room to calm down and talk about what was happening. Jeanne and Shana had been forced to tell the children that not only was it a question of whether Paul would come and live with them but also whether Jesse could stay. However, this was said mainly in passing as they still hoped to resolve the situation without Jesse — or the other children — having to really deal with such a drastically disruptive possibility. Jesse barely knew his father and was not exactly looked upon with favor by his rough, older brother.

Jill looked out the bay windows in the study and called out that the van from Channel 5 had just pulled up at the curb. Neighbors along the quiet street appeared at windows and doors.

In came the cameras. Up went strong lamps on skinny metal stands. A maze of cords and TV cables wriggled across the burgundy rug. Inordinantly long, black microphones were tested close to their faces as Jeanne and Shana sat on the couch next to each other, sneaking stolen hand-squeezes like school girls. Twenty-five year-old Dennis kept the children upstairs for the moment although they asked that Jesse come down and sit next to his mother.

Jesse looked delightful with his blond curls tumbling unconcernedly around his mischievous face like an impish Baroque putti. His smooth, small hand slipped into Jeanne's; everything in his behavior exuded security and a typical three year-old's obliviousness. Watching the news that night on their small black and white set, everyone broke into laughter at the sight of Jesse sitting next to his mother, pulling a long strand of bubble gum out of his mouth as she seriously answered ominous questions beside him.

The next two stations arrived almost simultaneously. The living room became warm with the heat of the strong lamps. The reporters and camera crew were amused and friendly.

As soon as the talking interview was concluded, they asked that all the children come down. The children, of course, were falling all over themselves to accomodate.

"Do something together. There should be some action."

"Music!" said Hannah.

And out came the instruments — the bongos and a snare drum, the $4 flea market guitar, two tambourines and Jeanne seated at her topless upright piano. The kids grabbed instruments, Dov first to the guitar, and in all their glory, Jeanne played her one standard boogie to their cacophonous accompaniment for the Nightly News. Jeanne looked over at Shana as the camera scanned them all and they both threw back their heads and laughed at the pure outrageousness of life.

CHAPTER SEVEN

Will This Court be the Battleground?

In the morning the sun seemed to cling to the horizon, dripping orange, and then let go, moving swiftly up into a once again clear blue sky. By 9:30 people began flowing into the Dali-esque emptiness of the plaza in front of the Alameda County Courthouse and up to the halls of the Third Floor, Department 15. At the curb, cables wiggled like rubber snakes out of the side and back of a television broadcasting van, a white needle sticking skyward out of a concave radar dish on top. Two smartly dressed reporters conferred with a young technician in jeans about the hundred people holding placards and milling near the front entrance of the stoic, cement County Building.

Upstairs, Jeanne's father threaded his way through the congested hallway with strained politeness. He opened the door on an equally crowded courtroom. He held his breath and looked flustered as he jostled for a courtroom seat with women dressed in blazers or unadorned working clothes. His lips narrowed with disgust as he resigned himself to a seat between a well-trimmed white man with a gold earring in his left ear and a large, forceful black woman with closely cropped hair. Knee on a seat, Joann's long curls bobbed as she rolled her eyes and joked sharply about the situation with a male therapist seated behind her. Suzi, Marya and Shoshana slipped quickly into the few remaining seats. Three reporters leaned chattily against the rear wall, pens and pads classically in hand.

The Respondent, Franco Benelli, slightly balding and pale, followed his lawyer into the room. Mr. Horowitz, in a striped suit and bow tie, threaded his way through the crowded aisle with his protruding and bulging briefcase. The Petitioner, Jeanne Jullion, touched toes with the black, high-buttoned boots of her lover, Shana, who was deeply engrossed in the consultations of four calm women lawyers gathered in a circle near the front banister. The long hands of the bold-faced clock signaled 10:00. The bailiff tugged on his uniform and moved to clear the aisle of those without seats. Completing his sweep to the back door, he returned to the front, squeaked an about-face on his black cork shoes and announced loudly over the pitch of continuing conversations:

"COURT IS NOW IN SESSION. JUDGE GORDON MINDER PRESIDING."

Out from the chambers he came, short, swift and well-groomed. Judge Minder stepped up behind his broad paneled desk and stood looking silently out at the packed courtroom from his high perch. He ordered the bailiff to clear the few remaining individuals who had slipped in near the door. He remained standing, scanning the full and silenced courtroom with a sharp and yet almost bemused look. His eyes clearly noted the press along the back wall.

Slowly, judiciously, he took his seat in his brown, high-backed leather chair. He began to speak and with suprising fawningness addressed the court.

"I would like to greet the members of the press that are here today," he cooed. He picked up a pen and began rocking slightly in his chair. He continued: "I have a great deal of respect for the manner in which the press covers the events that happen in this community. I find that it is done with accuracy and fairness.

"However, I must remind the press and those present that this is a case of Family Law concerning divorce and the custody of minor children."

He rocked forward, clacking the pen down on the desk. He picked up a piece of paper and surprised the court by beginning to read a prepared statement.

"Due to the contested nature of the proceedings and the Petitioner's action to involve the media," he read, "a separate lawyer had been appointed by the court to safeguard the children's rights — Mr. Gertmenian, Esq.

"Secondly," his voice escalated, "the Petitioner, Miss Jeanne Jullion, has tried in vain to sway the court by making demands on the court and attempting to garner support from individuals in high standing in the community. I will not allow this courtroom to become a battleground for the testing of the validity or non-validity of any particular social, political or sexual persuasion. To that end and in the interest of the minor children involved,'' he concluded, ''I order that these proceedings be closed to the public and all documents be sealed and kept confidential to the court proceedings.''

NO, chorused both men and women present. Jeanne's heart sank. Judge Minder turned his chair toward the bailiff and said, ''Bailiff, would you please clear the courtroom.''

There was a moment of stunned inaction by the courtroom as a whole, an instinctive and collective refusal to move. The bailiff stood up. The Respondent and his lawyer gave one nervous squeeze to each other's biceps, congratulating themselves. The bailiff came forward, arms churning. Jeanne turned in her chair and caught Shana's eyes. Joann put her arm through Shana's and turned her towards the aisle. The bailiff closed the doors behind the last person and pulled down the shades over the small window on each door.

The room was restored to its ominous dimensions of the first hearing. The glow of the crowd's energy faded like the coals of a fire. Jeanne felt a lonely fear seep back into her heart. The five remaining people settled down at the long table before the judge. Mr. Gertmenian, a pleasant, middle aged man, sat at the center of the table between the opposing sides. Jill cleared her throat, rose to her feet and summoned Jeanne Jullion as her first witness.

CLERK: Do you swear to tell the truth to the best of your ability, so help you God?

JULLION: I do.

CLERK: State your name.

JULLION: Jeanne Jullion.

CLERK: Take a seat next to His Honor.

Jill led Jeanne through a presentation of the situation, during which Mr. Horowitz's objections became progressively more frequent and, at times, blatantly obnoxious. At times Jill could not help but respond directly to his insinuations and distortions of facts, only to be reprimanded by the judge for 'arguing the objection'. At times Jeanne would just sit there in the witness chair waiting to be told, after the dust had cleared, whether or not she could or could not answer a question she couldn't by that time even remember.

Jill concluded her questioning with a final, impromptu question.

LIPPITT: I have one further question. You heard the judge's statement that he made when he cleared the courtroom about his questioning whether or not our use of the media was in the best interests of the children. Would you share with the judge the considerations that you went through in authorizing the use of the media?

Mr. Gertmenian looked up and the judge swung around lightly in his chair, waiting for an answer. Jeanne leaned forward.

JULLION: Yes, I will. I thought about this aspect of it, what will this do to the children. It was only after I was informed of the results and the recommendation by the Probation Officer to take Jesse away from me and to not give me Paul that I felt that I could not come into this court just on my own, that Jesse too would be removed from me. I felt that the issue of my lesbianism has entered into this evaluation and this recommendation, and I truly felt that I needed the support and concern of the community.

Silence hung in the room. She added one more statement and stopped.

JULLION: And I did it in the most responsible way that I could.

JUDGE: Will you mark that, Miss Reporter.

LIPPITT: I have no further questions, Your Honor. However, would it be possible to recess before Mr. Horowitz begins his cross-examination?

JUDGE: Yes, we will recess for 15 minutes.

Cigarettes met the lips as the hands met the door.

"They're out!" came a voice from the adjoining witness waiting room.

Franco and Armin Horowitz emerged from Department 15, puffy like roosters. Franco sneered at Jeanne as he passed, exuding satisfaction at the judge's reprimand of their actions and his move to close the courtroom. Joined by Jeanne's father and talking loudly, the three men moved down the hall, now vacant of the excitement of two hours earlier.

Shana hurried out of the witness waiting room. A group of women quickly circled Jill and Jeanne.

"Jeanne," Joann asked to one side, eyeing the greyish hue of her cheeks, "do you want me to get you something from the snack bar?"

"Yes, milk. There's not much time though."

Jeanne loosened the button on her borrowed slacks and drew on her cigarette, waiting through Jill's recap as long as she could before she erupted with the question —

"But Jill, what does 'marking the record' mean? What was that about?"

"What do you mean? What are you talking about?" Shana's questions cascaded on the heels of Jeanne's. Being shut out of the proceedings that were affecting her life so deeply was almost more than she could stand. Jill recounted the judge's actions and then concluded, "I don't know. He's up to something but I don't know what."

"I'm scared about Horowitz's cross-examination," Jeanne muttered, glancing down the hall at the posturing men. "I hate this."

"You'll do fine. Don't let him get to you." *Easier said —*

Behind her, the bailiff's voice barked that court was resuming. No milk, only last swallows on a second cigarette. Her head reeled a bit as they drew themselves away from the warmth of the women and re-entered the patriarchal hollowness of the courtroom.

Judge Minder signaled Mr. Horowitz to begin which he did with an aggressiveness meant to unnerve.

HOROWITZ: Miss Jullion, did you take JESSE with you when you went for your press conference at the Glide Memorial Church?

JULLION: No, I did not.

HOROWITZ: Did you take either of the children to any press conferences that you had?

JULLION: No, I have not.

HOROWITZ: Did you contact the media?

JULLION: Yes, they were contacted.

HOROWITZ: I assume Jesse —

JUDGE: Wait. Before the question is lost, he asked you if you contacted and you said they were contacted. Who contacted them?

JULLION: Friends of mine actually contacted the media.

Horowitz resumed like a dog on a scent.

HOROWITZ: Was it your initial idea to do this contacting?

JULLION: Yes, it was.

HOROWITZ: So the idea to get the media, the television and the newspapers, was your initial idea, is that correct?

JULLION: Yes, I felt it was in —

HOROWITZ: Just answer the question if you would ''yes'' or ''no''.

JULLION: Yes.

HOROWITZ: And Jesse last night, which television shows was he allowed to watch?

JULLION: He saw the one where they were playing music on Channel 7.

HOROWITZ: You feel it was important that Jesse see this, is that correct?

JULLION: The children were very anxious to see themselves on TV.

HOROWITZ: My question was: Did Jesse —

JULLION: Did Jesse what?

HOROWITZ: My question was: Did Jesse observe that?

JULLION: Yes, he did.

HOROWITZ: And you are talking in the cumulative when you refer to the children. I assume you are referring to Miss Ascher's children as well, is that correct?

JULLION: I am referring to our whole family, yes.

HOROWITZ: And did you have discussions with Jesse prior to allowing the television film crews to come to your home?

JULLION: Not an extensive one. We talked to all the children.

HOROWITZ: Could you tell the court what you told Jesse?

JULLION: I told Jesse that TV cameras were coming to take pictures of our home, that we — they wanted to see what our home was like, that it concerned whether he would be able to continue to live with me.

HOROWITZ: Had you previously discussed with Jesse that the Probation Officer requested or suggested that perhaps the custody of the two children go to Mr. Benelli?

JULLION: I told him last Friday that we were going to speak to the judge about where would be the best place for him to live, and that I was concerned — Dr. Nestor advised me that, given the Probation Officer's recommendation, that it was necessary to in some way forewarn Jesse in case the decision should go that way.

"Look at yourself," Dr. Nestor had counselled her as she left his office. "You're having a hard enough time dealing with this and you're an adult. You've got to prepare him. You've got to prepare him for the fact that he might have to leave you."

Back at the house, Jeanne walked distractedly into the living room, hooked her foot around the black piano bench and scooted it out to sit on. She sat with a hand on each knee until Jesse burst into the living room from outside.

"Jesse," Jeanne started, as if a statue were speaking. "Jesse, wait a sec. Com'ere, honey."

"Oh, hi, mom," he changed direction abruptly and crashed into her legs. He hugged her thighs tightly. Jeanne's strong hands spread wide like paws and clamped around his short, round thighs. She scooped him head first and dishevelled into her lap and he laughed and laughed. Tilting him back in her hands, she took a long look at him. Slowly she raised him up straight, sitting facing her on her knees.

"Oh Jesse," she began, "I hate to tell you this but I really gotta talk to you, honey." She smoothed his curls back off his tanned forehead.

"Listen, honey, listen to me carefully. You know your daddy and I don't — live together as a family anymore."

Jesse started to listen to his mother. His pudgy fingers opened and closed over her hand.

"I want you and Paul to live with me but now a judge is going to decide that."

Jesse was listening real carefully now, waiting for what she was saying, hand opening and closing over hers.

"We go back to the judge tomorrow. It'll take a few days to talk to him. Jessie, listen. I don't want this, believe me, I don't. But there's a chance, a chance that maybe you'll have to go live with your father.''

Jesse didn't say anything, and then announced, "But I don't wan' to," as if that were that.

"I know, but if that's what the judge says, then that's what has to happen."

"No!" He pushed her away. "No!" he squirmed down out of her lap. "I don't wanna go. I want to stay here with you."

"I know," air gushed out Jeanne's mouth, "I know. I'm doing everything I can. But it's hard."

Large tears appeared suddenly in the corners of his eyes.

"But we'll see," she tried to brush away the damage, go on with the day, the play, as if. But the blow had landed, the first tear had been made, to be followed by the tears, the confusion, the wetting.

"I don't want to go!" he yelled again. "I wanna live with YOU."

"I know that, Jesse," Jeanne repeated. "I understand. Your father's the one who needs to hear it…"

"I'm going to call Daddy."

"Huh? Wow, well, I guess you could. I don't know if he'll listen.

"I'll tell him," Jesse asserted with confidence.

The phone call, uselessly written off as something his mother had put him up to. Leaning against the doorway, she had watched her small son's worried face change as he was distracted, lured, teased away from what was on his mind.

HOROWITZ: And did Jesse make a phone call to his father at your request?

JULLION: No, it was at his request.

HOROWITZ: Jesse is the THREE year-old?

JULLION: Yes.

HOROWITZ: That was a telephone call then where he asked his father not to take him, is that correct?

JULLION: Yes.

HOROWITZ: You were present when that conversation took place also, were you not?

JULLION: Yes, I was.

HOROWITZ: Miss Jullion, before this case started, didn't you tell your husband that this is a very sensitive matter concerning custody and it should be left to the Probation Officer and to the judge?

JULLION: Yes, and I have done my best to stick by that.

HOROWITZ: And then about a week and a half ago you called your husband and said that this is such a sensitive matter that it shouldn't be left to the Probation Officer and the judge, isn't that correct?

JULLION: I feel that ultimately my husband and I should resolve this.

HOROWITZ: Would you please respond to my question?

JULLION: What was your question again?

JUDGE: Read the question, Miss Reporter.

JULLION: Yes.

HOROWITZ: So you changed your mind. And am I correct that the change was because of the fact you had the Probation report?

JULLION: No.

HOROWITZ: You certainly believe that Jesse and Paul should live together, don't you?

JULLION: I decide what I feel is in their best interest on an individual basis. I think Jesse should stay with me. I think that is unquestionable. I see that my oldest son is in need of an extended period with me. If you are trying to lead me down the path of saying that the children should be together at all costs, and if that means removing Jesse from his mother, then I think that is a secondary bond which does not override the primary bond of him to his mother.

HOROWITZ: You believe though that Paul should be removed from the father, isn't that correct?

JULLION: I think he should live with me, at least during the school year, and have as full a relationship with his father as possible. I'm not trying to obstruct that.

HOROWITZ: Miss Jullion, do you want this hearing to be open to the television cameras?

JULLION: This hearing? No, I don't see where that is in anyway indicated.

HOROWITZ: I assume you plan to talk to the press about this afterwards?

JULLION: I want to be sure of what Judge Minder said at the beginning, which I'm not very clear on. If he is recommending we do not talk to them, I will abide by that.

HOROWITZ: As I understand it he hasn't made that order. And with that assumption in mind, do you plan to talk to them?

JULLION: I don't have any plans of contacting them on my own. If they ask me what the result was, I feel they have the right to know what the result was.

HOROWITZ: You would tell them, is that correct?

JULLION: Yes.

HOROWITZ: Did you advise the people that interviewed you where your husband was employed?

JULLION: No, I did not.

HOROWITZ: Have you any idea how they found out where he was employed?

JULLION: I believe that I did mention it to the reporter from Channel 5 and then I realized that it was a mistake and I didn't give that information out again.

JUDGE: Excuse me. Did you do it once, though?

JULLION: Yes, I did.

HOROWITZ: Did you ever tell any of the channels to call his place of employment?

JULLION: No, never.

HOROWITZ: You know where he works?

JULLION: I think it's called St. Joseph's Seminary.

HOROWITZ: Did you know his teaching contract is up for renewal at this time?

JULLION: Yes, I think he's told me that.

HOROWITZ: Did he tell you it has to be read to the bishop for approval and signature?

JULLION: No.

HOROWITZ: Do you feel it's to the best interest of the children to have your husband's job jeopardized in that regard with this exposure?

JULLION: In no way was I trying to jeopardize my husband's employment.

HOROWITZ: Let me refer you to the article in the Examiner. Read for the record, Miss Jullion, this part down here staring with "Benelli, age 34..."

LIPPITT: Your Honor, may we have a slight break so I may read this article? He's been cross-examining. I haven't been able to pay attention to both.

JUDGE: Certainly. Yes, in fact we'll take our noon recess, until 1:30. You may step down.

Oh my body aches, Jeanne realized as she slowly pushed herself from the blue upholstered chair. Black robes swooshed and exited behind her.

Women came out of the waiting room.

"Let's go to Grandma's for lunch," Sheila suggested.

"What's Grandma's?"

"It's a gay restaurant, right across the street. They serve lunches. It's run by gay men."

"Right across the street from the courthouse?"

"Yeah. Judges eat there all the time."

Mr. Horowitz resumed after lunch by waving the morning issue of the *San Francisco Examiner* in the air.

"Your Honor, could I have this marked?"

Judge Minder opened a large ledger in front of him. "That will be Respondent's. A. Any objection to it going into evidence, counsel?"

Jill proceeded to register an objection which was quickly overruled. Mr. Horowitz forged ahead.

HOROWITZ: Now, Miss Jullion, tell me how many people were in the courtroom today for your cause.

JULLION: I don't know how many.

HOROWITZ: Would you estimate it was over 50?

JULLION: I don't know what the courtroom seats — 40, 50. I don't know.

JUDGE: Rather than ask the witness to express an opinion, I'll recite for the record, and counsel will correct me if I'm wrong, that every seat in the courtroom was occupied, that at least 20 people were standing in the center aisle, and there were persons seated in the jury box. Now, would any counsel like to venture a different opinion?

LIPPITT: I would ask all this information be stricken as having no relevance on this case. The fact that the public has responded —

JUDGE: Please. If you want to make an objection, do so and tell me the grounds without arguing the motion.

LIPPITT: Lack of relevance.

JUDGE: Objection may be overruled. Let me ask you again whether what I stated is reasonably accurate with reference to what you people saw this morning.

"Reasonably accurate," Jill said flatly. Judge Minder appeared ready to take bets. Satisfied, the judge nodded to Horowitz to proceed.

"Now, we've heard a lot about your home in Oakland. Can you tell us a little about your external relationships, in other words, what is your relationship with your parents?"

Jeanne looked at Franco and shook her head. She shifted her weight in the chair and answered measuredly.

JULLION: My relationship with my parents is in great difficulty ever since I told them that I am a lesbian. They are older, they have a very rigid Catholic mentality and —

JUDGE: Mentality, did you say?

JULLION: Yes. And they are unable to accept this as a valid way of life for me. Since their objection comes strictly from religious grounds, I tried to facilitate a meeting with two Catholic priests who have a deep theological understanding of this issue and biblical sources on it, and they told me they would sit down with the — with their own parish priest to try to mediate, to open up some communication. But when a meeting was actually set up, my parents refused to got through with it.

Jeanne finished slowly, remembering her mother saying, "Well, I don't think we'll come."

"Mother, please! It's tomorrow. It's all set up. You can bring your parish priest like you wanted. Tomorrow, Sunday, at 6:30. It's important, Mom," she pleaded.

"I know it's important," she echoed a bit vacantly. "But it's not going to change our minds, I don't care what anybody says, Jeanne. It's unnatural and it's a sin. It just isn't moral."

"Mom, that's what the Catholic Church has taught you but the thinking in the Church is changing. These are Catholic priests. Please, let's just talk about it. It might help."

"Well, I don't think it will," she said flatly. "I don't care what they say, I know it's wrong and them saying different isn't going to make it right. I don't know what kind of priests they are anyway to be saying that."

"They are Catholic priests, Mom," Jeanne said, feeling a bridge of sand eroding away from under her feet.

"Well, I don't care if the Church does say it's right — it's still wrong."

The phone line whined in the ensuing silence.

"Why don't you come home, Jeanne, and stop this..."

"I don't feel I can come home — as me."

"Come home," she coaxed. "Just don't bring that woman. You can come home," she said, "just as long as... you aren't... who you are."

"So," Jeanne finished answering Mr. Horowitz's question, "I'm at a loss how to overcome this obstacle."

Jeanne noticed that Mr. Gertmenian appeared to have perhaps understood. Mr. Horowitz took a few steps, pushed his horn-rimmed glasses up his nose and burrowed on.

"What about your sister?" Again Jeanne shot a single look at Franco. "How is your external relationship with your sister?"

"My sister is equally condemning, also from a very rigid Catholic viewpoint. And I also made an attempt about two weeks ago to meet with her and her husband. I gathered some research together — she doesn't know any gay people."

"Could you — "

"And she and her husband refused to meet with me and refused to look at any of the literature," she finished flatly.

"About this literature, you also recently called your mother and told her you wanted to drop off some HOMO-LESBIAN literature, is that correct?"

Horowitz half laughed as he leered at the words. Jill's mouth dropped open and Jeanne twisted in the swivel chair. Jeanne looked over to Judge Minder who showed no objection to Mr. Horowitz's slur. Franco covered his mouth and snickered in his chair.

The incident hyperbolized by Mr. Horowitz was clear in Jeanne's mind. It had occurred months earlier during Jeanne and Shana's third and final visit to her parents' home. Conversation was not coming easily. Jeanne had seen a book put together by parents of gays and asked her mother if she would read a book if she sent it to her. Her mother laughed out loud and looked at her husband.

"No, I don't want any books like that in my house." Then she added, "Probably written by a bunch of homos anyway."

"Mother!"

"Well, they probably are," she repeated again with a single, loud laugh. Her cheeks flushed shiny red and she basked in a total camaraderie on the point with her husband.

Jeanne and Shana caught each other's eyes as they walked out past the pool in the condominium complex that evening — no more visits, they agreed. That night in bed, Shana kissed Jeanne's nipple and with both hands on her narrow waist tried to gently jostle these words out of her mind.

"A bunch of homos, eh. Is that what we are?" Jeanne muttered.

"Com'on, sleep," came the slurred reply.

"Eh," Jeanne spewed, "look out." That attentive brown nipple rolled across Shana's cheek. Jeanne stuffed a pillow behind her shoulders, summoned Shana back into her arms and kissed her.

"Thanks, Shana, for going through all this with me."

"Yeah."

"Really. Here, don't go away. Sleep in my arms." Jeanne wound her long arms around her tired lover's back and stroked the slope of her hips. Shana burrowed into the fragrant curve of her arm and her breast and fell asleep.

"No, you are not correct," Jeanne answered Mr. Horowitz curtly.

"Then gay literature?"

"No."

"What type of literature?"

"I did not call her and offer to drop off any literature," Jeanne replied uncooperatively.

"When is the time you got into the argument with your mother concerning the literature you wanted her to read?"

"In November — Shana and I made about three or four calls."

"And what was her response?"

Jeanne cleared her throat. "Her response was that 'They're probably written by a bunch of homos anyway'."

"And your response was to become irate, wasn't it?"

"No."

"You remember swearing at your mother?"

"No."

"You remember using the term 'shit'?" The word hung in the room.

"No."

"Do you remember your father telling you not to speak to your mother in that language regardless of what your feelings were on the subject?"

"Mr. Horowitz, on one visit to my parents' home — I really don't remember which — the conversation became extremely overheated and extremely emotional, and my father was using abusive language towards me. At one point perhaps I did say 'shit'. He objected and I told him that — "

" — you could use it any time you wanted?"

Jeanne glared at him and answered measuredly, "I reminded him he was using the same language and my mother was capable of telling me herself."

"Did they tell you you were becoming irrational?"

"No," she said, rejecting the hysterical woman label.

"Did you feel you were becoming irrational?" he cajoled in a quasi-intimate tone of voice.

"No more than they were," Jeanne said pointedly. Mr. Gertmenian smiled and looked down at his notes.

The cross-examination droned on endlessly, through real and fabricated incidences and issues. The impact of the morning show of strength had clearly worn off. Objections were being summarily overruled with progressively less concern for how anyone might feel about it.

"You are not going to pay taxes, you told your husband, isn't that correct?"

"No, I haven't told him anything of the sort," Jeanne answered wearily, wondering how the judge would ever sort out fact from fabrication. Horowitz continued, never seeming to run out.

HOROWITZ: Because Mr. Gertmenian and Miss Lippitt weren't here at the last hearing, can you tell us in summary, again, what your view of society is today?

JULLION: That's a very broad question.

HOROWITZ: Let me ask you specifically, have you told your husband you don't feel society has any values you want to relate to?

JULLION: That's absolutely incorrect, and I did not say that at the first hearing either.

HOROWITZ: And you also didn't testify at any time that you ever told your husband you wanted to go underground?

JULLION: No.

HOROWITZ: I have nothing further.

Mr. Horowitz's questioning came abruptly to an end. Judge Minder motioned to the children's lawyer.

JUDGE: Do you have any questions, Mr. Gertmenian?

GERTMENIAN: Yes, I do.

LIPPITT: May I inquire whether Miss Jullion would like a break?

JUDGE: Do you feel in need of a recess?

JULLION: I am in need of a cigarette.

JUDGE: We're going to be recessing for the day in a few minutes. If you are uncomfortable —

"No, then I prefer to finish," Jeanne answered, wanting her part over with. *What a relief to have Horowitz's cross-examination finished,* she thought to herself.

Mr. Gertmenian began with questions that were clear, simple, not devised for distortion or entrapment. He seemed interested in clarifying pertinent information — her intended work schedule, school plans for the children, TV and sports for the boys. Then he returned to the issue of the media.

GERTMENIAN: I think you testified you felt it was necessary to go to the media because you couldn't come to court alone.

JULLION: That's right.

GERTMENIAN: What effect did you think media exposure would have?

JULLION: I felt that by me coming here only as an individual lesbian and mother that my home was not being taken seriously and not being validated because it was headed by — the heads of the household are gay. And I felt that I needed the backing of the community to validate my right to have my home recognized as a good, viable home, even including the fact that I am gay, that Shana is gay.

GERTMENIAN: In the eyes of the Court, do you mean?

JULLION: Yes, in the eyes of the Court. The first hearing was dominated with where do you sleep and do I conduct sexual activities in front of the children. Questions that would never be directed to a heterosexual. You'd just presume a certain amount of common sense about such things. And I felt that the focus… on those myths and prejudices had to be removed and that the court should just look at my home as a home.

GERTMENIAN: What kind of effect do you think that media exposure will have on Paul?

JULLION: I don't know. I don't know if he has seen it. But what I opened up to the media was my home.

GERTMENIAN: Well, you opened up something more than that to the media, didn't you?

JULLION: What do you mean?

GERTMENIAN: Well, you opened up your cause, the cause of lesbian mothers to the media, didn't you?

Jeanne answered tentatively, not liking the bandwagon-sounding *cause*.

JULLION: Yes…

GERTMENIAN: Is that the cause of Paul and Jesse?

JULLION: No, but they are affected.

GERTMENIAN: They were brought into that cause, weren't they?

JULLION: Paul was not touched by it. But he was concerned because he is my child.

GERTMENIAN: I think you said that you did that to help your children. How did that help Paul?

JULLION: I am firmly convinced it is in Paul's best interest to be with me.

GERTMENIAN: I'm sorry. I'm having trouble understanding how you thought that helped.

JULLION: How does it help Paul?

JUDGE: That was the question.

The judge was clearly listening closely. Jeanne felt bewildered at the lack of penetration of her answers. Her mind felt sluggish, tired, groping.

JULLION: It helps Paul by — removing the lesbian issue and focusing on the quality of my parenting and the quality of our home and these are the grounds on which I'm asking for Paul.

GERTMENIAN: I guess — how did that eliminate the lesbian issue by putting the issue in the newspaper?

JUDGE: Mark that, Miss Reporter.

JULLION: I'm getting very tired. So let me try, see if I can say this better. Let me say it this way — I felt that by having a list of supporters whose integrity and public standing in the community, by — by having them support me in my right as a lesbian to be given equal consideration for custody of my children, that this would be helpful.

GERTMENIAN: Helpful to Paul?

JULLION: Yes, to Paul.

GERTMENIAN: Hm. I think you testified earlier that you've had discussions with Jesse about the possibility that he may go live with his father.

JULLION: This week I have.

GERTMENIAN: How did he react to that?

JULLION: He reacted by crying and he reacted by saying very strongly and clearly that he wanted to live with me, that he wanted to visit his father, but he wanted to stay here, that he didn't want to leave me, didn't want to leave the other children.

GERTMENIAN: After he got through with that, did he get over the crying?

JULLION: Yes, he got over the crying, but he has been wetting his bed, he's been wetting his pants and he's woken up at night with a stomach ache.

GERTMENIAN: If you lose his custody, do you intend to pursue the issue of your right to custody in the newspapers?

JULLION: I don't know if it would be pertinent. It would depend on whether I felt that the reason why I was denied custody was the fact that I was lesbian. If that were the case, then I think it would be justifiable. If that were not the case, I'm not interested in this, the limelight and notoriety. That is not, you know, why I'm doing it.

GERTMENIAN: Don't you think that noteriety can have an embarrassing effect on someone Paul's age?

Oh, that's what you're worried about! Being on TV that your mom's a — Shame, that's what you're looking for. YOU feel that it's embarrassing and shameful that I'm a lesbian and I'm their mother. Jeanne threw the ball back to him.

JULLION: Why should it be embarrassing?

GERTMENIAN: I'm asking what's your opinion. Could that be embarrassing to him?

JULLION: I don't see how he could be embarrassd that his mother — I am openly gay.

GERTMENIAN: I understand.

JULLION: And I don't consider that an embarrassment. The other thing I'm saying is that I love him and I want him to live with me and I don't think that's an embarrassment.

GERTMENIAN: You don't think noteriety, namely in the paper, pictures, television coverage of his custody, is something that could bring embarrassment to him?

JULLION: No.

GERTMENIAN: You think that's perfectly fine?

JULLION: I regret the situation as such. I really do.

GERTMENIAN: I don't think I have anything further.

Jeanne looked over at Judge Miner for a cue to get down. He took some papers in his hands and swung his tall, leather chair slowly around towards the witness.

JUDGE: Do you know what the JEANNE JULLION DEFENSE COMMITTEE is?

JULLION: Yes, those are some people who have come to my assistance.

JUDGE: You know they made demands on this Court?

JULLION: Yes, I do.

JUDGE: Who prompted that?

JULLION: Who prompted that?

JUDGE: Who prompted this Defense Committee to make demands on this Court?

JULLION: I felt that it was necessary that these — these issues be specifically laid out and brought to your attention.

JUDGE: Did you contact Congressman Stark?

JULLION: The Defense Committee did.

JUDGE: Did you?

JULLION: Not personally, no.

JUDGE: Did you contact Congressman Dellums?

JULLION: Not personally, no.

JUDGE: Did you contact Assemblyman Willie Brown?

JULLION: The Defense Committee did.

JUDGE: Did you contact Supervisor John George?

JULLION: The Defense Committee contacted all the parties.

JUDGE: All of them? You didn't contact any of them?

JULLION: I didn't do it personally.

JUDGE: Was it with your blessing?

JULLION: Yes.

Judge Minder laid the papers carefully aside and picked up his pen.

JUDGE: Who is on this Defense Committee? Their names, please.

JULLION: (Looking at her lawyer.) Uh, well there's Sheila Goldmacher, Suzi — I don't know her last name...

JUDGE: And where does this Sheila Goldmacher live?

JULLION: Pardon me?

JUDGE: Where does she live? What is her address?

JULLION: I don't know.

JUDGE: And where does she work?

JULLION: I don't know.

JUDGE: How about the addresses and places of employment of these others?

JULLION: I'm sorry but I don't know.

(Silence.)

JUDGE: Miss Jullion, you may step down. Court is recessed until 10 a.m. Monday morning. (BAM!) COURT IS ADJOURNED.

1

On Monday morning the five people resumed their places in Judge Minder's courtroom. Franco looked pale but rested and Mr. Horowitz sported a white bow tie. Mr. Gertmenian greeted everyone pleasantly and sat between Jeanne and Mr. Horowitz. Jill's auburn hair rested in long strands on the shoulders of her black suit jacket as she reviewed the Probation Officer's report once again. White ruffles spilled out the V of her vest as she studied the document. Jeanne felt comfortable in a borrowed herringbone blazer and dark slacks. She stretched out her legs under the table and suppressed a nervous yawn, relieved that her part of the proceedings was over. COURT IS NOW IN SESSION.

Jeanne's heart thumped as she saw Mr. Horowitz stand and ask that she retake the stand. Already sworn in, Jeanne climbed the three carpeted steps to the dark blue witness chair.

HOROWITZ: Miss Jullion, you recall when you lived in the commune on Benvenue? You recall that?

JULLION: The single parent house, yes.

HOROWITZ: Weren't you staying with another woman and your child, Jesse, in the same room in that single parent residence?

JULLION: No, I lived there alone with Jesse. Nobody ever lived there with me in my room.

HOROWITZ: My question is did you spend the night with another woman?

JULLION: On a couple of occasions, yes.

HOROWITZ: And did you have sexual acts with that woman on the premises at that time?

JULLION: I did not.

HOROWITZ: Is your answer you were not having relations during that period of time?

JULLION: That's correct.

HOROWITZ: And what was her name?

LIPPITT: I'm going to object, Your Honor. I think there's no relevance to this.

JUDGE: Well, the objection may be overruled. She may answer.

JULLION: Her name was Natalie, Natalie Zarchin.

HOROWITZ: Miss Jullion, did you happen to read *The Oakland Tribune* on Saturday?

JULLION: No, I haven't seen it.

HOROWITZ: Did you have any conversation with any representative from *The Tribune* after court here?

JULLION: No, I did not.

HOROWITZ: And it still made the front page?

JULLION: That's where they put it.

HOROWITZ: Your Honor, I'd ask that the article be introduced in-to evidence.

LIPPITT: I would object to its introduction into evidence, and I would ask for what it is offered as proof.

JUDGE: I think it may go into evidence. It will go in as C.

HOROWITZ: By the way, who is head of this Jeanne Jullion Defense Fund. Is that you?

JULLION: No.

HOROWITZ: Who is the head of it?

JULLION: There are several individuals working on a collective basis. There isn't a head.

HOROWITZ: Have you taken Jesse, or Paul when he's visited with you in the last year, at any time to church?

Oh christ, Franco. Jeanne swore to herself, looking over at him, remembering their agitated confrontations about religion, his proud anti-clericism clashing with her ecumenical spirituality. The thought that the Court would, of course, prefer to have the children brought up with religious training nagged quickly at the corners of Jeanne's mind, prodding her to lie. But she answered in fact.

JULLION: No, I have not.

HOROWITZ: Do you follow any religious denomination at this time?

JULLION: No, I do not.

HOROWITZ: Do you plan, if awarded custody of one or both of the children, to expose either of them to any religious background?

JULLION: Not at this time.

HOROWITZ: And if Miss Ascher happens to be residing with you and she happens to be celebrating Chanukah, you'll celebrate Chanukah, is that correct?

JULLION: We may participate by singing the song or watching the candles be lit.

HOROWITZ: What about the services? Will they participate in that?

JULLION: No.

HOROWITZ: And have either of the children, to your knowledge, gone to church with their father in the last year?

JULLION: I don't know.

HOROWITZ: I have nothing further.

Jeanne returned to her seat and there was a lull as the bailiff went to summon the next witness from the witness waiting room: Shana. She looked a matronly mother of four as she was sworn in. As she sat down in the witness chair and crossed her legs, her black patten, antique boot sort of jutted out in mid-air. Her choice of these boots had provoked a bitter, frightened argument with Jeanne earlier that morning.

"You can't wear those!"

"The hell I can't."

"Shana, you'll be testifying today. Those are too camp, they're too weird."

"They are not. They're dressy."

"Shana, please. The judge can't relate to — "

"The judge, the judge! First, Spence — no, first your parents, then Spence, now the judge. You're so paranoid about how we look, how this place looks, the kids — there's nothing wrong with being poor, which we are right now, and there's nothing wrong with the way we look, Jeanne, so lay off."

Jeanne stared at the pointed 1930's boots Shana was lacing up on the bed. "Sure, those boots are perfect — for the witch's shoes in the Wizard of Oz."

"Odds, remember? That's what we are."

Jeanne turned and pulled the door shut with a slam behind her. She was, in truth, terrified of her lover's appearance in court and the concoction brewing in one man's mind.

Jill smiled at her witness and began a tapestry of questioning designed to ignore Shana's identity as Jeanne's lover and focus on her as a mother, a mother of four. Her testimony was a purposeful string of vignettes, told with humor and warmth, about life with five and six children. A lot was said but little seemingly heard of these building blocks of children's lives.

Mr. Horowitz seemed to relish his chance at cross-examining

Shana, an opportunity missed at the first hearing. Some damage was done but his attacks met a worried but witty and unintimidated foe in the person of Shana Ascher. By noon recess, Shana was through.

After lunch Jill swung on the offensive by calling the Probation Officer, Fred Spence, to the stand. He would have presumably been called as a witness for the husband's side. However, rather than give Mr. Horowitz a chance to entrench the Probation Officer's opinions in the judge's mind and then be left to try to dislodge them, Jill had decided to call him as her own witness.

Jill smiled and handed him a copy of his own report.

"Now, Mr. Spence," she began loudly, turning her back and walking back to the table, "will you please turn to page one of your home evaluation..."

Jill mercilessly took the stammering witness step by step through every page of his report, noting one by one its discrepancies, double standards and bias.

LIPPITT: Why is it, Mr. Spence, that when you refer to the father's situation you use the simple, clear present tense — "is", "are", "have" — but when you refer to the mother's situation everything is "seems"? The children "seem" happy, "seem" well-cared for, "seem" well-adjusted? Do you have difficulty believing that children can be happy, can be well-cared for, can do just as well with a loving homosexual parent as they do with a loving heterosexual parent? Do you think, Mr. Spence, that children respond to labels or love? You are aware, Mr. Spence, are you not, that the younger child, Jesse, has never been separated from his mother, is that correct?

SPENCE: Yes.

LIPPITT: And how is he doing?

SPENCE: Fine.

LIPPITT: Speak up, Mr. Spence.

SPENCE: He appears to be doing fine.

LIPPITT: 'Appears' to be. I see. And did you contact Dr. Nestor for his professional evaluation?

SPENCE: Yes.

LIPPITT: And you are aware that the father secured a court order preventing Dr. Nestor from seeing the older boy and that the father refused to participate in any counselling or mediation attempts?

SPENCE: Yes.

LIPPITT: What is Dr. Nestor's evaluation of the one child he was allowed to see — Jesse?

SPENCE: He said he was doing well.

LIPPITT: Speak up, please, Mr. Spence.

SPENCE: He said he was doing well.

LIPPITT: Did he say he was doing well with his mother or exceptionally well with his mother, that he was one of the most well-adjusted children he'd seen in his twenty years of practice, Mr. Spence.

SPENCE: I — I don't remember that.

LIPPITT: Well, the Court will have a chance to hear from Dr. Nestor personally. But you, Mr. Spence, in spite of all this, you have recommended that this Court remove this child from his mother, is that correct?

SPENCE: Yes.

LIPPITT: Mr. Spence, tell the Court something. Did your supervisor have anything to do with the decision in favor of Jeanne's husband?

SPENCE: No.

LIPPITT: Hm. Then it is your conclusion as the best thing to do.

SPENCE: Yes.

Jill completed her interrogation. The men in the room all exuded a certain uneasiness at the dismemberment, so to speak, of a fellow male at the hands of, good heavens, a female. Perspiring and limp, Mr. Spence slipped off the witness chair and out the rear door. Looking at the clock, Judge Minder decided the afternoon hour was sufficiently tardy to recess for the day. His calendar was filled tomorrow and the parties were ordered to return and finish on Wednesday.

Jill and Jeanne pushed through the swinging doors and poked their grinning faces around the corner of the witness room.

"What happened? What happened?" chorused Shana, Joann and Shoshana, springing to their feet in the windowless room. "Is it over? Did we win?"

"No, no," Jill and Jeanne's faces clouded over momentarily. "But Jill demolished Spence," Jeanne announced. Jill tilted her head and grinned widely. They moved excitedly down the hall and gathered into a vacant elevator. Franco, thinking surely of his upcoming turn in the witness chair, hung back from the glow of the women's energy and waited with Mr. Horowitz for another elevator.

On the First Floor, the group chattered past the blind man's candy counter and out the front door. Arm in arm they crossed the street and dipped into the darkened interior of Grandma's Bar and Restaurant. Wine flowed with the stories of Shana's morning duel with Mr. Horowitz and Jill's afternoon work. One more day of testimony, Jeanne thought amidst the laughter, then we'll know.

Fatigue and the wine settled heavy on Jill. She faded back into her chair. Joann leaned back and beckoned to the smiling man at the bar for the check. Outside the sun hung low and red over Oakland, waiting for the women to reluctantly leave the precious hour of optimism and honeysweet taste of piecemeal victory. Warm and quiet, Shana and Jeanne headed the aged Comet home.

2

Tuesday morning's light stirred Jeanne's eyelids to creep open. *Ah, no court today!* She lifted Shana's sleeping arm and draped it around her neck like a stole. Jeanne wrapped herself around Shana's large frame and sunk into the softness of her sleeping body. *No court today.*

The door knob rattled and a knock was heard halfway up the door.

"Huh?" The door opened.

"Mom, I can't wake up Hannah. She's dead."

"Aaron!" came a muffled exclamation.

"Well, you know," he stood on one leg with a satyr's smile, "dead to the world."

"Oh Aaron, come here," yawned Shana. "Let me see what clothes you put on. God, go wash that face — "

"Yeah, I know, and comb my hair."

"Well, if you knew it already why didn't you just do it, hm? Your clothes look fine. Listen, try waking Hannah again. It's late. Whisper in her ear that it's preferable that I don't have to come up there."

"Huh?"

"Just go."

The heads of Jesse and Dov were moving along the foot of the high platform bed.

"Can we get up?" they popped up and pleaded.

"No."

"Yes."

"Alright."

"Oh, Jesse, you're all wet," Jeanne exclaimed as she scooped them up over the edge.

"Damn Franco," Shana swore into the pillow.

Jesse laughed brokenly. "You'll have to get down and go change, honey. Dov, let me see something. Did you remember to put some socks on?"

"I don't need socks."

"How can you wear cowboy boots with no socks? Doesn't that hurt your feet?" His favorite boot clung to his bare foot. Once removed, Jeanne looked at the pink width of his foot and the narrow taper of his beloved boots. "I don't know how you wear these, Dov. Anyway, with socks, you hear? Now, scram. And quiet in the kitchen, you guys. Let Dennis sleep. We all get to sleep. Get some granola for now — we'll fix eggs later."

The blue phone on the foot of the bed rang periodically, press and friends asking if they had a decision.

3

On Wednesday morning, Shana and Jeanne smoked a last cigarette together in the chill marble hall before Shana moved to keep her last day's vigil in the small adjacent room.

Dr. Nestor's eyes twitched perceptibly as he took the oath as the day's first witness. He squirmed slightly in the witness chair as if nestling a place in the sand at the beach. He smoothed his blue suit jacket and pant leg several times and then appeared ready to begin. Jill led him through his list of degrees and credentials. Horowitz picked and protested, hoping to disqualify Dr. Nestor as he had Dr. Wroblewski at the first hearing. Dr. Nestor's credentials and experience withstood his challenge, however, and he was accepted by the court as an expert in child and adult psychiatry.

LIPPITT: Dr. Nestor, you were only allowed to spend time with the younger child, Jesse, is that correct?

NESTOR: Yes.

LIPPITT: He has been in the exclusive care of his mother, is that correct?

NESTOR: Yes.

LIPPITT: And how would you rate his development, both emotional and social, in his mother's care?

NESTOR: Excellent, above average... In my professional opinion, it would be extremely damaging to remove this child from his mother's care. It really should be unthinkable...

Jeanne looked up at Judge Minder and realized incredulously that he was deliberately not paying attention! Stunned, she continued to watch him steadfastly ignore the key testimony being given. His testimony concluded and Dr. Nestor stepped down, nodding encouragement or sympathy to Jeanne as he passed, she wasn't sure which. After a recess, Jill summoned the next witness — Franco Benelli.

Franco's face jarred, pale as the day he was married. He approached the bench and stood, hand raised, in his best Italian suit, pledging allegiance to truth and his once-again-adopted America. His voice scraped out shaky and garbled from deep in his throat and watching him, Jeanne wondered bitterly how it had ever come to this.

Wisps of nostalgia, however, were quickly blown away as Franco's testimony began. The vehement anti-clerical was now the devout and obedient Catholic. Apple pie and all-American dad, he was hitting heavy on Church, football and TV. He spoke in a distressed voice and thick accent of his wife's turning away from "all the traditional values of American life."

Although over 100 questions had been prepared, Jill approached Jeanne at recess with an abrupt change in strategy.

"Listen to me, Jeanne," she began. "I've thought about it and I'm afraid that a grueling cross-examination will probably only engender sympathy for your husband in the judge's eyes. Jeanne, I think we should be more... cajoling. In fact, I strongly urge you to go over and speak briefly to Franco. Just talk a little bit before we go back in."

Perplexed, Jeanne stiffened. "Good god, Jill, what are you talking about? He's definitely going to take my children away from me if he can, you know that. He's also supported Mr. Horowitz in all his distortions, his surveillance, his milking the judge's prejudice. And now we should be charitable to him, let him off the hook?"

"Jeanne, I have the questions. I'll do it whichever way you want but think about it... "

"Christ, Jill, you're crazy. There's no time. We got Spence, we can get him. It's our only chance."

"Jeanne, I just don't think Minder's going to see it that way."

Jeanne looked over at Franco, pacing alone down the hall.

"Jill, what can I even say to him?"

Franco looked up, startled and suspicious at her approach. Jeanne said some half-sentenced regrets about the level of hostility and the black-haired bailiff called them back. Jeanne sat down and noticed Franco lean over and whisper to Horowitz. Horowitz whispered something back.

Judge Minder was surprised when Jill finished her mild questioning of the Respondent. The Petitioner's case was thus closed.

Mr. Horowitz rose. "Your Honor, I would like to call Mr. Benelli as my own witness."

More testimony ensued in which the witness woefully chronicled the aberrations of his former spouse and stressed that, for their own good, the children should be raised together in a proper middle class home, his own.

"And did your wife, in fact, approach you in the hall during this morning's recess?"

Franco squirmed slightly in the blue chair. "Yes, yes, she did."

"And what did she tell you?"

"She told me that if I would let her keep Jesse, she didn't mind if I kept Paul."

"What!" Jeanne exploded audibly. Jill's mouth dropped open in disbelief. The judge grabbed his gavel and eyed the women sternly. Like a dentist's drill held against a nerve, his final lie manipulated Jeanne's deepest pain, that of her separation from Paul, and it was too much. She let go, releasing a flood of feelings inside as if a dam had broken. They assumed frightening forms in her mind yet she told herself not to be afraid. She saw herself viciously stabbing him over and over yet sat quite still in her chair, eyes hidden behind tinted glasses, and wondered if Mr. Gertmenian at her left or Judge Minder whose gaze occasionally scanned her had any idea of the ferocity of the scaring images into which her anger had formed itself.

Then basically it was over. Her husband's lawyer called no witnesses, presented no expert testimony. Jill asked to make a closing argument and did. Mr. Horowitz obligingly made up one accordingly. Jeanne's fingers felt like ice as she stirred and crossed her arms.

"Mr. Gertmenian, as the court-appointed lawyer for the children, I would appreciate hearing your opinion on this matter."

Gertmenian rose slowly, reluctantly to his feet. He appeared very uneasy, torn. Jill and Jeanne held their breaths, listening to every word — which proved difficult.

"It appears to me, Your Honor," he began, "that the oldest son, Paul, apparently wants to stay with his father and is doing reasonably well there. I do not see that there is a compelling reason to change custody but he should be provided with significant time with his mother. That is clearly important to both of them. As far as the three year-old goes, uh, Jesse...."

His voice dwindled, his words became garbled, muffled and uttered amidst nervous glances up toward the judge. A very successful, well respected, articulate lawyer turns inarticulate. Mumble jumble, mumble jumble.

Mr. Gertmenian sat down. There was a brief silence as the five people at the long table turned their attention to Judge Minder for his decision.

Judge Minder reached over the brim of his high desk and asked his clerk for the items he had personally marked as evidence himself. Leafing through the papers he began slowly.

"I have considered charging the Petitioner and her lawyer and the members of this — Defense Committee — with contempt of Court for having levied demands upon this Court."

He paused. Jill and Jeanne sat perfectly still.

"I've decided not to do so, however," he continued. "However, I will say that both the Petitioner and her attorney exercised very poor judgement in thinking that they could sway the Court one way or the other by such tactics. I have, however, decided not to press contempt charges.

"As for the rest of this matter, there is evidence that I would like to review before making a decision. I will notify the parties in writing."

BAM! COURT IS ADJOURNED. He stood and walked swiftly in to the sanctuary of his chambers, leaving behind him a startled courtroom.

Numb, Jeanne turned to Jill. "What does that mean?"

"That means he'll write out his decision and mail it to the lawyers," she answered mechanically, staring straight ahead.

"When will that be?" Jeanne pressed.

"I don't know," she answered wearily. "If his clerk mails it tomorrow, maybe we'll get it Friday…"

Slowly Jill began shuffling papers into her briefcase. Franco smirked as he passed, evidently pleased at their close brush with being charged with contempt. Beyond this, he did not, however, look as if he felt any more assured of the outcome than she did.

"Well?" Shana beseeched them, no longer able to stand the waiting.

"He's going to notify us by mail," Jeanne answered in a monotone.

"*By mail?*"

"Yes," replied Jill, "they can do that."

A lone reporter was waiting, leaning up against the wall. He came forward.

"Did you get a decision?" he asked politely.

"No," said Jill. "Judge Minder said he'd let us know by mail."

"Okay. Thanks anyway," he said.

"Thank you," they said back.

Turning towards the elevator Jill said to Shana out of the corner of her mouth, "That creep tried to bring contempt charges against us. Against all of us. That's what he was up to. Didn't have the guts to do it, though. This community would be up in arms and he knows it but he had to say it — throw his power around, reprimand.

"That's why he didn't want to announce his decision today. Thought there might be the press outside. He wants to act as if it didn't phase him but we would never have gotten three calendar days for a custody hearing if we hadn't put that pressure on. Anyway," she said as the elevator doors swooshed open, "we'll just have to wait and see. Hard to tell what he's going to do. That goddamn Gertmenian. What the hell did he say anyway?"

"I don't know," Jeanne burst out in frustration. "He started saying how Dr. Nestor said Jesse was doing fine with his mother and then he just mumbled. Did you understand what he said?"

"No," replied Jill, "he sort of ate his words. I think he was afraid to say what he thought to Minder. He's been clear all along that there is no reason to remove Jesse."

"Goddammit," Jeanne swore under her breath as they pushed the door open and left the stale air of the Oakland courthouse. "Just like Spence. What happens to people's heads, Jill? What happens to people's heads?"

Her shoulders rounded and her gait slowed, "I don't know," she replied, shaking her head, "I don't know."

CHAPTER EIGHT

Meanwhile, in Dade County

San Francisco Examiner
May 24, 1977

A lesbian mother in Oakland has lost a battle for custody of her two sons despite wide support from feminist groups and East Bay politicians.

Following three closed courtroom hearings, Alameda County Superior Court Judge Gordon Minder has ruled that Franco Benelli be given custody of Jesse, 3, and Paul, 8.

Jeanne Jullion said the (younger) boy was taken from her home while she was in court seeking a stay on the order that gave custody of the child to his father. "We didn't even have a chance to say goodbye."

Her husband, Franco Benelli, from whom she has been separated for two years, took the boy Monday with the aid of his attorney, Armin Horowitz, and a police officer, Jullion said.

"He didn't even have his toys with him. He left without his shoes. They just whisked him out of the house."

Benelli was granted custody of Jesse in an order issued last Friday by Superior Court Judge Gordon Minder. Notice of the decision arrived on Monday, and Jullion promptly went to court to seek a stay.

It was while she was gone, she said, that the child was taken.

Nothing had been able to stop it. Five months work, up to and including the moment it was happening, several thousands of dollars spent and owed, and still it had happened. Jesse's single sneaker, the one they couldn't find and had left hurriedly without, lay around the house in mute testimony.

A cold shadow fell across the house. There was a closing down as happens when suddenly a loved one dies. It didn't help that the death had unspokenly been seen approaching for five months. Shana watched her lover rise slowly in the mornings and sit quietly on the edge of the bed. Jeanne crawled through the ensuing days, lost at his loss, moving mechanically through chores and a steadily increasing schedule of appointments. There was no word from her family except this letter from her mother:

Thurs. May 26

Dear Jeannie,

Well, tomorrow we leave for Copenhagen. Before we go I wanted to write you and let you know we'll be home about the 28th of June.

I heard the news about Jesse. I feel sorry for both you and Jesse but mostly for the child as he will really miss you. However, I think the Judge was right in taking him out of the environment he was in. I really don't believe the Judge would have done that only for the fact that the publicity was very bad for the children. It sounded like you were fighting for the issue rather than for custody of your children. Jeannie, for heavens sake, you are supposed to be a very smart girl. Can't you see that these people are using you for their goal of recognition? I hope you don't burn all your bridges behind you.

I am praying for you every day, Jeannie. I still love you very much and surely hate to see you going down the path you have chosen.

Well, I must close as we have much to do before we leave tomorrow at 2:30 p.m.

Love,
Mother

Judge Minder left town too, on a week's vacation. He left behind him a six-paged decision prefaced by a gag order forbidding disclosure of the reasons for his decision or transcripts of any of the court proceedings without further order of the Court.

After Jesse's abduction, Jeanne's attorney and Dr. Nestor returned to court. In Judge Minder's absence, a woman judge heard the motion and sharply criticized Jesse's removal by the police. She ordered that Jesse be allowed to return home for the three day Memorial weekend.

The change in Jesse was drastic. Both boys had been given odd and severe Marine haircuts. Jesse, thin-lipped, clung morbidly to his mother. In the car, Shana's four children babbled anxiously to him over the back of the front seat but his somberness quieted even them. Shana and Jeanne exchanged shocked, bitter looks over his head. Nights were punctuated with crying and stomach aches.

At the end of the three short days, everything within Jeanne rebelled at having to take him back. As one exit after another slipped by on the freeway, she felt a tight heaviness in her chest as if it were being filled with lead. Tears began breaking out of her control, blurring her vision. She pulled over.

"I can't stand it, Shana. Would you drive?"

Jesse had fallen asleep. She scooped him into her arms, the wetness of her tears spreading a dark spot on his shirt. Then suddenly a last hope broke loose somewhere in the middle of her grief. *Surely when he sees my anguish...*

"Go tell him that if he wants Jesse he's going to have to come and take him out of my arms. I'm not taking him up there," she announced hoarsely when the car came to a stop.

After a few minutes she heard footsteps and then her door opening. Her face felt grotesquely contorted with pain, her eyes wild, desperate. Her head shook slowly from side to side, like an animal. "No, you're not taking Jesse. You have Paul. Please, please."

She pressed Jesse hard against her, as if to stuff him back in her belly. She searched the face of the man she thought she knew so well. There was not a glimmer. His arms reached into the car. She pushed them away, peeling his hands off the waking child. Jesse cried, tears blinded her. As he pulled Jesse out of her arms, her uterus started contracting. It was excruciating, like a miscarriage.

1

May gave way to June. Lemon yellow, summer sun streamed through the high Victorian alcove in Jill and Sheila's legal
office on Valencia Street. It fell at a steep angle and caught the
tip of the orange Mexican wall hanging behind Jill's broad and
cluttered desk. The explosion of publicity around the case in
conjunction with front page stories on the Gay Rights struggle
in Dade County, Florida, generated an ever-increasing barrage
of calls. Thanks to Elizabeth, headquarters was switched to the
United Neighbors in Action offices on Telegraph Avenue and
the home phone number was no longer given out. Still a clicking on the line persisted.

"Jill," Jeanne stood in front of her, "everybody's saying
our line's tapped."

"Hm, I was wondering myself," Jill mused, leaning back in
her chair. "Well, last year my car was bugged — courtesy of
the FBI, I suppose. I was defending a lesbian woman facing
criminal charges. I got in the car one day and put the visor
down and something caught my eye up there. Sure enough it
was a tiny microphone about this big." Jill squinted and held
her fingers a half inch apart. "I gave them an earful and then
yanked it out!"

"But, Jill, what in the world would the FBI want with our case?"

"I don't know but the FBI monitors the Women's Movement
and whatever is challenging the system. Lesbians are the most
renegade women, independent and just fine without men. The way
this has gone, your case has accrued political dimensions and
a significance beyond your own personal situation. So who knows?"
Jill lit a match against the side of the metal ashtray and touched
the end of her cigarette. Exhaling, she continued.

"Now, we don't know for sure that it is a tap — although that's
certainly what it sounds like. But let's look at it this way," Jill leaned
forward over her desk. "We've been threatened with contempt,
Judge Minder wanted to know the names, addresses and places of
employment of Defense Committee members and now the gag order
he put in his decision — "

"That portion following, together with the reporter's notes or any transcript thereof shall be sealed and not divulged publicly without further order of the court," Shana chanted out loud by heart.

"Yes, so, as your lawyer, I advise you not to discuss matters on your telephone and you might be careful in the car as well. You never know, just to be safe. And don't forget, you aren't doing anything illegal, anyway."

2

The new puppy named Blue rounded the corner and sprawled belly up on the newly shined kitchen floor. The phone vibrated against the rough, green brocade arm of the sofa.

"It's Channel 2," Shana said, covering the receiver. "They want us to be on a program called ON THE SQUARE. It's a live, call-in show."

"Sure," Jeanne said, distractedly. "Write it down."

Channel 7 called.

"They want us to be guests on A.M. SAN FRANCISCO. It's a morning talk show. We'd be on with F. Lee Bailey!"

"They should be calling the U.N.A. office. Anyway, sure."

The morning of the interview was a splendid early summer day. Jeanne and Shana pulled out of the hurling traffic on Van Ness Avenue, parked and went into KGO-TV studios. Following a guide, they threaded their way through a black labyrinth studded with props and cables and came upon a hot, brightly lit set. Against a backdrop of the Golden Gate Bridge, red potted plants and a snow white sectional sofa, they stood in a line, smiling, as a man rode a camera towards them. Music welled and the exuberant voice of the announcer intoned —

WELCOME TO TO A.M. SAN FRANCISCO! WITH THIS MORNING'S GUESTS: PATTY HEARST'S LAWYER, F. LEE BAILEY, LESBIAN MOTHERS SEEKING CUSTODY OF THEIR CHILDREN IN AN OAKLAND COURT CASE, JEANNE JULLION AND SHANA ASCHER, AND

ASTROLOGER-FORECASTER, SHAWN FORESTER.
STAY TUNED AND A.M. SAN FRANCISCO WILL CON-
TINUE AFTER THIS IMPORTANT ANNOUNCEMENT!

Smile, two, three — and the red light on the camera went out.
Jeanne and Shana glanced quickly at the large color monitor before
it went dark.

Later at home that afternoon, Hannah burst through the front
door with Aaron, calling, "I saw you! I saw you on TV! The whole
class saw you!!"

"Hey, slow down," Jeanne and Shana chorused, motioning
them to sit down in the living room. Dov followed the commotion
and slipped into Jeanne's lap as soon as she was seated. "Now, what
happened?" Shana asked.

"Wel-l!" drawled Hannah, loving to tell a good story, "when
I got to school I really wanted to see you on TV. So I went up and
told my teacher that my mom and her friend — really like my second mom — were going to be on A.M. SAN FRANCISCO and
asked her if we could watch it!" she recounted, sinking back into
the sofa at the brilliant simplicity of her move.

"Well, what did she say??" laughed Shana with tinges of pride.

"She went out and had a TV brought into the room and the whole
class watched it!" Hannah answered triumphantly.

"What'd they think of it?" Jeanne asked a bit guardedly.

"Oh, it was fine," Hannah assured her, sensing her apprehen-
sion. "After the show we had this big discussion about custody and
it was real serious. Then all the kids asked me if I was going to be
a TV star like my mom!"

They all burst out laughing except Dov who sat dreamily in
Jeanne's lap, content that they were both home, not on the phone
or arguing, but actually sitting down so he could get a shot at one
of their laps.

"And you know what, mom and Jeanne?" Hannah continued.
"My teacher said to me afterwards for me to tell my mother that she
was really sorry about Jesse being taken and that if there was
anything she could do for you to call her."

"My god," Jeanne exclaimed softly. "That's amazing. Hannah, you did great!" Jeanne warmed at the glow of her apple cheeks
and drank in the freshness of her youth and optimism.

"But you know what?" Hannah mused on. "I hate the word 'lover'. I mean, I don't hate it but you know what I mean?"

"No! Yes!" Jeanne sputtered, "I know exactly what you mean. The same problem in court. 'Lover' sounds so... so... "

"Like sex," Aaron grinned.

"Exactly! It's all sexual, like homo*sexual,* and *sexual* preference," Jeanne concurred vehemently.

"Paht-nahs — " offered Dov.

"What, Dov?" everyone asked.

"Paht-nahs," he said slowly in his 'r'-less way of speaking.

"Partners," Aaron sparked.

"That's what I said," Dov protested. "Why don't you cawl yo-selves paht-nahs?"

"How d'ee, partner!" Aaron slapped his thigh and jumped lithe-ly into the air.

"Or mate?"

"Companion," Hannah offered dramatically in a mock English accent. "This is Jeanne, my travelling companion."

"Really," Jeanne concluded, "none of them fit. Same as in court. The word just doesn't exist yet, like in some ways we don't exist yet, have a place yet in people's minds, in the culture."

"Jeannie?" Dov asked.

"Hm?"

"I miss Jesse," he said with sadness.

"Oh Dov, why do you have to bring that up," Aaron bolted grumpily and headed towards the stairs. Among the children, Aaron most of all felt the failure of the efforts to have Paul come and live with them. Dov acted out his anger and bewilderment at Jesse's abduction, sinking into his fantasy world without the friend who had daily shared it.

"Cuz I do, Aaron," Dov retorted as his brother stomped upstairs. "Is this the weekend they come back, Jeanne?"

"No, no, Dov, it isn't. Remember, they were here last weekend. Ten more days... "

"Yeah," remarked Hannah with bitterness, "for a big 48 hours. They barely begin to settle down... "

"Okay, okay," Shana said irritably, jerking the conversation away from the inevitable theme. "Hannah, don't you have homework?"

"Mom, it's only 2:30!"

"Well then, change into some play clothes. And be sure to hang up that dress. It's from your Grandma."

3

As Jill prepared the appeal, the Defense Committee prepared a corresponding rally to be held June 11th in front of the San Francisco Court of Appeals. Details were hammered out at Tuesday night meetings. As it happened, that Tuesday, June 7, 1977, would be marked in America's history as Orange Tuesday, the day of the vote on the Gay Rights Ordinance repeal in Dade County, Florida. Four hundred thousand presumed homosexuals were exterminated under Hitler and, as the San Francisco papers reported, bible-wielding Baptist Anita Bryant had been sounding like she'd like to reheat the ovens.

THE SAN FRANCISCO CHRONICLE
JUNE 7, 1977

MIAMI

One of the strange things about today's election here is that in a real sense voters will be passing judgement on San Francisco when they go to the polls to decide the fate of Dade County's homosexual rights ordinance.

San Francisco had been on everyone's tongue — denounced from the pulpit over six months of Sundays as a modern day Sodom and Gomorrah and daily on the radio call-in shows as being in the political grip of perverts whose ungodly example should be a lesson to the rest of the nation.

San Francisco Sheriff Richard Hongisto, who left Miami yesterday after spending the better part of a week campaigning against repeal of the ordinance, said he was forced to spend half of his time defending San Francisco's good name.

Barbara turned on the radio at low volume during the Defense Committee meeting to listen for the results.

"The gay rights ordinance in Dade County, Florida, has today been defeated by an overwhelming 2 to 1 margin — "

What?

That's what San Francisco said.

The meeting adjourned and Jill, Jeanne and Barbara drove towards Castro Street.

"Listen — "

They rolled down their windows on the night air and heard chanting and whistles. They glanced up Market Street at the next intersection and could see buildings and people strobed by red and blue police lights and city blocks full of people marching.

THE SAN FRANCISCO CHRONICLE
JUNE 8, 1977

> In a raucous, impromptu demonstration here last night, more than 5,000 persons marched and chanted through downtown streets to a hastily organized Union Square rally to protest the landslide anti-gay vote in Miami.
>
> One of the parade's leaders characterized the event as an "exorcism of some of the hate that's been thrown at us."
>
> The noisy but non-violent protest began at 10 p.m. when several hundred gays gathered for a candlelight vigil at Castro and Market streets.

Barbara parked the car and grabbed her emergency first aid satchel by its army green shoulder strap.

"You nurses," chided Jill.

"This satchel's been to many a demonstration," Barbara's round, young face spread into a grin.

The chants reverberated in the night sky and the three hastened their steps to the corner of 18th and Castro. Linking arms, they stepped off the curb and into the surge of jubilant, taunting gays. Jeanne was recognized and her arm swung into the air in a clenched fist. Boxes of candles from Cliff's Hardware were passed down the street and lit. Those in the street coaxed and prodded the clusters of grinning onlookers billowing out the doors of Castro's many bars.

SAN FRANCISCO CHRONICLE

> ...The crowd started walking through the surrounding neighborhood chanting, "Out of the bars and into the streets." Its ranks swelled and continued to grow as the demonstrators turned south on Market Street, went north on Polk Street and wound over Nob Hill.
> The demonstrators held hands, hugged, sang "We Shall Overcome" and waved candles...

In *The Mayor of Castro Street,* Randy Shilts, a reporter for the *San Francisco Chronicle,* records the events of that night:

> Over the next two years, such shouting mobs would become a common occurrence in the city, but police were dumbfounded at the first spontaneous eruption of long-buried anger.
> They feared a riot and called on the one person who they knew had credibility with the militant crowd, Harvey Milk. "Keep 'em moving," Harvey shouted. "We've got to keep 'em moving."...
> For three hours, Harvey led the crowd over a five mile course.

Up Nob Hill, three, four, five miles from Castro to Union Square. Tinny, megaphone voices brought surges of cheers that rose and sank under the palm trees. Harvey Milk raised his bullhorn and announced prophetically, "This is the power of the gay community. Anita's going to create a national gay force."

> ...At the Union Square rally, leaders armed with megaphones led the crowd in chants of "No More Miamis" and "Fight Back".

Again Jeanne was recognized and was pushed forward through the crowd towards a raised, cement abutment. Men leaned down precariously from the crowded ledge and shirt-sleeved arms pulled Jeanne up off her feet and onto the narrow wall.

"Here's a megaphone. Push the red button in. You can go next."

A bank of TV lights snapped on directly below her. Jeanne looked out at the crowd through the bluish white glare and saw with a start that the crowd was all men. Or so it seemed. She stared out at the row upon row of well-groomed heads of smiling and jostling gay men and wondered suddenly, *how can they relate to what's happening to me? do they care?* They looked so gloriously, studiedly single.

ANITA SUCKS ORANGES, a hoarse, inebriated voice rang out. Laughter rankled through the crowd. Her turn, Jeanne pushed hard on the red lever.

"Sheriff Hongisto did not have to travel all the way to Dade County, Florida. It's happening right here in his own backyard, in the San Francisco Gay Area — " laughter at her inadvertent but apropos slip, " — in an Oakland courtroom. I have lost custody because I am a lesbian. The courtroom had been closed, a gag order imposed and the Oakland police accompanied my husband and his lawyer to my home to take my three year old. He was taken barefoot without any of his possessions and without a chance to even say goodbye to his mother. Well, I have no apologies to make because I am lesbian and... I want my children back." Jeanne continued haltingly. "The vote in Dade County will translate to just this in our own lives — you can lose your kids, or your housing, or your job because you're gay. I don't believe I have to be straight to have rights in America. I don't believe that is what this country is about."

Applause, some cheers.

ANITA SUCKS ORANGES, the same raspy voice rang out again. Braced on out-stretched hands, Jeanne squeezed down off the ledge and rejoined Jill and friends. They made their way out of the congested plaza area. Realizing the impromptu march had taken them miles away from Castro, they began walking down Powell Street to catch a bus on Market. People drifted through intersections oblivious of lights.

"JILL!" A group of women shouted from the curb. Jeanne recognized Shoshana among them and waved. As Shoshana drew near, Jeanne's arms automatically unfolded in pleasant expectation of a hug. She found the ease with which lesbians embrace such a warm and welcome bonus to her new "lifestyle." But strangely, Shoshana pulled back, leaving space between them.

"Shoshana, is something wrong?"

Jeanne was startled by her slightly embarrassed response.

"Hey, Jeanne, you know, now I feel like you're famous... important... "

"Hey, Shoshana... " Jeanne exclaimed softly. She glanced down at her second-hand clothes as if to find traces on her person of this transformation Shoshana perceived. An empty cablecar clamored by in back of them. The group was drifting on and they were pulled apart. Jeanne walked silently behind them, taken aback.

THE MAYOR OF CASTRO STREET

After the rally, the crowd made a silent march back to Castro Street, where a thousand of the still angry protestors decided to simply sit down in one of the city's busiest intersections. The police wanted to move in with a show of force, but, talking over a police loudspeaker, Milk cleared the street with the promise of still another demonstration the next night. Even Harvey's most adamant detractors conceded that only his presence had averted a riot that night.

By the time Jill, Jeanne, and Barbara arrived, the intersection at Market was clear and traffic flowing normally. The droves of people returning from Union Square had simply moved down and occupied Castro Street instead. They sat down everywhere, as if in a giant outdoor living room.

"You know what?" Jeanne said over Jill's shoulder as they swung down out of the Market Street bus. They stood at the top of Castro looking down the occupied street towards 18th.

"We may be thinking the same thing," Jill replied. "Barbara — ?"

"Gotcha. The new flyer, n'est-ce pas? Now I just happen to have 500 in my back seat from the meeting tonight. I'll get some and meet you in front of the theater, okay?"

JEANNE JULLION LOSES HER CHILDREN, the yellow banner read. Joann brought the bold, yellow flyer to the meeting that night, freshly typeset and donated by Up Press, a women's collective in Palo Alto. The crisp print spelled out the consequences, on a personal level, of the overwhelming mandate Anita Bryant had received that night. Jill, Barbara and Jeanne wound slowly through the clusters of people until the yellow sheets were gone. They talked to more men than women and the support was the same.

The next morning the noted photograph of Harvey Milk speaking through a bullhorn was on the front page. The next night...

THE MAYOR OF CASTRO STREET

...five thousand marched in Greenwhich Village, four hundred in Denver, and another crowd surged from Castro Street past City Hall and through the city's wealthy neighborhoods. Thousands more took to the streets on Thursday and Friday nights, shocked and angry. ...It had been easy to forget that most of them had not been attracted to Castro Street, they had been driven there; the forces that had driven them to seek sanctuary were finally getting organized. On Friday night, after a City Hall rally, one thousand sat stubbornly at Castro and Market. ...And three thousand marched again on Saturday night. The next morning, as Catholic worshippers went to St. Mary's Cathedral, they faced five hundred silent demonstrators lining the long wide plaza to the church entrance, standing in vigil to protest the Dade County archbishop's support of Anita Bryant's campaign.

4

CIVIC CENTER PLAZA
JUNE 11

The day of the rally broke clear and cloudless. At noon, Rosie and The Riveters leaned forward into three microphones and in close militant harmony sang driving, *a cappella* ballads to open the rally. Change rattled like castanets in colored collection cans. Men and women sold white fundraising buttons bearing a lavender triangle and inscribed Support Jeanne Jullion — Bring The Boys Home. Children's presence was strong, complete with homemade placards in bright colors reading Strong Kids Can Deal With Reality and We Love Our Gay Moms.

Bobbi strained the tight muscles in her arms pushing the wheelchair of disabled activist Kitty Cone up the steep ramp at the rear of the platform. A powerful speaker, Kitty held down her notes with her heavy left hand and delivered a sweeping political analysis tracing the oppression — in jobs, custody, housing and education — of all who do not fall within the mainstream of white, heterosexual, able-bodied, middle class America.

"The Court's action is a truly dangerous precedent — that children can be removed because the parent is gay, is poor, on welfare, is not 'religious', is perceived to lead an 'alternative lifestyle', lives in a non-white neighborhood, that a middle class setting is *a priori* superior to a working class home regardless of parenting and ignoring all bonding. This decision must not go unchallenged."

The voice of the rally outside, however, did not penetrate the high, columned facade of the San Francisco Court of Appeals behind it. The appeal never crossed a judge's desk. It was read by a law clerk. In his or her opinion, no error in point of law was found. Appeal and request for stay — summarily denied.

Jeanne and Shana stood before Jill in her office. The former seemed thinner, the latter heavier, and both faces showed the marks of unyielding strain. Jill could feel the tension between the two women.

"This is only temporary custody, Jeanne," Jill moved from behind her desk to console them. "We've got another shot at it — the Interlocutory trial. And another thing — it won't be before Minder. A new judge. I admit there isn't much to pick from on the Oakland bench at the moment but it will be a different judge."

"When? When can we get back into court?" Jeanne asked tensely. Curls billowed forward on the crown of her head. Jill frowned and began massaging her left hand with her right. "Maybe August... "

"August!?"

"The court calendar is about eight months slow. We'll have to check to see if your first lawyer filed for the Interlocutory back at the beginning when she got the case. If she did, maybe August, September.''

You mean he'll be gone the whole summer, Jeanne reeled.

''What judge is going to give them back to me after they've been gone that long!'' she exploded. ''This is just what they want — they'll just stall and stall, won't they, Jill? *Won't they!* I can't believe this, I just can't believe this is happening. Well, I can't take it, do you hear me? I want my kids back! *I'm getting out of here!*''

Shana threw Jill a distraught look, then hurried to catch up with Jeanne who was running down the stairs two at a time out into the summer that stretched long before her.

''I want to get out of here. I just want to take them and go.''

''You're not leaving without me.''

''Would Paul even want to come with me? Maybe Gertmenian's right. Maybe's he's been with his father too long. But I really don't believe that. Franco'd hunt me down if I took both of them. But I couldn't just leave Paul behind.''

''You're not going to let them break up this family, too.''

''But Shana — ''

''Listen, I have the Winnebago. It sleeps eight. We could sell the Comet, keep the kids on their weekend visit and — ''

''Sure. Two dykes and six kids in a big, green Winnebago. Now just how far do you think we would get. How fuckin' far do you think we would get?''

''There's still the trial. I love you. There's still so much we have to do together. Don't leave me. Please.''

5

Jeanne, Shana, Dov and Reuben rounded the corner of the UNA office on Telegraph at 66th Street. The side door of the building grasped at its frame before giving in and opening. Oversized, it swung open more like a gate to a courtyard than a side door to a building. Shana picked up Reuben with a sweep of her arm and the four of them clammered up the stairs. In the corridor, Shana let Reuben make a benign but rapid drop to the cushions of the maroon sofa without breaking her stride.

"Stay with Reuben," she told Dov as she strode ahead into the office. Slower and distracted, Jeanne followed into the room whose walls were lined with desks and ringing phones. The office was doing as much work for the Jeanne Jullion Defense Committee as its regular tasks of neighborhood canvassing for under-funded services, primarily nursing home care.

Connie spun around in her chair, her head tilted customarily to the side. Her tanned face was attractively framed in a deep brown crewcut. She welcomed the two with a smile.

"Well, hello, Shana. Hi, Jeanne. How are you two doing?"

Sensing the tension, she wished she hadn't asked. She quickly went on.

"Have a seat. Listen, at the staff meeting this morning, we began to talk about doing a joint benefit for UNA and the Defense Committee. UNA would produce it. After expenses, we'd split whatever money there was."

"Hm, sounds good," Shana nodded, glancing at Jeanne.

"Well, JJ," Connie turned to Jeanne, her easy Western cadence bordering on a drawl, "do you have the datebook I gave you ready?"

She reached around on her desk for a list of engagements written on a pink notepad. "You know," she interjected, "We've been telling people to call the Gay Parade Organizing Committee about you speaking."

"I can't believe you're not on the list of speakers," piped up George, a short, well-dressed man with handsome dark eyes. He leaned against Connie's desk and greeted Jeanne and Shana.

"I know," fumed Connie. "What with Anita Bryant and her Save The Children campaign, it's downright ignorant they aren't having Jeanne speak about this case." She laughed out loud at her own vehemence. "Anyway, East Bay Gay Day *does* want you to speak, on this Saturday."

"What about me?" snapped Shana.

"What do you mean? They didn't say. They just said Jeanne

Jullion.''

"Right, Jeanne Jullion, Jeanne Jullion.'' Shana squashed out her cigarette in the ashtray.

George moved slowly off. Connie rose a bit stiffly and handed Jeanne the pink list. She put it in her pocket.

"Defense Committee meeting this Wednesday as usual?'' Connie asked as a matter of course.

"Always is,'' said Shana heavily.

The ride home was short and silent. They pushed through the front door and into the coolness of the house. Reuben's eyes were at half mast as he sucked two fingers like Aaron and leaned sleepily against his mother's neck.

"Here,'' Shana pushed him off her shoulder towards Jeanne, "would you put him down for his nap? Com'ere in the kitchen, Dov. I'll give you a bottle to take upstairs for your brother.''

"I want some yoguht,'' he whined, looking tired as well.

"Alright, alright, but eat it at the table.''

Jeanne came slowly down the stairs and slumped uneasily onto the scratchy cushions of the green brocade couch. Exhausted, she dreaded the argument she knew was coming. Words were already coming as Shana rounded the corner of the kitchen.

"Jeanne, can't you see what's happening? All they want is you, the star. Miss Shirley Temple. Jeanne's lost her kids. *This family* has lost one of it's kids.''

"I know, Shana — ''

Dov flapped slowly through the living room and to the stairs, bottle in hand. Suddenly, Reuben started yelling from upstairs, "Mommie! Yeanie! Mommie! Yean — ''

"Reuben, shut up!'' screamed Shana from where she stood. She rubbed her forehead roughly. "Dov's bringing your bottle right now. Now go to sleep!''

Reuben seemed to accept the curt answer and in a second Dov arrived with the goods.

"Here, Reuben,'' Dov consoled his brother sweetly, "your bottle.''

Reuben reached for it with both hands through the side of his crib and then rolled over on his back, drinking.

"I think Mommie and Jeannie awh going to have anothuh ahgument,'' Dov told told him. He turned and confessed out loud, "I'm tiwad.''

He brushed back the long strands of his blond hair and sleepily slipped out of his thongs at the end of his bed. Jesse's stuffed animal, Eeyore, lay on the floor under the bottom bunk. Dov's broad flat feet curled over the metal crossbars like a monkey. Although Jesse was gone, Dov always slept up on top.

''I'm gonna sleep, too,'' he decided. Diving forward, mid-bed, he fell asleep.

Shana's feelings were at the center of an issue that was rocking both the Defense Committee and the legal strategy of Jill Lippitt, their attorney. In the Defense Committee, the consensus of opinion had been steadily moving away from defending them as a family unit in favor of focusing on the mother's individual right to have her children.

Jill's father had succumbed to cancer six weeks earlier. As she drove the long stretch from San Francisco to Los Angeles to spend time with her mother, she gave a great deal of thought to the legal development of the case at hand. From Los Angeles, she wrote Jeanne and Shana a long letter.

Dear Shana and Jeanne,

...As I see it, the question isn't Jeanne's right to raise the boys, or Jeanne and Shana's right to make a family together, but rather the boys' right to be with the person who is the most important person in their lives — and that happens to be Jeanne. The fact that your household is a positive environment is icing on the cake. Somewhere around Bakersfield I fully understood just how far apart we are moving...

Shana, I wish you could see that as much as you love Jesse and Paul, as much as you personally feel·this is a family affair and should be fought as such — we are not fighting for your right to have this lesbian co-parent ''adoption'' acknowledged by the courts. What you want is for the courts to give their approval to lesbian families. What I want is for the court to give children the right to be raised by the parent who best fosters their growth, regardless of sexuality, external benefits or social approval. It is, moreover, children's right to not be used as pawns for the system to punish their mothers for stepping out of what the state believes to be a woman's place.

You say the court should look beyond the "psychological parent" — I hearti-
ly disagree... You are asking the court to go much further than it needs to —
to approving lesbian households. That battle will be a long time in coming,
and we will not win that one until many lesbian mothers have broken the ground
first... It is not that I don't agree that lesbian families like yours are truly
good for children — it's just that that's not what we're going to court to prove...

Time for struggle on this issue is running short, however. The case must be
prepared. With me or without me, you're going to trial in August. You must
now formulate your plans and move forward. If you can see it my way —
I'd love to fight alongside you. If not, then I'll be rooting for you all they way.

Love,
Jill

6

An afternoon in late June, Jeanne and Shana sat on the patchwork
quilt and tensely discussed the upcoming week's schedule. Shana
bitterly noted Jeanne's full schedule and, again, the slippage of focus
from them as a family.

— Shana, I think Jill's right. I know you care for and have fought
for my kids —

— Our kids. This family.

— What family? What family? Jesse and Paul are gone, and your
kids haven't gotten anything but stress for months. They need you,
Shana.

— They need you, too.

— But I don't have anything to give them now. I'm a wreck.
Just look at how much there is to do, — she slapped the open,
blackened pages of her appointment book, — this house needs a
break. Your kids need a break.

— I'll help you.

— Help them. You gotta let go. You can't be at every speaking
engagement there is. And I have no choice.

— Then let's take the kids and get out of here.

— What kind of life would that be, always looking over our
shoulder... ?

— You're just scared. Of Franco.

— How 'bout of *jail*. I can't take this anymore. Jeanne jumped off the bed like a spring. I've gotta get out of here.

— No, you're not going.

— Yes, I am.

— You're not leaving us.

They both reached for the door.

— What damn good is *this* to anybody?

Jeanne yanked the door open and it flew against the wall. Shana struggled out of the room. The unsettling sound of adults losing control spilled into the hallway. Upstairs the children's play became distracted and then ceased. Some toys still in hand, they milled out of their rooms and into the hall along the banister. Slowly, step by step, they shuffled collectively down the stairs, whispering and glancing at each other's eyes.

Shana reached out for what she knew was slipping away. Jeanne twisted out of the way. Jeanne's arm flew around against the oak hallstand by the door. Her hand fell down and closed around the glass knob of the heavy candy dish on the table.

She picked it up and smashed it down on the hallstand again and again and again. A piece of glass bit through her palm.

"Ow, my hand," she turned in pain. A few drops of blood fell in perfect circles on the linoleum floor. Startled, she glanced up at the frozen faces of the children on the stairs. An intangible limit had been exceeded. Looking at their stunned faces, she knew at that moment that she had to leave.

Dennis herded the kids quietly upstairs and then gently took Jeanne's hand and said, "Let's rinse it off."

"I can't go speaking tonight. I just can't," Jeanne shook her head with exhaustion.

Shana stood with a hand clasped over her mouth and eyes frightened. "Don't worry," she muttered, "I'll call somebody."

Half an hour later Ruth Hughes was at the door. Dressed smartly in black cords and a red crewneck sweater, she laughed with indomitable good spirits.

"What's this I hear — that Jeanne Jullion cut her wrists?"

"O for christ sake," Jeanne bellowed from the kitchen, " I did not! It's just a nick." As Ruth rounded the corner into the kitchen, Jeanne extended her hand for verification.

"Goddammit, did you really hear that, Ruth?"

Ruth's laugh rolled around in her throat as her dark eyes took in the situation.

"Listen, Ruth," Jeanne continued, "it's getting late. I just can't go speak at the Live Oak Theater tonight. Lilith, the theater group, is doing a benefit performance. Could you go and just say what's happening — not this! — and pass the can?"

"Sure," replied Ruth, laughing, "but they're expecting to see Jeanne Jullion. They sure are going to be surprised to see my black face! But you know I *love* being Jeanne Jullion! Say, are you really *the* famous Jeanne Jullion? Is that really you?"

"Ruth!"

"Hm, all is not harmony in the Lesbian Family of the Year, is that what's happening?"

"O Ruth, shut up," groaned Shana wearily.

"Alright," her laugh resounded again heartily in the yellow kitchen, "now don't worry. I'll go right now. It's after 7:00. You take the night off and, for christsake, take care of yourselves. Tomorrow's the parade, Gay Day '77, you know. Are you two speaking after all?"

"Yes," Jeanne replied with a headache, "the Committee got so many calls, especially from women, that they called U.N.A. and said to call off the troops — she'll speak, Shana, too."

"Ha! Well, rest up. They're expecting a whole lot of people, what with Anita Bryant on the warpath and all. A gay man was stabbed to death by youths in the Mission — you know about that?"

Everyone nodded.

"Well, the march may reach a quarter of a million, can you believe that? Anyway, rest up," she reiterated. "You have to be JJ tomorrow. No surrogates. Take care — I'm going."

7

VROOOMM!! VROMM — VROOOOMM!!
Sunday, June 25th, had arived.
VRROMM — VVRROOOOMMM!!!
Market Street reverberated like a sound tunnel. At the head of

the parade, fifty laughing, tank-topped women on motorcycles revved their engines, a roar beckoning to the crowd. High-pitched yells
swelled in response, witch calls, a roaring mix of feelings cut through
the air over the bikes' thundering. The calls scaled the sides of the
downtown office buldings, soaring in continuous, piercing intensity until VRROOOMM!! the roar crested and broke in the air.
Fists in the air, Dykes on Bikes rolled slowly forward, signaling the
start of the 1977 Gay Freedom Day Parade.

An estimated 250,000 had gathered with particular resolve to
commemorate the Stonewall Rebellion of 1969 in New York City.
Angered by police harassment at the Stonewall Bar, gays, with drag
queens in the forefront, took to the streets for an unprecedented
four nights of rebellion. Each June since then, gays commemorate
that 'first' revolt and the beginning of a bonafide political movement. Until this year, however, the Gay Day Parade in San Francisco was primarily a gay men's event, a taking to the streets on
foot and aboard floats, men cross-dressing in their most outrageous
fantasies, an annual party winding through designated streets to
smirking but silent police escort.

This year, however, was not a party, hardly a parade and definitely a march. The violence of Robert Hillsborough's stabbing death
at the hands of youths in the wake of Anita Bryant's resounding
victory jarred many people out of the closet, out of bed, out of the
house and into the downtown area that morning. Many hundreds
of lesbians from all walks of life were in the streets that day, lesbians who in preceding years had considered the celebration irrelevant to their lives and had, in years past, been angered at the grotes-
que stereotyping and parody of women displayed in gay men's drag.

In 1977 there was also an increased awareness that marches were
simultaneously occurring not only in other American cities but in
Europe as well. In Barcelona, ten thousand marched and were fired
on with rubber bullets and tear gas by La Guardia Civil in the first
gay demonstration in Spanish history. The march ended behind
barricades and, as in San Francisco, was preceded by the murder
in the streets of a young homosexual man. Charter planes arrived
in San Francisco from London and Amsterdam. The sobering
urgency of the political situation had forged a new solidarity. The
pressure had met up with healthy and pliant muscle that would fight
back. 'Come out with joy,' urged a thin and tough, brown-eyed

candidate for San Francisco Supervisor, Harvey Milk.

Applause rippled out concentrically as two women in their forties unfurled a street-wide banner, painted with the words LESBIAN MOTHERS' RIGHTS — JEANNE JULLION DEFENSE COMMITTEE. Sheila, mother of three, steadied the pole and laughed raucously to Connie, lean and tall, on the other end. Jeanne ducked under the banner and bumped into Marya.

"Oh, I'm glad I found you," Marya exclaimed, her long, narrow face somewhat flushed. "What a crowd this is! Here, these are from the Defense Committee for Robert Hillsborough."

She laid a large bouquet in Jeanne's arms, like a fragrant child wrapped in green crinkly paper. "They'll be laid on the steps at City Hall. I'm going to go up and march with the Women's Center. Good luck with your speech."

"Thanks, Marya. Is your son here?"

"No, too many people. He's with his father."

Bobbi appeared from out of the crowd in faded jeans and tee shirt. "I just went over to the hot dog stand. It looks like there'll be few food concessions. We have 2000 hot dogs and I bet we'll sell them all."

"Yeah, 'Wienees for Jeannie'!" quipped Joann.

"No — o!" Shana and Jeanne moaned simultaneously.

"No, it's true," laughed Shoshana in a deep voice. "That's what they're going to say. The men will love it!"

"Hey, look out — we're moving."

Marya turned to go. "Jeanne, Joyce will be taking the overflow money from the cash box over to Pam's apartment on Noe. Her motorcycle's the only thing that can get through this crowd."

"Com'on," Elizabeth announced, threading arms with Jeanne and Shana, "let's go!"

A yell rolled out of their throats and they began to advance up the center of Market Street. Suddenly, a lithe young man appeared before Jeanne, startling her. Tanned and naked to the waist, he was of exquisite beauty, like a young, mythological figure that had just stepped down from the side of an urn. He reached up to Jeanne who was taller than he and placed a lei of lavender orchids over her head. Wordless, he smiled and left. They hung down in heady fragrance, resting on top of her armful of memorial flowers.

The parade route seemed disappointingly short given the intensity of the event and the feelings surrounding it that year. Anger bristled and rippled through the marchers as nudges and nods pointed out the presence of combat police banking the final, right angle turn into Civic Center Plaza. The police stood legs spread, four deep, in complete riot array. They were seen as a reminder of an at best inhospitable power structure.

But the sun coated the marchers as they moved from the close downtown streets out into the spaciousness of the city square. The police show of force passed like a cold shudder. In all its French Provincial grandeur, City Hall glinted impressively in the sun. On the first floor balcony, Jody, the Parade Coordinator, waved with amazement and pride at the spectacle that would file past for the next four hours.

It came in wave after wave and in many moods. There were city blocks of solemn silence, ripped only by a snare drum's somber beat. Thousands marched under towering, wordless placards of the faces of Hitler, Mussolini and Anita Bryant and a fourth that read: WHEN THEY CAME FOR THE JEWS, I SAID NOTHING. WHEN THEY CAME FOR THE HOMOSEXUALS, I SAID NOTHING. THEN THEY CAME FOR ME.

Then blocks full of music, sensuality and joy that seemed like an extract of Rio on Mardi Gras night.

Jeanne moved through a solid corridor of spectators to the steps of City Hall. She leaned over and laid the bouquet on the memorial mound of flowers for Robert Hillsborough that ruffled over the cement steps.

The parade swung left at the end of the plaza and diffused out into the central, tree-lined area. The long rectangular pools that stretch out in front of City Hall glistened green and inviting in the afternoon sun. Handsome young men in seductive shorts, choosing not to resist, waded slowly in.

Smoke spiraled up from the committee's barbecue pits. Women hawked WIENEES FOR JEANNIE! BUY A HOT DOG AND HELP PAY THE BILLS! Business was booming. Ravenous marchers were being fed as fast as the hot dogs could be readied for sale.

A new member of the Committee, Joyce Garay stood in full leather next to the booth. She flicked her ponytail to the side and smiled into the camera of a documentary film crew asking her questions about the case. As the cash box filled, she was summoned to the back of the booth.

"Joyce, we've got to get rid of the cash," said Mary Pat, another new volunteer. They scooped the cash into a paper bag and, rounding her shoulders, Joyce pushed it down inside her leather jacket like a balloon. Throwing a leg over her bike, she straddled her motorcycle and revved the motor to scatter a path through the crowd. Joyce's deliveries throughout the afternoon carpeted Pam's living room floor with currency and pools of change. The Finance Committee's total from the food sales, buttons and collection cans topped $2500 by the end of the day.

Dazed by the day's intensity, Jeanne sought a place on the grass. Signs had been spotted throughout the march saying SUPPORT JEANNE JULLION that the Defense Committee had not made. Slick, stick-on banners were seen tagged on other signs, on cars and floats, on the backs of men's leather drag. Overwhelmed, Jeanne wanted to recede. Surreal slices of yesterday's drops of blood on the floor regularly cut through the festivities. The still photograph of the kids' stunned faces on the stairs. Feeling weak, she leaned back and pulled the notes for her speech out of her pocket.

The program at the mammoth event was running behind schedule. Four, then five o'clock passed. The warmth of the afternoon was quickly being supplanted by the chill of San Francisco's evening fog. Jeanne and Shana sat stiffly on the rear edge of the broad speakers' platform. Suddenly, the wind lifted Jeanne's notes from her fingers and shot them spiralling across the stage. She lunged after them, recovering the three small sheets. Finally they heard their introduction.

The shivering crowd gathered around the platform was an anticlimactic fraction of the original march, a thousand people, perhaps two. Jeanne and Shana stepped up to the wind-buffeted mikes. Jeanne's legs trembled inside the columns of her pant legs as Shana punched out her speech. The crowd loved it, applauding frequently. Jeanne concluded her own, arm in the air, saying, "Our children are not negotiable." Shaking overtook her body as they climbed down the wobbling aluminum stairs from the platform. Cheers faded behind them.

8

The dull realization that she had to move out had been with Jeanne since Saturday. Monday morning Jeanne and Shana drove down a quiet street in North Berkeley and for almost two hours tried to explain the cumulative entanglement of their emotions to a therapist. No good. They decided to separate.

That afternoon as Shana was out on errands, Jeanne climbed the stairs.

"Aaron? Dov? I need to talk to you a minute."

As she sat down on the top step, Dov lifted her arm and slipped on her lap before his brother emerged from his room.

"What, Jeannie?" Dov asked.

O god, she thought, arms encircling both of them, *my other children.*

"Listen," Jeanne began with some difficulty, "you know your mom and I haven't been getting along?"

Slow nods, "Uh-huh... "

"And I even hurt my hand?" she looked at Aaron's face, eyes big. He slipped his two fingers reassuringly in his mouth and paid close attention. "I don't think it's doing any good me being here. I've been real upset ever since the custody thing started and especially since they took Jesse. It's going to take a long time to get him back — if we can get him back. We're going to try. I think I should move out so things can cool down here and get back to normal."

Silence.

"Jeannie, don't leave. I don't want you to leave."

"And I really don't want to go. But it's better," she said wearily, resting her cheek on Dov's silky blond head. "This is no good, for any of us. But listen," she said, trying to break the depression settling in around them like fog, "it doesn't mean we won't see each other or be talking to each other," she offered. It fell flat to all of them. Again there was silence.

"You know what?" Jeanne said.

"What?" they answered in unison.

"I love you."

"I love you, too," slurred Aaron.

" ...love you, Jeannie," Dov echoed softly.

"Give me a kiss. I'm going to go now. I'd better just go. This is hard."

Jeanne lifted Dov back up on his feet. She pulled herself up by the banister. She glanced briefly at I LOVE YOU JEANNE on the wall by the little boys' door.

''Com'on, guys, pick up your rooms. My god, they're a holy mess,'' she muttered hoarsely.

Jeanne went downstairs, through the house, to the dining room closet. She carefully extracted her blue suitcase from where it had been stacked last October. She walked back into the bedroom and swung it up on the high, quilted bed. *Snap! Snap!* It yawned open in faded baby blue silk. *Same baby blue case I packed for college, for Florence, for Ravenna...*

She walked into the closet and took her most frequently worn clothes, shoes, a few papers. *Snap! Snap!* She reached back in the closet for her jacket. The hanger bent reluctantly, then sprang like a metal arrow. She turned her back, leaving it where it shot. She dragged the case off the bed and walked out into the hall. She glanced up the stairs, kids' sounds filtering down. She stood still, last gulps of sounds, colors, textures, smells — the feeling of home.

She opened the door, swinging her heavy suitcase out onto the porch. The wind chimes shuddered as she closed the heavy beveled glass door behind her. She stared a minute at the fading paintings and sign behind the glass — WELCOME TO THE HOME OF JEANNE, SHANA, HANNAH, PAUL, AARON, JESSE... and left.

CHAPTER NINE

Keep the Faith, Baby

A narrow, blue and burgundy Victorian stood independent of its neighbors in a mainly black neighborhod near Sacramento and Ashby Avenue. A white woman with slightly pudgy cheeks and nose and thin, wavy hair answered the door.

"Hello, are you Lois or Trudy?"

"Lois."

"Hi. The landlord, Ricki, said you'd be showing the apartment downstairs for rent... ?"

The apartment was a dim, low-ceiling converted basement. The floor was concrete with a thin thriftstore carpet. Red, blue and yellow stained glass panes in the front windows cast a sick, brownish light into the living room. Jeanne stood with her hand resting flat on the low ceiling overhead and said, "No, this is not what I need."

"Would you like to see the place in back? It's for rent also," Lois said as she yanked the door closed behind her.

"Sure, I only saw the ad for this one."

As they rounded the corner of the Victorian, Jeanne was startled to see the tip of a high A-frame rising over the top of a tall, redwood gate. As the gate swung back, the rest of the structure was revealed.

"Wow," Jeanne murmured, swept with love at first sight.

"You'd never know this was back here. It's beautiful! If this was up in the Berkeley Hills, the rent would be outrageous."

"You're right. But Ricki is also a reasonable landlord."

Inside Jeanne looked up at the long, high windows that rose up to the peak of the A-frame. A free-standing brick fireplace separated the living room from the kitchen. She mounted the stairs that wound around behind the fireplace. Her love was sealed as she moved through the cool, open loft with two skylights and a second bath. A door opened out onto a vertiginous balcony above a garden and fenced backyard.

The kids would love this. Downstairs Jeanne eyed the wrought iron bars on the window.

"Ricki put those up and also this alarm system." Lois flipped a brown switch near the front door, triggering a fierce and abrasive alarm. She silenced it quickly, laughing. "It rings in both apartments in the front house and ours rings back here."

"Good," Jeanne agreed with mixed feelings inside. The sun showered in and fell in long rectangular patches on the empty floor. How unnatural to think of the threat of violence. Yet now violence was the subject of her work — a CETA position at Bay Area Women Against Rape.

I've never lived alone, I mean totally alone, Jeanne realized. *I wonder what this place would feel like at night...* A shudder brushed through her. *A woman living alone, small children visiting every other weekend. Exactly the M.O. of the rapist named Stinky who has been striking in southwest Berkeley, unapprehended for almost two years. Skilled burglar and entry artist... knife from the kitchen... subjugation... uses the children to make the woman submit... ugh, I wish I didn't know so much.*

Jeanne shook her head and stepped onto the long, redwood porch in the front. She moved around to the side and back of the house and stood knee-high in the tall grass beyond the garden. She drew in a long, sweet breath and marvelled how there could be such a strong sense of country around a place that was so close to city streets. Jeanne discussed the matter with Jill and then rented the hidden cottage on Russell Street.

After she had moved in, Jeanne went to play volleyball at an open game near Telegraph Avenue that happened every Saturday. Later that afternoon, she emptily made love with a woman she knew casually. Next door there was a litter of very black kittens, born in the country and, now weaned, needing a home. Having a new home and needing family, Jeanne knelt down and cupped two of the black, furry babies to come home with her.

As she opened the cardboard box and put each of them out on the carpet at home, they wobbled and bumped into each other as if they had been at sea for days. Jeanne smiled. They sprang up on the back of the faded, pink couch, nestled into each other like mirror images and immediately went to sleep as if they had always lived there. *Okay. Mellow little creatures, aren't you.*

Jeanne tossed the cardboard box onto the back porch, feeling a bit less alone.

1

August sun, fire-sign Leo, candles and evening fires — two and a half weeks with my children at the end of the summer.

It had been more than two years since Jeanne and her oldest son had so much daily time together. Their two-and-a-half week summer visit had now arrived. The sun melted away their initial nervousness and the days flowed liquid and healing. It seemed that they both felt soothed by the resumption of daily closeness while Jesse and his mother fell back into step with each other as if the past two wrenching months had been but a beat that others had forced them to miss.

Everyday they went to the beach. When the sun got heavy in the west, they returned home and started barbecue coals in the pit in the yard. As darkness gradually blanketed the tall A-frame, they withdrew indoors to yet another fire — logs and scraps from the mudflats along the Bay, set to burn in the fireplace. Jeanne watched as Paul lit the many little candles each evening and arranged them throughout the long living room.

Then, from the iron belly of the faded pink couch, out came the hide-a-bed, their favorite. Lying on the bed in front of the fireplace and to the endless strains of Paul's favorite, Linda Ronstadt, the three of them played games and talked until another day of summer's moratorium had passed.

After they fell asleep, some evenings Jeanne would not rise and climb the stairs to her room in the loft but stayed with them instead, drifting off to sleep between them. Soaked in their warmth and soothed by the rhythm of their sleeping breaths, the three of them slept, fused together like the melting coals of the nightly liquid dying fire.

On the last day, the sun shone no differently and the dragonflies were as fat and blue, yet cold was seeping in around Jeanne. Jeanne and her children lay in the morning sun on their last trip to Lake Temescal the day her husband was to pick them up.

At 4:00 Jeanne pulled the borrowed car to a stop to drop off Bobbi and her nephew, Adam, who had frequently joined them on their outings. Anger bumped sluggishly inside her chest and tears began falling of their own accord in rivulets down her cheeks.

"Don't cry, mommie," Paul urged comfortingly. He leaned his curly head against her arm and wrapped his arms snugly around it.

"I can't help it, Paul," she replied, flustered and short of breath. "It isn't fair. Only two and a half weeks? It makes me angry — and it doesn't make any sense."

"Goodbye, Jeanne," said Bobbi, closing the door. "Call me when they've left and I'll come over. Goodbye, Paul. You take care. Bye, Jesse."

"Bye, Bobbi," they answered in unison.

Looking trim in his pink summer linen shirt and beige slacks, Franco stepped in the open front door. He looked tanned and relaxed. Paul startled Jeanne by blurting out immediately, "Dad, I want to stay another three weeks with Mom. Please?"

Jesse nestled close to Jeanne's side on the couch at his father's approach and piped up in a low voice, "I want to stay here."

Instantly, Franco glared at Jeanne, presuming that she had staged this mutiny. He dismissed the idea flatly.

"No, Paul, school starts next week. Do you have all your things?" he summoned, clearing this throat and anxious to depart. "Come on, Jesse," he said, reaching towards him on the sofa, "we'll talk about it later."

"How about talking about it now?" Jeanne threw in.

Franco glowered back at her in response and with combustible disdain.

"I don't want to discuss this in front of the children," he replied with a bothersome tone of adult custodial superiority.

"I think we should talk with them," Jeanne decided to pursue the issue with no expectations. *He took Jesse with the police two months ago, he took Jesse out of my arms ten days later and I have no illusions but that he will indeed take them again today.* So she continued anyway.

"This is a decision that affects them, you know. It's not where you are going to live or where I am going to live. It's where *they* are going to live. Shouldn't they have a say in that?"

"Come on, kids," he said, fluttering his hands as if to dismiss such a presposterous notion. "We'll talk about it later."

"We'll talk about it later, we'll talk about it later," Jeanne mimicked under her breath.

Jesse hung back against Jeanne as she buttoned an errant button on his shirt and kissed him goodbye. He picked up his bag and walked to the door as if his feet were tugging through wet cement. The promise of "dinner at MacDonald's" lured him into moving faster.

"I had so much fun, Mom," said Paul sincerely, looking up at Jeanne. She looked at him, bag over his shoulder, tanned and handsome. *My world-travelled son,* she thought. She felt her face soften its tension into a warm smile. She unfurled her long arms and wrapped them around him snugly.

"Thanks, Paul. I did too. I love you so much."

"I love you too."

"Then that's what we've got."

2

In late summer the legal team was joined by another dark curly head, a tenacious lawyer for whom respect was growing on the progressive legal and political scene, Mary Morgan. Mr. Horowitz successfully conducted a long series of delaying tactics, including trips abroad and a "schedule too full" to permit scheduling of the Interlocutory trial. August became September. Then October. The children stayed with their father. Still no trial date set.

September, however, did see preparation for the trial begin. Jeanne was told this process was called discovery.

Mary Morgan sat in her small, glassed-in office with legal folders pulled out of vertical files and stacked in piles on the rug. Her incisive blue eyes scanned several pages of a 16-page document that had just arrived from the offices of Armin Horowitz, Esq. Re: Jullion vs. Benelli. Dressed in a tailored cotton shirt and attractive matching grey cords, Mary dialed Jeanne's number at Bay Area Women Against Rape and, as it rang, knelt over the stack of material Jill had forwarded to her new co-counsel. Her blue eyes sparkled behind her wire-rim glasses and she smiled irrepressibly as she began to talk.

"Jeanne, how are you doing? I just wanted to tell you that we received the interrogatories from Horrible Horowitz. We'll start going over these at the legal meeting on Wednesday at 4:00, okay?"

"What are interrogatories, Mary?"

"They're written questions we have to answer and they'll be used in trial. We'll be preparing some for your husband, too. It's part of discovery."

"Huh. Alright," Jeanne said vaguely. "See you Wednesday at 4:00. Your office or Jill's?"

"We'll be meeting at my office this week."

At the first two hearings, the examination of Jeanne's life had taken the haphazard form of questions of any nature put to her on the stand plus surveillance. Now with the discovery phase, she quickly saw that the scrutiny and dissection was to be much more open and frighteningly systematic. The process was twofold: interrogatories (written questions) and depositions (oral testimony taken under oath). All information contained therein could be cited and introduced into evidence at the final trial.

On Wednesday, Jeanne walked up a short alley in the Financial District called Jesse Street. She entered a red brick office building that was dwarfed by neighboring high-rises. She sprinted up two flights of stairs to the loft-like offices of Susan Jordan and Mary Morgan, Attorneys-at-Law. The secretary with short cropped hair smiled and motioned her into the high-beamed orange conference room and continued typing. Jeanne sat and began reading the interrogatories:

1. Please set forth the full and complete address of each and every residence where you have resided from January 1, 1975 to date:

2.   (a) Please set forth whether you resided overnight at any of the addresses with any other third person in said residence in the same room in which you slept during the periods indicated for each and every address:

(b) The name and address or place of employment of each and every individual who so resided overnight at any of these residences:

(c) The dates to the best of your knowledge on which said persons slept overnight in the same room where you slept...

3.   Please set forth the reason or reasons why you left each and every address commencing January of 1975 to present:

4.   Please set forth the present address of Shana Ascher.

If she is not presently residing in the same residence where you reside please set forth the reason...

Jeanne threw the document down on the long, polished table. "Do we have to answer all this?" she fumed. She rose to her feet impatiently and began pacing. "It's pretty clear what their 'case' is going to be — right back in the bedroom! Plus *instability*. I broke up with Shana, our 'long-term monogamous relationship' we swore to at the hearings — oh, will Horowitz have a field day with that one — plus I've moved five times in the past two and a half years. I hate it," Jeanne glowered. Her stomach smoldered. She looked from Jill to Mary's face and back again. "I hate it," she repeated uselessly, dropping back down into the upholstered chair.

They waited silently as she chewed her anger and calmed her exasperation. They then set to work.

Shana was the first to be served a subpoena. She was to report to Mr. Horowitz's offices in Jack London Square in Oakland to have her deposition taken. A court reporter was present and Jill and Mary briefed and accompanied her as her attorneys. Eyes puffy and not looking well, Shana pulled a chair back, sat down in the drab and unadorned conference room and lit a menthol cigarette. Mr. Horowitz spread out a sizable mountain of papers, smiled and began.

Q. When did you first meet Miss Jullion?

A. About a year and a half ago.

Q. Where?

A. It was at a picnic.

Q. After you met Jeanne at the picnic, do you recall if you had relations with her that particular day? When I say relationship, some type of a sexual relationship?

A. With whom? With Jeanne?

Q. With Jeanne.

A. Oh, no.

Q. Approximately how long after you met her was that?

A. Many months after.

Q. Do you have any idea of how many times you had sexual relations with her either in your home or in her home?

A. No, I don't.

Q. More than 10.

A. From when I first met her to the present? There is no possible way I could make an estimate.

Q. Are you able to say if it was more than 10?

A. Yes, it's been more than 10.

Q. Are you able to say if it's more than 20?

A. I guess it would be safe to say it's more than 20.

Q. Would you say it's more than 30?

A. I would say it was more than 30.

Q. Would you say it was more than 40?

A. You know, I didn't keep count so we could go on like this forever. I really don't know.

Q. I understand that. I just want to get your best idea.

A. I can't give you any better answer than that.

Q. Do you think it was more than 100?

A. I really have no idea.

Q. Can you tell me what these acts consisted of generally, not specifically?

A. Well, why don't you tell me what you want and I'll tell you if it took place or not.

Q. I am just asking you to generally describe what acts took place between you and Miss Jullion.

A. Loving acts.

Q. I'm not talking about holding hands.

A. That's my answer — loving acts.

Q. Describe that a little further. What do you understand the term 'loving acts' to mean? Different people have different definitions. I just want to find out what you believe is encompassed in that.

A. Touching, kissing.

Q. Is that basically it?

A. Yes.

Q. Am I correct that those acts or whatever conduct between you and Jeanne that you call loving acts would take place either in her residence or yours or in a residence that you shared jointly?

A. Yes.

Q. You wouldn't go to a motel or an outside location generally, is that correct?

A. No. Yes, that's correct.

Q. You wouldn't go do these acts in a car or out in a field or anything like that, is that correct?

A. Definitely not.

That's more your style, Shana thought to herself. She twisted her cigarette out and looked over wryly at Jill and Mary.

Q. Generally, always in the home?

A. Yes.

Q. When did you and Miss Jullion start living together initially?

A. October of 1976.

Q. When did Miss Jullion move out?

A. It was sometime in the beginning of August.

Q. Can you tell me the reason for that?

A. Well, it was because it was mutually decided that the stress and the trauma of the custody case and Jesse's being ripped off from our home was very detrimental to the home situation.

Q. Tell me what the effect was on Jesse.

A. He was very upset. He wanted to stay in our home.

Q. Anything else?

A. He began to wet the bed when he began to feel pressure from his father. He very much wants to be back with his mother.

Q. Tell me how that manifested itself, to your knowledge?

A. He talks about it incessantly.

Q. Tell me what he says.

A. He tells us all the time, has told us in the past, that he has spoken to his father about it and tells his father that and his father doesn't listen to him and he doesn't want to go back there. Does he have to go back and how long will it be before he has to go back, why does he have to go back and so forth. He said he wants to get a new judge, and he wants to speak to the judge and tell the judge where he should live.

Q. Tell me, have you been over to see Miss Jullion since she left.

A. I have seen her.

Q. That's not my question. Have you gone over to see her?

A. Where she lives?

Q. Yes.

A. Yes, I've seen her where she lives.

Q. Did you have any kind of sex relations with her or love relationship when you went to visit her?

A. No.

Q. Why's that?

A. Because we were no longer living together and no longer sexually involved.

Q. I believe you said at the court hearing that you were deeply in love with her. Is that a correct statement of what you said?

A. Yes, that's correct.

Q. Are you still deeply in love with her?

A. No.

Q. Can you tell me, if you know, the reasons why you are no longer deeply in love with her?

A. It was necessary for me to make a distinction between

the type of relationship that we had and what our involvement with each other would be in the future due to my prime concern, which is my children.

Q. Tell me what it was that you noticed in your children that caused that.

A. My children were very emotionally distraught after Jesse was ripped off and they required my full attention. They were very upset that Jesse had been removed and were afraid that the policeman might come and steal them.

Q. Can you describe what you mean by the term Jesse being 'ripped off'? I'm not sure what that term means. Maybe you can describe what the term — "ripped off" — means.

A. Stolen. Forcibly removed from the home.

Q. You believe Jesse was stolen from somebody?

A. Yes.

Q. And you also believe he was forcibly removed from the home?

A. Yes.

Q. Did anyone tell you there were court orders that the child could be removed?

A. Yes.

Q. And you still believe the child was stolen?

A. Given the manner in which he was taken, yes.

Q. How did you form the opinion that somebody was stolen or ripped off if you weren't there?

A. By the fact that neither Jeanne nor I was present in the home, and neither of us was informed of the fact that he would be removed, or when he would be removed, and when he was taken without any of his permanent belongings, without a chance to say goodbye to any of us, and without even having his shoes on. To me that constitutes stolen and ripped off.

3

The Presiding Judge of Alameda County Superior Court sat high at the end of the cavernous marble room, the county's court calendar open in large ledgers in front of him. Jill Lippitt and Armin Horowitz walked through the swinging doors and approached the end of the long chamber in step. Then Mr. Horowitz burst out, "Your Honor, this is that lesbian mother case, the gal that's been on TV and in the papers."

"*Mr. Horowitz!*" Jill exploded. "Do you wish to try this matter now or shall we set a trial date to do so?"

"*Your* client has been trying this matter in the press," Judge Lindsay angrily retorted at Jill. "What does your client think she is doing, counsel? *We have an independent judiciary!*"

As Presiding Judge, he was in the process of setting trial dates for the month of November, the ledger open in front of him. The calendar for the next year had not even been set out yet. Nonetheless, he roared punitively from his end of the room — "Trial date is set for *January*. January — let's see — 17th. And your client, counsel, is advised to cool this matter out. *Good day.*"

As Jill Lippitt and Armin Horowitz walked down the marble corridor of the Courthouse, Jill looked over her shoulder and said, "Mr. Horowitz, you are a disgrace to the legal profession."

"Why, Ms. Lippitt, I am what I am — a paid prostitute."

"You, sir, are also a disgrace to the Jewish race."

"Why, Ms. Lippitt, I am going to Israel this month."

"Good," replied Jill dryly, "I'd say it's time that you meet your Maker. I'll pray that you see the light. Good day."

It was another blow.

"January." Jeanne reeled at the news. "January 17th? You mean that we must go through the holidays like this?"

At least we finally know, she tried to console herself. *By late January it will be over.*

4

Unable to resist, Jeanne left the Bay Area Women Against Rape office in Berkeley early and headed her used car onto the Nimitz Freeway towards downtown Oakland. Mary Morgan was defending another lesbian mother, another aftermath of Judge Minder's work. Her client, Lynn Ransom, had received such short notice of her husband's move to secure custody that she had appeared in court without having a chance to secure an attorney. Judge Minder summarily awarded custody of the children — a boy and a girl, ages nine and eleven — to the father for the summer. Now, for the Interlocutory, Lynn had fortunately drawn a well respected and independent judge whose eyes nonetheless followed Jeanne carefully as she unobtrusively slid into a back row seat of the proceedings in progress.

Shortly, Judge Barber called a recess and directed Mary Morgan to come into his chambers.

"Has there been any publicity on this case?" he demanded crossly.

"No, Your Honor," Mary replied respectfully, slipping one hand into her black blazer pocket.

"Good. There'd better not be," he warned and dismissed her abruptly from his chambers.

Jeanne returned after work the next day. Lynn, Mary and friends were waiting anxiously outside the courtroom, the trial drawing to a close. Judge Barber had called both her children into chambers.

The bailiff held the courtroom door open and the two well-dressed and somber children stepped out. They looked guardedly at both their mother and their father as a family friend quietly took their hands and led them to the elevator. The bailiff intoned that court would resume.

Judge Barber emerged from chambers in shirt sleeves. He neither donned his formal black robes nor did he resume his high seat at his table. Instead he leaned informally on the banister and simply spoke directly to the litigants and those present.

"Based on my conversation with the children, based on their wishes and my consideration of the testimony, I am ruling that the children be returned to the custody of the mother."

Jeanne's heart lurched and her eyes jumped back to Lynn. She watched her silently wipe the tears of joy that were running down her cheeks as he finished his statement and set visitation. Jeanne struggled hard to choke back her own tears, to contain a desperate envy of her moment of joy and resolution. *How can I ever match her well-dressed beauty and composure... how can I ever combat the court's image of me as a radical activist more interested in a cause than in my children.*

All those present stood and quietly applauded Judge Barber's courage and reasonableness and embraced and congratulated Lynn outside. Lynn looked over at Jeanne as if wanting to shorten her time, share her relief, and said warmly, "Oh Jeanne, you're next."

Jeanne mumbled something, excusing herself. She walked past the unavailable elevators and went into the cement stairwell, taking the steps two at a time, heading for the sanctuary of her car. There in the anonymous bowels of the municipal parking lot she slammed the car door and, leaning on the wheel, she set her sobs free.

5

The Defense Committee had dwindled to four or five regular members. Months earlier, Pam Miller spoke up during the weekly Defense Committee meeting and suggested that a Finance Committee meet separately to concentrate on fundraising and keeping the effort afloat financially. That was almost the last Jeanne saw of Pam and the women who joined her on the committee: Harvey Milk's successful campaign manager, Anne Kronenberg, Joyce Garay, Mary Pat Power, Devorah Honigstein, Jill Sanford and more. Nonetheless, for months this group of of women organized and coordinated fundraising and managed the account in the face of bills now estimated at $12,000 to $15,000.

The U.N.A. office on Telegraph Avenue continued to serve as a clearinghouse for contact with the community. Requests for

Jeanne to speak continued to come into the office in a steady flow. From Stanford University to the People's Cultural Center, from a socialist bookstore to Sociology classes at the Community College, Jeanne spoke at them all and passed the legendary colored cans that sat in the myriad bars, bookstores and gathering places of the Bay Area.

The high-energy staff at U.N.A. — led by Elizabeth who was also coming out — were also busy preparing a major fundraising concert by feminist songwriter Margie Adam and a dynamic women's jazz trio named Alive! It was scheduled at the Castro Theatre in San Francisco for October 16th. The Gay Student Union at Stanford where Jeanne had slipped dismally into a summer meeting two years earlier was preparing a benefit performance by folk songwriter and long-time activist, Malvina Reynolds for November.

Bobbi, straggly-haired, bony, soft and tough, stayed with Jeanne the night before the Castro concert. Earlier in September, Jeanne's love for and companionship with Bobbi had silently appeared in her life like a single desert bloom. Bobbi's unfaltering friendship, joy in Jeanne's children and scrappy anger at the world was a steady hand that Jeanne clutched almost daily. She watched and was sooth-ed by Bobbi's special relationship with Paul — her pointed humor, her gentle way of shaking his dreamy world, looking in, saying hi, poking fun at the loopholes in his semi-tough code of behavior, his fascination with Bruce Lee and what's cool.

For Jeanne herself it was grey mornings, curled in her arms. Bob-bi's kisses rained down on Jeanne's long body like the comforting pressure of the rain on the loft roof. Or, tossing the quilt down to the living room floor below, they'd lie naked in the giant patches of sunlight on the floor, Jeanne's muscles loosened under the soothing touch of a woman's hand.

But there were times when Jeanne thought she could bear no more. There were times when even Bobbi's strong arms around her, a dark beer and an old Nina Simone album couldn't calm her or allay her desperation. *If you are going to get through this, you're going to have to let yourself cry,* she had told herself early on. Yet sometimes tears only smoldered her anger and took her breath away. She'd look out wildly from bloated eyes and flee the house if alone there after dark. Or Bobbi would guide her to the giant paisley pillows on the living room floor to beat out her rage as an alternative to her racking headaches.

Cigarettes helped keep the lid on but worsened her health in every other way. Marijuana helped, love helped, speaking publicly helped, one day at a time helped, trying to make sense of it helped, but understanding it politically really helped most of all.

A stream of letters and donations came into the P.O. Box in the small substation on San Pablo Avenue, from the Bay Area and beyond. Sometimes the letters would stop her in her tracks outside the Post Office, letters like this one:

Dear Jeanne,

I just read of your problem and I wanted you to know someone else is with you. That whole deal makes me angrier than I already was. You see, I'm lying in my top bunk here in Central Prison in Raleigh, N.C. writing this. A couple of years ago I was sentenced to prison because I am a homosexual. Not unusual in this state.

The idea that one is less suitable to be a parent because of the most private part of his or her life is ludicrous. Tragic may be a better word... In fact I have known many fathers who themselves were primarily homosexual but lived in despair having not enough courage to do something about it. Both parents were unhappy and the poor kids were usually emotional "disaster areas."

But in your case, as in most cases where the parent refuses to be hypocritical, your only real problems are caused by the ignorance of others whose own hysteria should not be allowed to be a factor.

I can't help but feel you will win out eventually... but it just isn't fair that you should have to go through all this. I know the trauma of being separated from one's own son.

Under these circumstances I don't have much to spend but I did want to at least send these two dollars to add to your fund. I'm also enclosing a few stamps — I'm sure you will be needing a bunch. I also want to add my prayers and my love to you all.

Best of luck —
Peace
Ed T.

A letter from a mother in Illinois:

I am a poor mother so I can't send any money — but as a human, a mother, a woman I can send my support and encouragement.

Judge Minder and the Oakland Courts' attitudes and actions are inexcusable. They are <u>outrageous,</u> and I do feel a rage when I think about what they/he have done to you, your children, your lover and your life. You are not alone, they do it to a lot of folks.

But most people are afraid to stand up and fight back — that is why your struggle is so important, not just from the overall implications for other families but because you're not afraid, you're ready to fight back and you can inspire others.

Don't let them defeat you in their "system of justice". Fight back in <u>every</u> way you can.

Stay strong sister, for all of us!

Ande M.A.

A handwritten note:

I am a black man 76 years old. Read about you in the papers. Best wishes.

Wm (Bill) D.

Five dollars and a note on a yellow Meow Mix notepad:

Dear Jeanne,

Keep the faith, baby. Keep the baby, too. It's about time for some happy endings.

Love,
K.

From a father in Durham, North Carolina:

My situation, as a divorced father with "normal" sexual preferences, has been less dramatic. It has made me well aware, though, of the tyranny of domestic courts, and how such courts are used to promote the most repressive aspects of our society.

I am enclosing a check for $10.00 to help you in your legal fight. I wish you the courage to hang in, and I wish you justice, in the form of having your children returned.

Sincerely,
Bob B.

And a thousand dollars, no names...

Dear Jeanne,

We are a group of six women who have collectivized around a sum of money that has fallen into our hands as a result of class privilege... In consideration and in concern for our sisters who are actively struggling for rights that will promote our strength and visibility as strong and independent people, we would like to support your efforts to gain custody of your children.

We believe that small victories for one woman will lead to victories for all women.

In support of your work and the risks you are taking for us all,

Small Change

6

OCTOBER 17, 1977
CASTRO THEATER

On Sunday morning, Jeanne and Bobbi looked out the front windshield of the car at the marquee of the Castro Theater. JEANNE JULLION BENEFIT. Jeanne's mouth hung open like a little kid at her name in lights.

"What a tortuous way to fame," she jested, punching Bobbi's sinewy arm at the wheel.

Inside the Castro, white tablecloths covered long tables in the upstairs and downstairs lobbies. These were lined with wine, beer, and fundraising buttons. Elizabeth and her redheaded lover, Amy, laughed hilariously as they dropped grenadine-soaked sugar cubes into plastic stem glasses of champagne and orange juice and sold them as JJ Fizzes.

The lobbies continued to fill as the women technicians completed a final check of the sound equipment before opening the doors for seating. Women sat casually on the red carpeted steps, one swaying a small infant on her knees. Greetings met Jeanne as she moved through the warm woman-energy that was transforming the commercial theater into the intimacy of a living room.

A woman with long black hair, and a key clip on the belt loop of her black cords opened the doors to the theater. Fifteen hundred streamed in to take seats. Butterflies batted inside her stomach and Jeanne began searching the crowd for Hannah. She spotted her flushed cheeks and long wispy blond hair as she talked excitedly with Sheila.

"Hannah," she waved, "com'ere a second. Listen," she began, hugging her warmly, "you know, I'm nervous about speaking."

"Oh Jeanne, you'll do great. You've done so much of this."

"Yeh, I know but I still get nervous. I had a thought. Would you come up on stage with me, Hannah?"

Her blue eyes widened.

"You don't have to say anything but it would make me feel better to have you up there with me."

"Sure!" she gushed, stars bursting in her eyes.

I need to find a quiet spot to gather my thoughts, Jeanne thought as Hannah disappeared to tell her mother and Aaron. She spotted the black-haired woman with the dark eyes by the front doors.

"Is there a dressing room of sorts?" Jeanne asked.

"Yes, that door over there by the drinking fountain."

"Thanks."

Jeanne slipped into the tiny room and slumped down in a wooden chair. She heard Suzanne, Rhiannon and Carolyn of Alive! humming and singing soft warm-ups close behind her. The door opened again and Margie Adam and her manager, Boo Price, came in. As they bent their heads in conference, Jeanne looked at Margie's light brown curls and thought distractedly, *we look like sisters.*

Jeanne heard applause. The program must have begun. She went into the theater and slowly walked down the darkened aisle to a seat at the side of the stage. Hannah appeared out of the dimness, having watched carefully for her return. She slipped onto her knee. Two MC's, Ollie, and Sabrina Sojourner, were dressed sharply in a tuxedo and long gown respectively, garb that they would reverse at the intermission. They finished their introduction — "the reason we're here today, Jeanne Jullion."

The audience sank back into blackness as Hannah and Jeanne stepped up on stage and into the spotlight's glare. Hannah stopped next to Jeanne but Jeanne reached over and pulled her right in front of her, wrapping her arms around her and feeling strong and soothed.

"Thank you," Jeanne began into the microphone. "I'm very glad you're all here. Believe me, I am *very* glad you're all here.

"My name is Jeanne Jullion. And this is Hannah. This is the nearest thing to a daughter that I have," she said fondly, stroking Hannah's long hair back off her forehead so they could see her. Hannah beamed, her dimples deepening into shadow.

"I also have two sons," Jeanne continued slowly, "Paul, who will be 9 in a couple of weeks, and Jesse, who turned 4 ten days after the police r-ripped him off from my home.

"As I am sure you know," she continued, "I am lesbian and I am a mother. I have been involved in a custody struggle for my children in the Oakland courts since last February.

"We all know why we're here," Jeanne's voice welled up from some deep pool of anger in her chest. "We're here to celebrate our strength and our resistance. I have lost temporary custody of my children out of a three-fold prejudice: prejudice against me as a welfare mother, as a lesbian mother and a mother who has chosen something other than the nuclear model set up for us — what the court refers to as my 'alternative lifestyle'."

She took a breath. Hannah's body felt warm, snuggled back against her own.

"Why do they fear us so much? Why was the courtroom closed," Jeanne demanded, "a gag order issued, my son removed by the police without even notifying me when he was to leave, without even his shoes or jacket or a chance to say goodbye?

"They *say* their fears are in the children's best interests. They *say* they fear that our children will have 'gender confusion', that they will not know whether they are a boy or a girl, yet our children show no such confusion. This has been verified by both professional studies of the children of lesbian mothers and by individual psychological examination of, for example, my own children.

"They *say* they fear that our children will grow up gay — horrors! To the courts and to most straight people, unfortunately, that is a horror. But to put their mind at ease, 99 percent of gay people were raised by heterosexual parents — it is not contagious. An estimated 10 percent of the human population is homosexual — always has been, always will be — and so some of our children may, in fact, be gay. If they are *hetero*sexual, they will grow up knowing that human sexuality also encompasses homosexuality and will hopefully be free of the intense homophobia which afflicts most people. If they are *homo*sexual, they will have a chance to grow up free from the self-hatred and crippling confusion that most of us have known. In either case, it is not grounds to take our children away from us.

"Lastly, and what was cited most often in my case, is stigma. They fear that our children will be teased and stigmatized by being raised by a lesbian mother. Well, as the kids say themselves," Jeanne squeezed Hannah, *"strong kids can deal with reality*. Prejudice abounds in our culture but it is no solution to take our children away from us. The only way we're ever going to end prejudice is not by bowing to it but by facing it for what it is.

"These are the things they *say* they fear. But I think what they fear goes deeper and is more political. They fear us because we are lesbians, and in a society that insists that a woman be dependent on a man and preferably within a nuclear family, women who stand alone and strong and complete are a threat. The system has a very deep, vested interest in seeing that mothers raise their children in the predominant values of this society.

"These values are a cult really, a cult of imagined superiority — the superiority of being male over being female, of being white over being black, brown, red or yellow, of being middle class over working class, of being heterosexual over homosexual. Quite frankly, these are not values that many lesbian mothers choose to foster in their children. To the contrary, much of our parenting energy goes into raising our children free from the racism, sexism and

violence of this culture. Thus, the Court, when faced with a decision, will opt to take the children and place them with the other
parent or in a foster home where the Court is assured that they will
be properly socialized. For being a lesbian is more than sexual insurrection; it is political insurrection.

"As long as women are kept alone and isolated, we will be
relatively powerless. But women are breaking out of that isolation
and fighting back. Just as Inez Garcia and Yvonne Wanrow and
Dessie Woods fought back against their attackers, the men who
would rape them. Inez Garcia, Yvonne Wanrow and Dessie Woods
should not be in jail," Jeanne punched out each word. "These
women are not criminals," Jeanne snarled. *"The criminals are dead
— they killed them."*

Jeanne's arm curled protectively around Hannah as she said this.
Applause thundered in the ornate hall, reverberating everywhere.
House lights came up slightly. As people gradually retook their seats,
Jeanne summed up.

"The cost of this case is now estimated at $12,000 to $15,000.
We will raise the money. Yes, and we will play all their legal games.
And we will make it to January 17th, the date the judge punitively
set for trial. We will do all of this but I tell you, in the end, we want
— " Jeanne's voice faltered, wondering herself what were her
chances for — "justice."

The word scraped out of her throat. She then thanked Alive! and
Margie Adam for performing the benefit and Ruth, Amy, Elizabeth
and the staff at U.N.A. for producing the concert. She thanked those
present. House lights came up further. People stood and applause
filled the gilded theater as a steady resolute force.

Jeanne turned to leave. Hannah stepped gingerly over squiggly
black electrical cords. The applause continued unabated and for
a second, Jeanne turned back into its flow. She felt suspended in
the arms of this focused outpouring of support. In a subliminal instant, her body's pores stretched open like a million parched mouths
as she let this sweet ocean swirl over her. Doubting they could know
how much it was true, she stepped back to the mike and said in the
midst of their applause, "I couldn't do it without you."

7

The two young male cats had grown black and sleek and extremely affectionate, almost canine in their responsiveness to their mistress' moods. They squeezed under the tall redwood gate and loped towards her at her return from work. One had a white spot on its forehead and was chosen and named Diamond by Paul. Its brother was likewise all black except for a white patch on its throat. Jesse named his cat Mr. Bow Tie.

The cats coiled and purred against Jeanne as she sat down on the donated pink sofa after work. She eyed her watch and then dialed the number of the daycare in Mountain View where they had learned Jesse attended.

"Hello, Friendship Daycare."

"Hello," Jeanne responded, "my name is Jeanne Jullion and I'm Jesse Benelli's mother. I'd like to come down and visit the daycare and see how Jesse's doing."

"Oh. I see. Yes, well, we'll have to call Mr. Benelli and get his permission. I'm sure it'll be fine but we do have to get Mr. Benelli's permission."

For two days Jeanne waited for permission to see Jesse.

Dressed smartly for the visit and intending to stop by her parents' home as well, Jeanne had one hand in the pocket of her long amber slacks as she stepped out into the play yard of the daycare center. She spotted Jesse sitting astride a Big Wheel, looking at nothing in particular. She smiled at the sight of him and stood still, waiting for him to notice her.

"Mommie!" he squealed, clammering off the vehicle and lunging into her arms. *Ah, how good to hold him.*

Jeanne sat for over an hour on the bench, holding him and talking to his playmates. Later, she stepped into the Director's office and inquired more closely as to Jesse's adjustment. Afterwards in the car, she jotted down what the Director and his favorite teacher, Gail, had to say about the outgoing, exceptionally well-adjusted child of a few months earlier.

> He started in September. We're very worried about him. He just stood by himself, didn't say anything, didn't interact. He clung to me and especially to Gail. He would

wake up from his nap crying fitfully, afraid of monsters, scared. He was like that for two months. We were worried but didn't talk to the father and he never asked other than how and what did he do today.

Mr. Horowitz prepared the Director for testimony before calling her as his witness at the final trial. Somehow, by the time she testified in January — whether by his coaxing reminders that the mother is lesbian or her personal fears — the above report on Jesse's behavior four or five months after he had been taken had shriveled to "Jesse was doing fine. He had a normal adjustment period when he joined the daycare in September."

8

Once again Jeanne paced around the long conference table at Mary Morgan's office.

"It just isn't fair!" she exploded in the pre-trial legal meeting. "We could call a demonstration that would blow the Courthouse off the block. It doesn't have to be the day of trial," Jeanne argued. "It could be the weekend before. Two weeks before."

"It depends on whether we want to do that... " Mary replied cautiously.

"*Yes!*" Jeanne exploded again, "I *want* to do that! I've been speaking at, for and before every group in the Bay Area for months. Now it's my turn, *my* ass is on the line. It's time they show up for me and we all know they will."

"You realize what the Court thinks of you already," Mary reasoned skeptically. "You know what they're going to base their case on. There hasn't been any media stuff since last summer. They don't know where you've been speaking. You've turned down those couple of above-ground, national publicity inquiries. If we don't call a demonstration we'll at least have a shot at downplaying their argument that you're a self-aggrandizing activist and secondarily a mother."

"I know, Mary, but I'm afraid if I go into Court without that support that I'll get fucked over just like before. It *scares* me to go back into Court, to go in alone, with nobody knowing what's happening.''

"The ACLU is preparing an Amicus Brief and will argue that the Courtroom not be closed,'' Mary continued. ''But even if it's left open, I think we should seriously consider whether we want anybody in the courtroom anyway. It also depends on what judge we get.''

journal
january 9

i think i'm going about this
wrong
back-assed
mangling our precious energy with
my fears
being so scared
scared of losing Jesse all over again
a police-less raid on my empty house
empty for eight months now
eight months!

A lurching elevator crept up to the second floor of a modest office building on Market Street near Powell, the offices of a group of feminist therapists. The old scratched, steel door rolled slowly to the side. Jeanne took a seat on one of the unmatched chairs in the room to the right. At 5:00 a smiling woman with dark eyes and long wispy black hair summoned Jeanne into a windowless room furnished with oversized pillows. Since August Jeanne had met weekly with Marcia Stein, therapist and daughter of long-time political leftists. Trial was next week and this was their final session.

"Marcia, Marcia, it's being so hard,'' Jeanne wasted no time beginning. "We can't call a demonstration. I have to downplay all the speaking. Dress up. I tell you, it's killing me. I'm scared of letting go of the only leverage I felt I had... ''

"Jeanne,'' Marcia leaned forward, understanding immediately the crossroad her client was at, "all that really did happen. The impact of this case, the connections you made, the talking to all sorts of people that you've done and their understanding of what was happening to you is real. I never thought I'd see on the front page of the paper and on the evening news a dyke and her lover saying they're lesbians and mothers fighting for their kids.

"But Jeanne," she continued in earnest, "all oppressed peoples have their survival mechanisms. They go in and bullshit and kiss ass when they *have* to but inside they know who they are and what's happening. You're dressing up for them, Jeanne. And you know that ultimately it's all drag anyhow."

Jeanne leaned back against the bright patterned pillows. The tension inside her loosened somewhat.

"Your case has done a lot to break down myths about lesbians," Marcia continued, departing radically from her usual quiet role in this, their last meeting before trial. "It's made people start to deal with us as mothers — those who have children from marriages and those of us who, as women and as lesbians, are now choosing to have children as does any other woman on earth."

Marcia paused with a sparkle in her dark eyes and then said, "Jeanne, I want to share something with you. My lover, Carol, is pregnant."

"What?" Jeanne said in wonder, drawn out of her cloud of worry, moved by the spark of new life on its way.

"And what you've done has meant a lot to us, a lot to a lot of people. So, I want you to put that in your pocket when you go to Court!" she laughed.

"You know, Jeanne, there's no telling what's going to happen in Court," she added seriously. "But please, don't think so linearly because change doesn't happen that way. It's awareness. It's expansive."

The two women sat in the windowless room, their eyes met in silence. There seemed little else to say. Their work together was over. They stood peacefully and embraced.

Jeanne stepped out of the office building into the orange-rose glow that frequently bathes San Francisco at sunset. A palpable fear still went with her but she felt calmed — and ready for trial.

CHAPTER TEN

The Trial

The trial lasted five days. It was dull, grueling and ponderously repetitive. Again it was clear that it was Jeanne that was on trial. So for five days the proceedings plodded back and forth through Jeanne's recent life while Mary, Jill and Jeanne worked stubbornly to train the focus onto parenting and onto Jesse and Paul as two separate children with separate and distinct emotional histories and needs.

They drew Robert Kroninger as judge. Known as moderate, somewhat indecisive and legally scrupulous, Judge Kroninger immediately asserted himself on the issue of lesbianism. He summarily refused to allow any testimony on the issue or on any concerns as to its possible effects on Jeanne's children.

"The fact that one parent is homosexual and the other heterosexual is of no more weight than what brand of cigarettes each parent smokes," he ruled defensively.

Jeanne, Jill and Mary were not convinced. They knew how deeply imbedded the issue was in the case and were prepared to confront and challenge the fears rather than let them lie. Jeanne had been interviewed by two experts of international standing: Wardell Pomeroy, co-author of the Kinsey Report, and Dr. Richard Green, recipient of over a million dollars in grants from the Department of Health, Education and Welfare and the National Institute of Mental Health for his studies of human sexual and social development. The focus of much of his work had been children. Both were prepared to testify. But while Dr. Pomeroy makes his home in San Francisco, Dr. Green had been flown in from New York as their expert witness.

Appearing to be in his early forties, a clearly intelligent man of medium build and stature, Dr. Green sat patiently in the witness chair, waiting to see if Mary Morgan's careful efforts to have him testify would be successful.

"Your Honor," Mary finally conceded, "I understand that you do not wish to hear testimony on the issue of the mother's lesbianism and its possible effects, if any, on the children. However," she shifted her approach, "Dr. Green is a highly qualified psychiatrist and has conducted a psychiatric evaluation of Ms. Jullion which I would like to enter into testimony."

"Well, alright, counsel," Judge Kroninger answered guardedly. "He may testify only as to his psychiatric evaluation of the mother."

"Thank you, Your Honor." Mary proceeded.

MORGAN: Now, Dr. Green, in order to demonstrate to the Court your qualification as an expert witness in Psychiatry, can you tell us what your occupation is.

GREEN: I am a physician and psychiatrist in the Department of Psychiatry at New York State University at Stony Brook.

MORGAN: Have you been the recepient of any kinds of awards in the area of Psychiatry?

GREEN: During my medical school training at Johns Hopkins, I received three Public Health Service training awards working in the area of Sexual Role Development in children. The year I spent in London, 1966-67, was by a United States Public Health Service Special Fellowship, again in the area of sexuality at the University of London. For five years at UCLA I received a research studies award under the auspices of the National Institute of Mental Health, which is part of the Department of Health, Education and Welfare. Again this was for study in the area of sexual development in young children. Additionally, I received a number of grants from HEW and NIMH totalling in excess of one million dollars. This has been research money again primarily directed at the area of human sexuality with the principal focus being the study of sexual identity or sex role development in young children.

MORGAN: I see. And are you a member of any psychiatric professional organizations?

GREEN: I am the President of the Society for the Scientific Study of Sex, founding President of the International Academy of Sex Research, a fellow of the American Psychiatric Association, a member of the Southern California Society for Child Psychiatry, a member of the Society for Biological Psychiatry, the American Association of University Professors, Southern California Psychiatric Society and a few others.

MORGAN: Now, Doctor, have you conducted any studies which have been the subject of any articles in scientific journals?

Mary looked directly at Dr. Green with her sharp blue eyes and the experienced witness quickly grasped the intent of her question. He proceeded to expand slightly on each of his published studies. Without upsetting the judge, he carefully proceeded to communicate the substance of his research and findings:

— that sexual identity develops in early childhood;
— that the children of homosexual parents appear to be heterosexual in the same ratio as in the general population (i.e. 90%); and
— that no study to date has been able to demonstrate any adverse effects on children being raised by their lesbian mothers or gay fathers.

Mary nodded and walked around the end of the table in the silent courtroom.

MORGAN: Dr. Green, have you had an opportunity to conduct a psychiatric evaluation of Jeanne Jullion?

GREEN: Yes, I have.

MORGAN: Could you tell the Court what is your professional opinion of the mother in this case?

GREEN: Yes. She is an intelligent and candid woman who shows no signs of pathology... She also appears to be holding up well under the obvious stress of the custody proceedings.

Jeanne sucked furiously on a cherry cough lozenge, trying to suppress a crooping cough and look healthy and well-adjusted as he finished his impressive though abbreviated testimony. Mary then left it to Mr. Horowitz to bring out the third concern with having a gay parent: stigma.

Rising to cross-examine, Mr. Horowitz strode over to the clerk's desk and picked up his collection of newspaper articles on the case from last May and June.

HOROWITZ: Dr. Green, are you aware that there has been considerable publicity on this case by the Petitioner?

GREEN: I was told there was something in the paper last year.

HOROWITZ: And on TV?

GREEN: Yes, I guess so.

HOROWITZ: Do you think a parent is acting in the children's best interest to publicize the fact that she is gay and there is a custody battle going on?

GREEN: I'm not sure I can answer your question.

HOROWITZ: Don't you think that a child would be teased, stigmatized, embarrassed?

GREEN: It really depends on how the parent handles it.

HOROWITZ: You don't think he'd be teased or stigmatized at school or in the neighborhood?

GREEN: Oh yes, he might very well be teased. Kids are teased about many things — their race, about wearing glasses, about being skinny or fat, having a big nose, something. What you have to look at is how the parent helps the child deal with it.

HOROWITZ: But don't you think it would be preferable to place the child with a heterosexual parent and spare him that pressure?

GREEN: Not on those grounds alone. If the homosexual parent is well adjusted to his or her identity, is intelligent and sensitive in helping his or her child deal with possible prejudice, it need not be a problem. In fact, it can be an opportunity for the child to learn valuable lessons about coping with life. So whether it is a positive or negative experience really depends on the parent.

Unable to eke out anything defamatory from the highly credentialled witness, Mr. Horowitz wisely retreated and the witness was dismissed to catch his return flight to New York.

1

Crumpled newspaper crinkled open slightly as Jeanne reached back on the sofa for a book of matches. Driftwood leaned over the paper teepee fashion, waiting to be lit. Mr. Bow Tie pushed affectionately against her leg as she squatted to strike a match. A fine black dust sprinkled down out of the chimney onto the wood. Jeanne stopped. Another mist fell. Then chunks of soot rained down.

"What the — ?" Jeanne exclaimed with a start.

More cinders fell along with bumping and scratching sounds. Jeanne dropped the matches and squinted up into the chimney. No sooner did she see a long black bushy tail than Diamond unceremoniously tumbled down atop the carefully laid fire, followed by a rain of chimney soot. Driftwood rolled helter-skelter and Diamond bolted past her knee.

"*Diamond!* Goddammit, how d'you get in there! Do you realize how close you came to getting roasted?"

Diamond ran as she followed him into the kitchen, shaken. He scooted around the corner and bolted up the stairs to the loft. Lithely he leapt out onto the beams that ran across the open ceiling of the living room. Jeanne rounded the disheveled fireplace and glared up at the still agitated cat, actually damn glad just to see him. Mr. Bow Tie, tail swishing, elegantly joined his brother on the redwood beam.

Jeanne bent down and grabbed the book of matches.

"Diamond... ," she swore up at him again.

Fire reassembled, she glanced up at the two lanky black cats before touching the match to the first corner of crumpled newsprint. Fire roaring through the paper, she stood and stuck another match for two votive candles on the mantle. She touched the wick of a rose candle and prayed for Jesse, the wick of the musk candle and prayed for Paul. The light flickered warmly across the kids' pictures on the mantle and the fire heated the legs of her jeans. She tossed the matches on the end of the mantle and stretched out on the faded pink sofa. She knew the trial would conclude sometime the next day.

She stared at the candles, given to her at last Saturday's pre-trial party, summoned in lieu of a pre-trial demonstration. She had felt the need to have a coming together before the trial was at last to begin.

The long table in Sue Cook's Berkeley home was covered with steaming potluck specialties, from spaghetti in clam sauce to Shana's copious chocolate mousse, shaped in the form of two sumptuous breasts.

"Thanks for doing the deposition, Shàna," Jeanne stepped up beside her at the buffet and laid her hand lightly on her shoulder.

"Oh, that's alright," Shana nodded.

"I hear you did great."

"You know, somebody's got to keep him honest... "

"Yeenie! Yeenie!" Jeanne looked down to see two year-old Reuben grinning and threading his way to her.

"Reuben," she scooped his light little body up in her arms.

"The kids are doing well," Shana told her with a smile.

Later everyone gathered in the living room. They sat and locked hands in a circle around rose and musk candles lit on a mahogany table in the center. They joined together to mark the culmination of a year's work and hope for the coming week.

Hallie Iglehart, pioneer in the recovery of women's spirituality, author and lecturer at the University of California and the United Nations, had crafted a ritual for the evening. Joined by a woman named River, she took out a spool of rough magenta yarn, hand-dyed and woven by women in Scotland. They walked around the circle, weaving it in and out among the women and children. The yarn was then cut between each of them. A piece of magenta yarn, reminder of their collective effort, would be kept and worn by each of them until the trial was over.

Jeanne lay staring into the fire, gently fingering the rough yarn that Natalie had braided into a bracelet for her that night. She knew testimony was almost over. Mr. Horowitz had announced that he had subpoenaed her father and sister to testify the next day. And Jesse's daycare director.

Diamond and Mr. Bow Tie suddenly appeared and leapt silently up on the sofa in two quick beats. Lean and lovely, they advanced slowly, then silently sprawled on top of her. She laid a hand on each of their warm, purring bodies and whispered that tomorrow it'd be over.

2

The borrowed Spanish leather clogs clomped loudly on the wooden steps as Jeanne left her house the next morning for court.

She had saved an attractive three-piece suit and white, high-collared blouse for the final day. As she walked towards the gate, she squeezed the right pocket to check for the polished stone that Connie had slipped her for good luck. A wide Italian leather bag that Anna had given her years ago for her birthday now served as a briefcase. Shooing the cats back towards the house, she latched the tall gate behind her. Jill was waiting in her yellow Vega at the curb, motor running.

When they got to the third floor of the Courthouse, Jeanne cleared her throat and said, "Jill, would you look in the witness waiting room and see if my dad or sister are there?"

She reported back. "No, they're not."

"Hm."

The last day of testimony began with Mr. Horowitz calling Jeanne to the stand for one last pass on his familiar themes. He then asked if it was true that she had telephoned her father the week before.

JULLION: Yes, it is.

HOROWITZ: Is it true that you threatened him if he came to testify here?

JULLION: What? I did not!

JUDGE: Now just a minute. Your counsel will speak for you. Let your counsel make an objection.

Legal double-speak rolled on with Mr. Horowitz eventually abandoning the question. It seemed a distraction for what he said next: Mr. Jullion was sick and would not testify today. Neither had he in fact summoned her sister.

Jeanne looked with silent relief at Jill and Mary. The threat of her family testifying had loomed as a last hurdle following the testimony of their psychiatrist (very hostile), the first Probation Officer Fred Spence (repeat performance) and the new Probation Officer whose report similarly concluded that "permanent custody be awarded the father with reasonable visitation for the mother."

Mr. Horowitz leafed through his yellow notes and tossed a few more warmed-over questions at the witness and then said that was all. Mary rose to her feet.

MORGAN: Ms. Jullion, tell me. In the past several months since the initial publicity at the time of the second hearing and then relating to Jesse's removal and the appeal, have you turned down any offers of publicity?

JULLION: Yes, I have.

MORGAN: And would you tell the court what they were?

JULLION: Well, let's see. CBS has called several times from New York wanting to do a story — including the children — and I said no.

MORGAN: Why was that?

JULLION: Well, I felt that there were specific reasons for the publicity last May and June. National publicity later on would not have helped.

MORGAN: Were there any others you can think of?

JULLION: *Playboy Magazine* called for an interview and we rejected their offer.

MORGAN: Why was that?

JULLION: For much the same reasons. In addition, given the nature of the magazine, there were additional factors in deciding against it.

MORGAN: Thank you. I have nothing more, Your Honor.

JUDGE: You may step down.

By lunchtime, only one witness was left to be called, the director of Jesse's daycare. Jill, Mary and Jeanne sat at a linen-covered table in Grandma's Restaurant across the street where each night friends had gathered for a debriefing on the day's proceedings. Jeanne pushed away the scarcely touched bowl of soup in front of her and turned to Mary.

"Listen, Mary — no, eat. But about your closing argument. This is really what I want you to say. It's so clear in my head, I wish I could just say it myself."

Patiently, Mary moved her plate to the side and reached down for her yellow legal pad.

"Just like we've been doing all along, we've just got to distinguish the two kids and talk about them individually. It all boils down to certain realities about them and what they've been through and not my sexuality at all... "

The afternoon was grey and overcast as they slowly walked back across the street to the Courthouse. With fifteen minutes left before court was to resume, Jeanne stayed on the elevator and went to the Women's Lounge on the Fifth Floor. Without turning on the light, she lifted her bent feet out of the high-heeled clogs and lay down in the dark on the vinyl couch. She curled up, coughing and numb, staring at the black wall.

After the daycare director's testimony, a final recess was called. Mary, Jill and Jeanne paced their own paths along the now familiar hallway as Franco paced his. There was nothing left to say. The judge's face had been uniformly inscrutable throughout, giving no indication of what assessment he was making of the five days of testimony he had heard. The usual ten minute recess stretched to fifteen minutes... twenty. Then Jeanne felt a warm release of tension.

"Jill," she motioned, coughing, "things are going to be okay. Somehow I think they're going to be okay."

Jill's red eyebrow arched with skeptical weariness. "Ah, I hope so, Jeanne."

COURT IS RESUMED, the bailiff barked one last time. Jeanne and Jill's hands locked. Jeanne reached up and tucked the piece of magenta yarn out of sight in the neck of Jill's blouse. *Is our odyssey nearing its end?*

The five participants resumed their places at the long table. Minutes crawled by slowly as they waited in silence for Judge Kroninger to at last emerge from his chambers.

BAM!

Mary glanced at the final notes on each of the children and scooted back her chair to rise for her closing argument. Suddenly scared, Jeanne grabbed her arm.

"Mary," she whispered sharply, "if we lose — " Jeanne hesitated, looking into her blue eyes, "I don't want the kids to go to Italy." *Not that much loss, not gone that far, not yet.* "Please."

"Okay," Mary answered *sotto voce.* Jeanne let go of her arm and she rose to address the waiting courtroom. Judge Kroninger interrupted her immediately.

"Now just a minute, counsel. I don't want to hear a lengthy reasoning about lesbianism," he stated defensively. "I don't care if the Petitioner's love object is a sewing machine. That's not relevant here."

A bit dazed by the bizarre nature of his analogy, Mary replied simply, "I was not planning to talk about lesbianism, Your Honor."

"Well," he continued shortly, "perhaps I can save you some time and energy by telling you what my considerations and opinion are so far and then, if you want to make some closing remarks, you may do so if you wish."

Mary sat back down next to Jeanne.

"I think there is no doubt that both parents are good parents. Both intelligent people, incomes relatively the same. Either parent is probably capable of raising these two boys.

"The children," he went on, "from the testimony that I've heard, appear to be doing reasonably well in the custody of their father.

"I think what has tipped the scale in favor of the Respondent," he nodded towards Mr. Benelli, and his voice began to rise, "was the Petitioner's lack of good judgement in taking this whole matter to the press. Your client did not exercise good judgement on behalf of her children by doing so," he unbudgingly reprimanded. *NO, it isn't fair.* Judge Minder, newspaper print swam in front of Jeanne's eyes.

"So," he concluded, "I have not really seen compelling reason to change custody and my opinion at the present is that custody of both children should remain with the father.

"Now, counsel, if you wish to make some closing remarks, you may do so."

Jeanne could feel Franco and Mr. Horowitz's muffled congratulations to each other to her right. Mary slowly put the cap on her pen and looked at Jeanne. She glanced at Jill. Jeanne felt her rise and begin speaking. She felt as if someone had placed the cold metal nozzle of a shotgun to her chest and pulled the trigger. Jeanne's heart felt like a hawk, shot and falling, feathers twisting.

Jeanne could hear Mary's voice... about Paul — a child who had been through many cultural changes in his life, without his mother in Italy at age 6, left continually with his grandparents, his father promising he would return from America in 11 days and gone three months, his mother asking that he live with her during the school year, live with his father during the summers, in Italy if they wish...

Breath snorted loud and jagged through Jeanne's nostrils. Her jaw locked, couldn't hold on any longer. Her chest heaved out of control, face felt wet. She took off her lavender glasses, dropped them on the table loudly. Her face bent forward into her hands, no hope of controlling her chest's wracking. She felt Jill's hand gripping her arm, slipping tissues into her lap. She felt the judge's eyes on her.

Jesse — Mary's strong loud voice forged on — a child who had never been separated from his mother, whom Dr. Nestor considered one of the most well adjusted children he had seen in 20 years of practice, who Dr. Nestor had urged not be disrupted and removed from his mother, taken by the police and placed at age 4 with the father, now doing only moderately well, the Respondent's own psychiatrist admitting he now has significant fears... of fire... of monsters... of the dark. This exceptionally secure child now stood for weeks in the corner of the play yard, not speaking or interacting with others.

"There is no reason, Your Honor, why he has to be made to cope with the stress of being separated from his mother... who wants him very much."

The courtroom was quiet as Mary sat down. Mr. Horowitz rose. Obviously feeling that he had won, he waxed magnanimous and conciliatory in his final remarks.

"Your Honor," he began philosophically, adjusting his bow tie, "in the course of this litigation I have been impressed with both parents of these two fine children. I have been impressed with the Respondent in working with him over the past year and I have been impressed with the Petitioner. I was particularly struck with her intelligence and sensitivity in reading her letters which she wrote to her husband during their separation. She obviously is a mother who loves both children very much. I can only hope that now that this long, antagonistic court battle is over that both parents can put aside their differences and work out satisfactory visitation and reconciliation."

He sat down. Franco patted his arm. Jeanne reached for her glasses and looked up at Judge Kroninger through greyed vision. The judge looked uncomfortable, slightly distressed.

"Well," he spoke up with some hesitation, "as I said, I think both parents are probably fine parents and could raise these children. As the boys get older, I am sure that both will want to live with their father... "

He paused indecisively and then continued.

"But perhaps the younger child, given his young age, is in need of the nurturing he was receiving from his mother. Perhaps the younger child, Jesse, should be returned to his mother for a certain period and the Court will re-examine this situation — let's say, in June."

No, Jeanne grabbed Mary's arm, *we can't go through this all again in June.* Both lawyers argued further and both concurred in asking that the matter be resolved now.

"Then," Judge Kroninger spoke reluctantly and slapped his desk, "although in all my years on the bench I have never split custody of siblings, I order that custody of the minor child, Jesse, be awarded to the mother and custody of the minor child, Paul, be awarded to the father. I also declare this marriage null and void."

BAM!

"Now," he pressed on impatiently, "there does not seem to be much community property to be disposed of... "

Jeanne desperately grappled with the words she had just heard. *Jesse's coming home?* She sat like granite, afraid to look over at either Jill or Mary for confirmation, afraid to move lest something she would do should cause the tenuous balance to flip out of grasp. She heard the judge begin discussion of summer visitation.

"I am going to order that Jesse be allowed to visit his father for the month of June and the balance of this summer both children will spend with their mother." *Two months with Paul!* "In succeeding summers, each child will spend half of the summer with each parent."

Mr. Horowitz rose to his feet.

"Your Honor, since this matter has at last been resolved, my client would like to ask the court's permission to take the children to Italy to visit his parents during his visitation with the children. Permission was denied last summer and my client has dutifully left Paul's passport in my possession per court order since the first hearing last February. I would ask that it now be returned to him and permission granted for him to take the children to visit his parents for the month of June."

"No," Jeanne whispered to Mary.

"I know," she replied, standing. "Your Honor, I would like to ask you to consider a moment the bitterness of this litigation. My client is very concerned that if allowed to take both children to Italy this summer, he will surely not return. His parents have financed his part of the litigation and will bring pressure to bear for them to remain.

"My client also does not think it is advisable for Jesse, considering the stress he has already incurred this year, to be taken to a foreign country that far away from her so soon. Due to these circumstances, she is asking that this trip be deferred to next summer."

"Oh, I think Jesse will do fine," the judge dismissed her reasoning, smiling. "You have been telling me what a strong child he is. No, they may go. The passports will be returned."

"Then, Your Honor," Mary persisted, "would you have the Respondent post bond as assurance that he will in fact return?"

"Oh no, if he's not going to come back, a sum of money isn't going to make any difference."

Mary pressed on with care not to jeopardize his custody decision.

"Then, Your Honor, should he not return, would you then grant custody of both children to the mother?"

"Yes, counsel," he conceded, "I would. If he does not return, custody of both children will be granted to the mother."

Dates for their visit with their father were set and BAM! COURT IS ADJOURNED.

Jill squeezed Jeanne's motionless hand. Stunned, she looked at Jill for confirmation. Mary gathered the heavy binders into her case.

"Let's get out of here," she muttered under her breath. Outside in the hall, Jeanne stopped and looked at Franco. Still somewhat bewildered, she walked up to him.

"I don't know what to say except that I'm glad that's finally over. When can I pick up Jesse?"

Mr. Horowitz plunked his heavy briefcase down near Jeanne's foot and cheerfully stretched out his hand to her. In reflex, she shook it, feeling unpleasant to make physical contact with the man who had harassed and haunted her life for the past year.

"Jeanne," he said grinning as she withdrew her hand, feeling as if she'd like to wash it, "it's about time you two made peace. I meant what I said in there. And you have two really beautiful children. I've learned some things about me and my own son in dealing with this case. You know, I bet that within a year you'll be back together!'' he snorted. Jeanne told Franco she'd call to pick up Jesse and took her leave.

As the elevator door slid closed, Mary, Jill and Jeanne rolled their eyes at each other, dazed.

''Is it true?'' Jeanne finally could ask out loud.

''Yep, but let's get out of this place before something happens.''

The three women pushed the door open and left the stale air of the Alameda County Courthouse. The sky was grey and heavy. A small group of women were waiting outside of Grandma's. They waved, searching for some signal of the decision.

Afraid to yell, Jeanne waved back and nodded her head affirmatively. Some of the women broke into a run, dashing between on-coming cars, Bobbi and Shana included.

''What?!'' they exclaimed. ''What happened?''

Jill looked nervously over her shoulder and announced briefly, ''Jeanne got Jesse back and more than half the summer with Paul.''

Bobbi fell backwards onto a parked car, her face ashen, looking ill.

''You alright?'' Jeanne grabbed her arm.

''Yeah,'' she replied weakly. ''I can't believe it. God, let's get out of here.''

The women darted across the street and huddled into the dim interior of Grandma's. A barrage of questions tumbled one on top of another.

''What'd he say?''

''What happened?''

''I need to sit down,'' Jeanne muttered.

''Here, I'll get you a drink. What do you want?''

''Milk.''

Jeanne sunk down in a swivel chair. *Over, over, is it truly over? Seems like it's been this way forever. Jesse coming home? Paul two months together.* Her forehead felt numb. Her feet fell sideways out of her shoes onto the floor. She covered her mouth with her hands. Behind her she heard the turnabout recounted.

''He changed his mind! He changed his mind in the last 15 minutes. First he said both kids to the father and then Mary delivered her closing argument and he saw Jeanne crying — I think you finally became human to him, Jeannie, a mother — '' Jill rested her hand on her shoulder.

"Did you cry?"

Jeanne nodded her head *oh yes.*

" — and ole Horowitz thought he had it in the bag and started saying what a wonderful person Jeanne was — "

"Did he really? Ha! Go on! Go on!"

" — and he changed his mind! He said Jesse was in need of the nurturing — get that, the nurturing — can you believe a judge saying that? Anyway, the nurturing that he was getting from his mother and he split custody. I don't know. You tell me, but that's what happened."

"It's all those goddamn strings we've been tugging at all week!" Joann quipped. Laughter, women milled around, others arrived, tables were pushed together, champagne.

Jeanne stood up barefoot, still amazed and only beginning to thaw. She hugged Mary, she hugged Jill, Bobbi.

"My god, let's call the kids," Shana said.

Jeanne moved to the pay phone in the corridor near the restrooms.

"Hannah? Guess what?"

"Tell me, tell me!" she begged.

"We won! Jesse's coming back. And Paul will be with me for more than half the summer."

"But he's living with his father?"

"Yes," Jeanne's voice drooped, "but at least we got this. It's a miracle, Hannah."

Jeanne tilted the phone away from her ear laughing as a child's squeals came over the line.

"Jeannie, I've been pulling at my string every day. Now can I take it off!"

"Yes, yes, it's over."

Someone tapped Jeanne on the shoulder.

"Listen, we're going to spread the word. Everybody's to come to the Bacchanal at 9:00 to celebrate."

"Great."

Dimes flowed out of the bartender's till as dozens of calls went out from the pay phone.

As many as possible piled into Suzi's car outside. Suzi drove raucously across the Bay Bridge with San Francisco shining like a magical, jeweled city to their right. They dove down into her streets and screeched to a halt at the Artemis Society, a women's restaurant in the Mission below Jill and Sheila's law office. Hungry, they burst inside. More champagne.

Then back into the car and back across the Bay Bridge to the Bacchanal, a quiet wood-paneled women's bar just north of Berkeley. The door was propped open and as they crossed the wide street, someone called out — "Here they come!"

Applause and cries reverberated through the high, paneled room as they stepped inside. Jeanne's arm went soaring into the air with a clenched fist. She stopped and kicked off one and then the other clog and sent them flying overhead. Ollie, the manager, handed her an oversized bottle of champagne and she threw her head back and let it foam down her open throat — it had hit her, it had sunk in: *It's over and we won.*

As she lowered the bottle, she saw Natalie and Sheila sitting on two stools, beaming at her. She fell into their arms and hugged them in unadulterated joy and relief.

"Jeanne," came a tap on her shoulder, "congratulations." It was Sabrina, the other MC of the benefit concert. "Listen, KPFA has heard about the decision and they want to do a live interview by phone for the 10:00 news. Do you want to do that?"

Jeanne thought for a moment and burst out — "Sure, let the whole world know. Well, let me ask my counsel. Jill, do you think it's okay?"

"Yeah, I think so. Judges don't listen to KPFA — I wish they would."

At 10:00 Jeanne moved behind the bar and took the black phone Sabrina held towards her. Everyone quieted. A voice came over the line.

"Hi, Jeanne, congratulations! We'll start in a few seconds. Hold on."

Jeanne listened as the announcer gave a synopsis and then said to her, "Jeanne, how are you feeling?"

"Oh, I feel wonderful!" Jeanne exclaimed and the bar erupted in laughter.

"Many of our listeners have followed your case and supported you through these long months. Can you tell us what you think made the difference?"

"Well, I don't know. I'm still in a state of shock. But you know, even though the judge said he didn't want to hear about lesbianism, still we managed to get in some expert testimony. You know, it used to be that all they had to do was cry *lesbian* and your kids were taken away. But now we're saying 'Yes, I'm lesbian' and confronting them on what precisely they fear about us having and keeping our children.

"And the fact is now there *is* research," she continued emphatically, not knowing from whence this clarity was coming, "there *is* expert testimony from extremely qualified sources which shows that their fears are not grounded in fact, that they are just that — fear, myth, prejudice."

The interview concluded and the music and dancing began. As the reality of it hit her again, Jeanne speechlessly slumped back onto a chair. Silently she gave herself over to the joy and relief that was swelling warm in her chest, washing hot up the back of her neck and cresting yellow and radiant out her eyes, cheeks, bristling to the tips of her curls.

Smiling she moved out onto the small dance floor. Her arms floated up and laced over the shoulders of her friends. Her bare feet pounded the cold floor as they drew into a close circle. They watched their own thighs rise and fall and Jeanne danced like she had never danced, not before or since. Her legs drove into the floor like pistons from the waist down as if to crack away the cement that stood cold and unyielding between herself and the earth. The women danced, danced fiercely, danced joyous, danced long into the night that was at last theirs.

Two weeks after the close of the trial, Armin Horowitz dropped dead of a heart attack while jogging at Lake Merritt.

BOOK THREE

CHAPTER ELEVEN

So the Rascal Flew the Coop

MAY 1978

The April wind bent the tall grass around the Russell Street cottage. The evening fog moved swiftly overhead, skimming up the face of the Berkeley Hills in long, grey rolls. Jesse, now a tow-headed four year-old, shuffled up the stairs behind his mother, peeling a banana as she fit the key in the door. Inside the phone was ringing. It was Franco and the questions were the same: to extend the trip to Italy to six weeks and to leave in May.

"Please, Jeanne, it will cost my parents a lot less if we leave in low season. They want to see the children. They — "

"They've paid every penny of your court case to get the children."

"Yes, but Jeanne, they haven't seen Jesse since he was one."

"I don't trust you, any of you. I don't think Jesse should be taking this trip this year. Too much has happened."

"Oh, he'll be fine. Also, please, if we leave in May, we can see the World Championship of Soccer. You know that's only once every four years. And Italy has a good team."

"Oh brother... "

"Please. Jeanne, the kids will go to the beach every day. They'll have good food, the best — you know my parents. Please, six weeks, Jeanne. Please."

"Franco, listen to me," Jeanne squinted as if peering down the sights of a rifle, "alright, I'll agree. You can leave early. But I am telling you, Franco, I am warning you. Don't mess around with this. I have no choice but to let them go and I'll cooperate but the same goes for you, do you hear me? No tricks, Franco, swear to God, don't mess around with this. We've all been through quite enough."

"Don't worry. I'll call my parents. Don't worry."

Don't worry. Don't worry.

Jesse was balancing on his knees on the edge of the sofa cushion.

"Gr-rr," she growled aloud. "Are you hungry, fella?" she asked, wiping a trace of banana from his cheek. "Wash up and let's get some dinner."

Thus in mid-May they gathered at the Pan Am gate at the San Francisco International Airport. Jesse clamped his legs tightly around his mother's waist and avoided his father's eyes. His brother stood silent and subdued in line beside his father. Franco held the passports and tickets tightly in front of his chest. Jeanne smoothed Jesse's hair a last time and rocked from leg to leg.

"It's only six weeks," she muttered in the warm crook of his neck. "Then you'll both be back. And you know what?"

"What?" he lifted his head slightly from her shoulder.

"When you get back — Paul, listen to this, too." She reached down and cupped her hand under his chin. "When you get back, we're going to go to the country for our vacation. Sally's land in Southern Oregon. I've been there once and it's beautiful. There will be dogs, all the blackberries you can pick and we can swim at the river every day. As soon as you get back, we'll go."

FLIGHT 642 NON-STOP TO NEW YORK IS NOW BOARDING AT GATE 98.

Jeanne's stomach clutched. Franco's lips drew thin. Jeanne looked at Paul, so quiet. Jesse tightened his small arms around her neck and then slipped down her leg to the floor. She opened her pack and pulled out a wrapped present.

"Here, Paul, this is something for you. I'm glad we'll finally have some time this summer."

From one instant to the next, all three disappeared from sight into the side of the waiting airplane. For Jeanne the disturbing waiting for their departure was over. The hourglass was turned. Now it was six weeks and counting until they would return.

1

GAY DAY 1978

It's hard to talk to a quarter of a million people. You find yourself shouting into the microphone, thinking that somehow you're supposed to project to the back of the crowd, sun-baked faces that faded into black dots in the distance, a good two city blocks away. Jeanne felt disconnected anyway. Then the announcer at Gay Day '78 did not do the background introduction that was planned. Standing at the back of the stage in front of City Hall, Jeanne was caught by surprise as he simply said, "And now Jeanne Jullion."

As she moved back through the crowd, a woman complained of her speech, "Same ole warmed-over coalition politics."

"I'm no oracle," Jeanne snapped in return.

The idea of selling hotdogs seemed warmed-over as well. Beer and food concessions had multiplied many times over from the previous year. The staggering 4000 defrosting hotdogs remaining at day's end were bootlegged into the freezers at the Department of Agriculture in Berkeley. Weeks later a notice appeared in the office newsletter: Would the owner of the hotdogs in the freezer please...

The day after the parade Jeanne grabbed her blue suitcase and climbed aboard a red van with a scruffy black dog named Clyde. Sally Smith, a tall, slim carpenter and one of the earliest tradeswomen in San Francisco, laughed loudly, turned on the engine and headed her van up stifling Interstate 5, north to her forested land in Southern Oregon.

2

A long sliver of madrone bark peeled off on its own and floated down from the high trunk like a light green, parchment butterfly. The midsummer heat held the leaves and cobwebs in glistening stillness. Clyde slept on his side, paws twitching, on the pine floor of the cabin in progress. Jeanne laid her hammer on top of the greyed woodburning stove and waited for Sally to finish her long cut with the screaming circular saw.

"Sally," Jeanne said cheerfully as the saw ground to a halt, "I'm going to run next door and use the phone."

Jeanne rested her hand lightly on Sally's shirtless back.

"I'm going to call Mom to see what time the kids' plane is arriving Sunday."

Preceded by a loping blond retriever that lived on the land, Jeanne ran swiftly down the fine dirt path that wound around the meadow's broad blackberry patch. Excited, she loped up six broken hillside steps to the women's land next door.

The white and green house was empty. Jeanne idly stroked the sunbleached hairs of her leg as she waited for the local operator to put her call through.

"Hi, Mom. Has Franco called you?"

"No," her mother's voice replied slowly. "No, he didn't call us. He called Sarah."

"Oh?" Jeanne hesitated momentarily. "What time are they getting in?"

"Well, Jeanne, they're not coming in. They're not coming back."

"Wha — ?"

Jeanne found herself standing.

"What do you mean, Mom, they're-not-coming-back?"

"That's right, Jeannie. I'm sorry. I guess it was the same day as that Gay Parade. He called and said he'd decided to keep both kids there, live there, in Italy. We went over to his apartment and his girlfriend, Lilli, was taking everything. The man next door bought the bunkbeds before he left, the woman downstairs thinks she's getting the car... "

The receiver went quiet, except for a roaring in her ears. She went out the back door, pushing the wooden screen door out of her way. Outside, her knees buckled and she doubled over in the long grass behind the house. One scream, then a second rang out in the still summer afternoon. Two hawks circled silently overhead.

The next day the red van wound back down the sweltering Sacramento Valley and ducked into the grey July fog of San Francisco. The following morning, Mary Morgan walked into Judge

Kroninger's chambers. He turned and said, "So, the rascal flew the coop."

Mary shook her dark curls slowly and handed him the transcript of his statement in open court that if the father did not in fact return, custody of the older child would be transferred to the mother.

"Oh, I don't believe in changing custody as a form of punishing a parent. However, I suppose I would consider a motion if it was duly filed before me."

In view of the fact that custody rulings of American courts have no legal weight in Italy, no motion was filed. By September Jesse no longer spoke any English and later could not apparently recall close friends such as Hannah, Dov or Jill.

3

Harvey Milk tittered like a kid on the ledge, peeking into the tarp of the booth behind him.

LIVE BANANA SPLIT — FRESH FRUIT COCKTAIL ONE DOLLAR

A gorgeous man lay in a pool of fruit as attendees of Circus Circus paid admission to further adorn him with fruit and whipped cream. Harvey laughed with glee as he sat relaxed on the ledge in the cavernous California Hall, site of the annual benefit for the counselling agency, Operation Concern. His contentedness with becoming the first openly gay City Supervisor in this or any other U.S. city was obvious. He spotted Jeanne.

"Jeanne," he called.

"Oh Harvey, hello."

"How are you," he asked jovially, taking her hand in both of his.

"Not so great, Harvey. I feel like Little Bo Peep. I keep losing my sheep."

"No... "

"Yes. The judge let him go to Italy for a visit and he won't bring the kids back. They're supposed to be with me this month and next."

The news rushed across his scraggy face like a cloud across the sun.

"Oh no, not after all that. What are you going to do?"

"Oh god, I don't know. Mary knows this hot shot investigator who could go over. But I'm thousands of dollars in debt from the case already, you know what I mean? I really don't know how much more my health can take of this. But one good thing."

"What's that?" Harvey searched her face with genuine compassion.

"It's brought my parents around, somewhat. At least we're talking. Eventually they might help me out financially, I don't know. But I'm really worn out. I thought it was over," she shook her head, "I really did."

"Oh well," she noticed his face and then tried to disperse the heaviness that raced over his good spirits, "we'll see what happens, Harvey. We'll see."

"I'm sorry, Jeanne. Good luck. Let me know... "

4

Jeanne's father stood stiffly beside his wife in the fashionable San Francisco apartment of a man named David. A Keith Jarrett album was spinning vertically at low volume on a hi-tech system that covered half of one wall. Jeanne's father eyed the high-paid investigator skeptically. Appearing to be in his late thirties and sweating slightly from residual malaria from a caper in North Africa, David looked like a miniature Peter Ustinov.

"I only travel first class and there's only one hotel I'll stay in in Ravenna, the Hotel Jolly. But I told Mary Morgan that I'll do this almost at cost. It's my contribution to the Women's Movement," he chortled. "I'm usually hired by the father's side, as Mary has had the opportunity to find out."

Jeanne's father grunted, uncomfortable with the whole situation, seeming on the verge of an outbreak of red-headed exasperation.

"Now just how do you think you're going to get Jesse back?" he demanded of the younger man.

"Well it's too bad it's not still summer— it'd be easier. But when I'm ready, the mother will have to come over. You realize for me the charge would be kidnapping. For her, not necessarily, even though the American custody decree isn't worth the paper it's written on over there."

David eyed Jeanne and Sally, standing in Levi's and Birkenstock sandals to the side. He slowly poured a chilled white wine into long stemmed glasses and offered them all some. Jeanne and her mother declined.

"Now, you just want the younger child, is that correct?" David turned and asked Jeanne, as if he were making sure which package he was to pick up.

"Yes," Jeanne replied in an undertone.

"It'd be easier to get the older one."

"David, it doesn't work that way."

"Well then, when I get there," David continued, "I'll notify the U.S. Embassy in Florence of the situation. However, they cannot help us. Although your daughter has told me about the children's life there, still they've got to be out of arm's reach at some point. I only need about twenty seconds. Of course, now it's a problem that Jesse is losing or has lost his comprehension of the English language. But Jeanne will have to be with me or close by — hidden, of course."

Jeanne's father glanced over at his daughter with an even more heavily furrowed frown. Jeanne's fingers burrowed into a half-empty cigarette pack and she fished one out.

"Me, too," Sally motioned.

David continued to cryptically take note of the four individuals in his pleasantly cool apartment and continued.

"Anyway, I'll get him into the car and get us away from there. Car rentals hate me," he remarked with amusement. "I'm not adverse to blocking the street with one car to get to our second one."

Sally shuddered and reached for her glass. Jeanne's father shook his white head as if it were preposterous, risky and potentially very costly to his pocketbook. Jeanne's mother seemed not to have heard and echoed her husband's question.

"But how will you get him out of there?"

David looked at Jeanne and then sat his glass down.

"May I remind you all that I have done almost one hundred of these cases and some of the names you would find in Who's Who? All I can tell you is that the only children I was unable to get lived on an Argentinian walled estate and went horseback riding with armed guards."

David was, nonetheless, unraveled by Ravenna. Even in the posh hotel, the bitter cold of an early winter bit through his clothes and blanketed the coastal town in a sheen of snow. After five days, David retreated to London, ill with pneumonia. The confined nature of the children's lives had not been underestimated by Jeanne. Jesse was, in fact, inaccessible.

After a week, Jeanne received a call from London.

"Come to London, Jeanne, and we'll go to Milan. I consulted with a very prestigious investigator there. An older man, very refined and distinguished. He says he'll accompany us to the Benelli home in Ravenna. He can be very persuasive."

Ashen with worry, Jeanne leaned her curly head heavily on her hand.

"Well, I can see he persuaded you," Jeanne replied wryly. "But David, nobody's going to walk into the Benelli home and convince them to pack Jesse's suitcase and send him away with us. Tell me, does your distinguished friend know, for example, that I am a lesbian?"

"No, there's no need to tell him that. Just dress up. You can dress like a girl for a few days, can't you?"

Jeanne bit the side of her cheek.

"I have a friend here and she can take you shopping for skirts here in London. Just get on the plane."

"David, be realistic. Franco may even have newspaper clippings. We'd go there and — if we get in the front door — they'd start telling him I'm lesbian, radical, unstable and the whole thing will blow up in our faces. I can't spend thousands of my parents' money for something that's not going to work. And I'm not well. I don't know if I could take it... "

"Then come and we'll rent a van and sit in it for ten days. But I tell you, he's put in the car inside the courtyard and driven to a Catholic nun's school. The grandfather takes him by hand to the

gate and walks him inside for the day. Same in the evening. Even
Saturdays. The older boy sometimes rides his bike outside but not
with this weather.''

Jeanne shook her head slightly as she listened to him itemize the
children's schedule as if it were new information. *It's taken too long,
the only chance was at the beach.*

The next evening Jeanne slowly packed and boarded a British
Airways flight for London. Shortly after take-off her body became
damp with weakness. Nausea swept over her in gusts. The back
of her head felt like it would crack with pain. Very ill, she disembarked in Seattle and wired David that he was through.

5

SAN FRANCISCO
NOVEMBER 27, 1978

- — Have you heard?
- — Heard what?
- — Harvey Milk's been shot.
- — Shot?! Shot?? Is — is he okay?
- — He's dead, Jeanne. The mayor's been killed, too.
- — What are you saying? What's happened?
- — This morning in City Hall. They've arrested Dan
  White.
- — Dan White, you mean —
- — Yes, the Supervisor. Ex-supervisor, actually. Mayor
  Moscone wasn't going to give him his seat back on the
  Board. He thought Harvey had something to do with
  that.
- — Oh no...
- — He hated queers. Harvey knew he was dangerous.
  Called him a real closet case. But this —
- — No, no.
- — Ex-cop. All American Dan.
- — No.

— People are gathering at Castro.

The march that evening along the by now well-worn route from 18th and Castro was like no other. The thousands of people who came were so hushed by the assasinations that the clear night sky seemed like the giant black vault of a church over the procession. Not a breath of air stirred. A river of candles glowed undisturbed for ten city blocks down the slope of Market Street. Tapers were raised high, then lowered in silent, collective waves of stunned emotion.

At City Hall Joan Baez sang on the broad front steps as the craggy bronze face of Abe Lincoln's statue, draped in the melting wax of dying tapers, looked solemnly on.

6

As the red van wound back up the dormant Sacramento Valley to the Oregon mountains, Jeanne felt that she was truly fleeing.

The walls of Sally's cedar cabin now were finished and Jeanne retreated inside. She continued writing a chronicle of what had transpired, but consciously broke with being 'Jeanne Jullion'.

Months later, when she came back from the country, every corner in Berkeley seemed to snag her with memories of the kids. She left the East Bay behind her and relocated in the flat below Jill's in the sunny patch of the Mission District in San Francisco. Comforted by the sun, the Latin language around her, church bells that still tolled and Spanish families strolling on Sundays with dressed up children, she flew on the wings of these similarities to the life of her children in Italy far away.

While moving mechanically through clerical jobs downtown in the bowels of Bechtel and the Pacific Telephone Company, she kept contact as best she could by phone. Jesse said he wanted to come back. Paul asked her to come there to Italy. And both Franco and his father, Nuncio, promised to send her a ticket in June to come and visit her children and see, as Franco insisted, "how well the boys are doing."

However, by February Nuncio conceded to Jeanne on the phone that Jesse was, in fact, not doing well.

"*Jesse non sta bene, non sta bene,*" he admitted. "He is sick, *poverino,* all the time. But it is his spirit that is down."

"*Babbo,*" Jeanne beseeched him with the affectionate term meaning Dad that she had once used with him, "can't you see what you're doing to him? Let him come back. Please."

"That's Franco's decision. Not my responsibility."

"*Merde, babbo,*" Jeanne swore, "all the money comes from you. He couldn't make it a month with two children without you. You are doing this too, *babbo.* Please let him come home."

"No, Geemie, come in June to visit. We will send you a ticket. Come and visit. We'll send you a ticket."

7

In May, Dan White went on trial for the November 27 murders of Mayor George Moscone and Supervisor Harvey Milk. On Tuesday, May 22, the jury announced a verdict for the double killings: manslaughter. San Francisco erupted. Gay anger would not be polite this time.

At 10 p.m. when Jeanne reached the turmoil in the plaza in front of City Hall, the police were chomping at the bit. Middle-aged street hippies were throwing bottles and thinking that the Sixties were back. The police were lined up on McAllister Street and stood silhouetted against the backdrop of their burning automobiles. Nine police cars, all neatly angled at the curb, were going up like roman candles. One after another, the sirens wailed eerily of their own accord as the fires reached and fused their insides.

"Burn 'em all." Jeanne shook her fist in the air. "Burn 'em all."

"So if you're White, it's not called murder," a tall man beside her yelled hoarsely at the police formation.

"Com'on, you cocksuckers, com'on," many policeman yelled this and more.

Suddenly a wedge of police was set in motion to sweep the northwest corner of the plaza. Jeanne looked up to see a raised club and helmeted policeman towering over her. With both hands she grabbed the top of her head and bolted through the crowd. Fear flushed through her like a fluorescent light. She had already seen that night what damage their nightsticks could do.

When she finally sensed that she was out of danger, she slowed and cautiously circled back through the crowd. *Harvey, Harvey, I know you're here.* She felt him there in the night air, dismayed and distraught, a Jewish angel swishing by overhead, calling no, no, this is not what I want. *It's alright, Harvey, alright to be this angry.*

The next night, teacher and community spokesperson, Sally Gearhart, stood on the platform at the top of a packed Castro Street at what was to have been the long-planned, commemorative 49th Birthday Celebration for Harvey Milk. She said quite bluntly of the fury of the night before, ''We have no apologies to make.''

June came. June came and Jeanne's ticket to Italy did not.

''Oh no,'' moaned Jeanne's father when he heard that the Benellis refused to send the ticket that had been promised for a year. ''Listen, Jeannie, let me talk to your mother. Maybe we can help you with the ticket. You should go see the boys. But be careful.''

With her parents' help, in late June Jeanne boarded a flight to Milan.

CHAPTER TWELVE

Skylab is Falling

The train clacked hurriedly down the tracks south from Milan. Soldiers, children and a tall American woman hung out the open windows for a breath of air. Piacenza. Parma. Bologna. Cut wheat lay dry and yellow on thick fertile fields. The cultivated land fit together like pieces of a well-crafted puzzle, every corner combed and planted. Cypress and olive trees traced elegant lines over the rolling foothills of the mountains that run down the country like a spine.

The train began to slow its high pace as it entered the periphery of Bologna. Iron screeching, it eased to a halt in a massive brick terminal. Jeanne yanked her suitcase down from the netted rack overhead and, wiping sticky humidity from her forehead with the back of her hand, pushed and excused herself through the crowded corridors and luggage to the nearest door. She awkwardly swung down the vertical iron steps and quickly dipped down into the cool cement underground tunnels to a secondary track marked Ravenna-Forlì.

Jeanne pulled open a door on a green, second class coach and the breath of provincial life seemed to come out. Heads turned. Unpadded wooden seats sat at stiff unyielding angles. A slow down. Heightened curiosity.

Jeanne arrived in Ravenna unannounced and immediately boarded a bus out of town to the resort area of Marina di Ravenna. She checked into a modest penzione near the sea.

A red haired woman with a line of silver at the hairline handed her the long skeleton key to her room at the second floor. Straining with both hands, Jeanne pulled the strap raising the heavy metal shades and leaned out the single window of the neat, narrow room. She drew in gulps of air heavy with salt and pine. Crescents of hyperkinetic swallows spiced through the evening air. Jeanne smiled at them, flying hungry through life, careening like bats, mouths open to catch anything.

Paul, Jesse — she called on the salty wind, savoring their nearness, making a welcomed arrival into their same time zone. *My god, Jesse's had two birthdays here. He's six. Paul's almost 11. Should I call? Would they not come to the beach if I did? Wisk them away again? I'll wait — one more day.*

1

The next morning Jeanne's legs were shaking like palsy as she walked down the white sand path through the pine forest to the beach. The Adriatic stretched out in a thin green line. The crowded beach was speckled with bodies as far as the eye could see.

She rounded the dunes and arrived unannounced at Bagno Trieste, one of many concessions and locale of summer provincial life. Quivering in the slight sea breeze, she walked between the metal tables and chairs of the concession the Benellis had frequented each summer for twenty years. The concession where she had strolled, pregnant with Paul, arm-in-arm with her mother-in-law, Anna, ten years earlier.

"Have Paul and Jesse Benelli been coming to the beach this week?" she asked in a shaky voice at the bar. The young couple who were the new managers of Bagno Trieste eyed her inquisitively and answered politely —

"*Si.* It's a little early. They should be coming soon."

Jeanne rented an umbrella and lounge chair in the first row, number 8, laid in the sun and waited.

Within a half hour, the Benellis arrived.

"Momma!" exclaimed Paul, stepping across the sand and into her arms. He laid his tanned cheek against her chest, his wooly head now shoulder high.

"Momma!" called Jesse, spurting across the sand. Their bodies came together hard, no longer fitting together naturally. Tittering, Jesse shrank away. His eyes skittered around as he spoke in clipped little phrases studded with spurts of nervous laughter. Pale and thin, recovering from a tonsilectomy, within a half-hour Jesse was taken back to the house in town.

In the ensuing days, Paul seemed alternately comfortably close with an unbroken intimacy that jumped back in time, and then distant and polite, as if addressing a distant, visiting relative. His friends beckoned. Preadolescent, his life was now and his life was here.

"Go, Paul, go play. Your friends are calling," Jeanne released him from their card game by the sea. Jeanne watched his long legs twist through the sand. *I wonder what you think.*

Jesse too would flutter away from her — on the beach, in the sea. Jeanne's arms reached longingly starved for him through the green water but taut he struggled away, preferring the waves that crashed on his shoulders, they too begging him to play. He heeded their call as Paul his friends' and her arms went empty and unsatisfied.

The days of the first week passed under the close sentry eyes of both Franco and his father. Jesse danced at the end of the string to the long satin Chinese kite Jeanne had carried from San Francisco. His body gained color. His old smile at times flooded his face.

"This is a kite, Jesse. *Un aquilone,* a big eagle — "

" — that will take us to America!"

"Yes! Yes!"

As the days passed, Jesse circled closer and closer to his mother. A sudden squall compressed them all into the humid interior of the bar. Jesse sat next to his mother, playing cards with his brother and grandfather.

"How is the food at your penzione, Geemie?" Nuncio inquired.

"Only so-so, I'm afraid. You need a buzzsaw to cut the meat. But the tagliatelle are good and last night we had a wonderful plate of fresh deep-fried fish. Those little ones, you know? With lots of lemon. I want the kids to come and eat with me this week."

"How long do you plan to stay, Geemie?"

"Two weeks."

"Anyway," Jesse announced unexpectedly in a strong voice, "I'm going back with mama."

2

In late afternoon, after the children had returned home for the day, the sun hung stubbornly high before beginning to fall to the West. It gave a shimmering Byzantine background to the historic umbrella pines of Dante's beloved forest, his consolation in bitter exile from Florence. A wash of evening pink began to tinge the white sand of the long beach. Some regulars remained for the evening at Bagno Trieste. Lavinia, a trim, bronzed beauty in a glimmering green bikini, smiled at the solitary American and took her arm.

"*Una passeggiata* — a walk?"

"*Si,* gladly," Jeanne replied.

They linked arms and began a wide arc around young boys in bikinis gracefully playing soccer.

"How do you find your children, Jeanne — May I call you Jeanne?"

"Certainly. Well, Jesse seems changed. Thinner, more nervous. Paul and he don't seem to get along very well."

"You know, this must be very difficult for you. I understand how you feel. Last summer, we all knew the children were supposed to go back to America. Especially Jesse."

"What did they tell Jesse? How did he react?" Jeanne asked, listening for the precious detail she could not get from the Benellis.

"Well," Lavinia said slowly, glancing back up towards the bar, "they weren't very honest with him. You know," her hand scooped wide circles in the air, "they kept telling him, '*la mamma viene, la mamma viene*' — your mother's coming. But Jesse's smart, he's *fantastico.* Everyone loves him, but really loves him here... "

"But what did he say and do?"

"*Poverino,* what do want him to do? He couldn't even speak to anyone except his father and brother. Then he'd stomp and say in his broken Italian — '*Mia mamma in America. Mia casa in America.* I'm going to America.' He was angry. He was rude to everyone. He got in trouble."

"Really?"

"Yes. In fact, signora, what he did was — spit at everyone."

"Spit?"

"Yes, he couldn't really talk — so he'd spit."

"*Dio mio* — "

"*Sì,* but you see he attached himself immediately to Lina. You know, she lives alone with her mother. She is good — *buona, gentile.* She would take his hand and go for walks, long walks on the beach and in the evenings. She'd bring him things from the stationary store in Piazza dei Caduti where she is a clerk. He'd always stop in there to see her. It's not far from the Benellis' house."

The gentle waves of the light green sea trickled up to their feet. A few remaining children clamored by with bucketfuls of shells. A group of young couples jostled by them, clad all in string bikinis.

"What happened with the spitting?" Jeanne coaxed Lavinia to finish.

"Well, like I said, he is very close to Lina. She finally made him stop. She said one thing and he quit," she recalled, shaking her head slowly.

"What did she say to him?"

Finger in the air and with a familiar Italian obliviousness to what she was saying, she echoed Lina's words —

"Stop or I won't love you anymore."

3

The midafternoon sun baked down on the patchwork canals and reclaimed marshlands surrounding Ravenna. Jeanne stepped out of the strong sunlight and under the cool portico of downtown Via Diaz, the two block commercial artery of the city. She passed the Libreria Longhi, friends of the Benelli family and a bookstore she had frequented often during her years there. She would say hello another time.

She continued on the route of the daily classic promenade and circled the intimate, 13th century Venetian piazza, couched like an open parlor at the center of Ravenna life. She turned down a side street and stepped into a Communist bookstore. She waited for a pale, lanky young woman to finish nervously shelving a series of white volumes and then asked if there was a women's center in Ravenna. Where did feminists meet?

Feministe, the tall woman bristled, rising upright like a tall stalk.

Jeanne quickly saw that the word 'feminist' had become a quarrelsome, politically spliced-up term. In 1979 it really only seemed to designate a specific faction of the women's movement in Rome.

The word '*compagne*' was the password Jeanne was looking for. No, there was no women's center in Ravenna. But, with didactic comments on the Communist Party's role in forming a postwar national women's organization, the tense woman directed Jeanne to the local office of the now autonomous *Unione delle Donne Italiane.* Or more simply known as UDI.

Jeanne re-crossed the central piazza that slumbered in summer languidity. She walked the short distance to Piazza Kennedy and approached a massive marble building built in fascism's flat, overstated, heroic style. Jeanne climbed the cool, musty stairs to the second floor offices of UDI, a vigilant national women's organization established by the Communist Party after World War II.

A short, attractive woman in a yellow dress with deep brown eyes looked over at the foreigner curiously. This was Lia, a vibrant and tenacious organizer of rural and urban women.

"*Buon giorno, signora,*" Lia greeted her with a smile.

"*Buon giorno, signora,*" Jeanne greeted in return. "I would like to talk to you a minute. Could we sit down? It's sort of a long story..."

Lia nodded, picked up her pack of American cigarettes and led her to a cool conference room, lined with posters from International Women's Days of the past six years. After listening, Lia hunched over the glass ashtray, bouncing her cigarette out and concluded, "We should first of all talk to Avvocatessa Aldiano. She is an excellent lawyer, *una compagna,* very sharp and totally for women. We can see what she would say about getting at least your youngest son back. If you want me to call, I'll call."

"Certainly."

"You are staying at the Marina di Ravenna? Can you come back in town tomorrow — let's say about 6:00 p.m. — without causing suspicion?"

The next evening Lia sputtered and laughed, searching for the next gear on the tiny, green Fiat 500 that belonged to the UDI office.

"I'm not a great driver," she laughed.

They lurched to a stop near an office building on a wide boulevard outside of the ancient town walls. Inside, a forceful, matronly woman in her forties quickly assessed the case.

"You are, then, an Italian citizen? You have dual citizenship?"

"That's correct," Jeanne replied. The official Italian translation of Judge Kroninger's decision that she had obtained from the Italian Consulate in San Francisco rested in the lawyer's hands.

"And your marriage is registered at the Courthouse in Ravenna?"

"Yes."

"Well, it is simple then," she declared, smoothing the document out on her desk. "We simply have to file this divorce and custody decision here and it will be binding as is in Italy as well as in the States."

"It will?" Jeanne exclaimed.

"Well, of course, this is Italy and we are dealing with the court system," she qualified. "So nothing is really that simple. It is slow — it could take two years."

Jeanne drew in a short breath.

"It will cost about two million lire — what's that, about $2000. Don't worry. Pay as you can," she waved that consideration aside. "And they will try to delay and, of course, bribe the judge. They will challenge this court order and try to get custody changed to them, I imagine."

"Porca miseria," Lia swore, "not so simple, *avvocatessa.*"

The three women sat some moments in silence in the gathering evening twilight. Lia then reluctantly articulated a possible alternative.

"Avvocatessa Aldiano, Jeanne has thought of perhaps trying to leave Italy with one or both boys."

"Do you have passports?"

"I have an old valid one of Paul's and a picture for Jesse's."

The women looked at each other. The lawyer then spoke up.

"Entre nous, I think you're right. Take the children. Give me power of attorney and after you're gone, I will deal with the paper work."

4

The fine sand sucked at her feet as she tried to hurry up the beach to Bagno Trieste. She glanced at her watch: 11:25. The night had been spent on a train, travelling to and from the American Embassy in Florence. With some reluctance, the Embassy had issued her a passport for Jesse.

"I wish you hadn't told me this," said the thin-haired Embassy bureaucrat in his fifties. "I will pretend I haven't heard. You will never make it from Ravenna to the Swiss border. If caught, an Italian judge will confiscate your passport. He can hold you in jail indefinitely. He can bar you from ever re-entering Italy and, therefore, ever seeing your children again. If you are caught, remember — we can do nothing for you."

On the return trip, the stretch of track from Bologna to Ravenna, a low priority route, seemed interminable. She held her bag with the passports and legal papers against her belly with both arms as she dozed restlessly.

I have no compunction about scooping up Jesse and running. But you, Paul — after all these years I shrink from just grabbing you, not even giving you any choice. I just want to say — You're coming home with me!

No time to return to the penzione. She stayed on the bus from the town past Bagno Trieste and then began walking back up the beach as if she were coming from her hotel. Anna continued to read behind large oval sunglasses as Jeanne approached. Puffing slightly, Jeanne nodded *'Buon giorno'*.

Trembling from expresso and no sleep, Jeanne peeled off her damp shirt under her umbrella. She stepped out of her slacks and hung them on the rungs of the wide umbrella above her. Men's eyes ran the sinewy length of this foreign divorcee's body. Jeanne tucked her glasses under the awning and beckoned to Paul who was coming down the walk towards her. Clasping hands, together they ran towards the sea and splashing, collapsed into the warm, churning waves.

That day, Wednesday, the Benellis decided to remain throughout the afternoon at the beach. With permission, Jeanne and Jesse took a long walk down the beach towards the pier. Buttressed with huge cubes of cement, the pier extended far out into the mild sea. Five prize fishing cabins dotted its length with electric drop nets dangling off their front balconies.

Jesse clamored along a less stable, adjoining pier. He jumped on the wooden slats that were rolling in the green waves beneath, looking back happily at his mother. *How simple it would be to keep going, if only a car were waiting.*

They ran races back to Bagno Trieste, turning heads as they went. The magic of their closeness had returned in full.

As they returned, Jeanne noticed Franco walking towards them, full steam and fully dressed.

"Jesse, go get dressed. We're leaving," Franco ordered out of breath, as they all converged at umbrella number 8. Jesse hesitated, digging his toe into the sand.

"Go on, I said," Franco snapped. Jesse looked up at his mother and she nodded. Jesse left slowly, then broke into a run towards the changing cabins.

"What's up?" Jeanne asked slowly, pulling her long towel down from the rung of the umbrella.

"Never mind. The children are leaving for camp Saturday morning," he announced cryptically.

"Franco! That's a week early. I've come all the way from — "

"I don't care. They're leaving," he yelled, his dark eyes narrowing at her. "And they will not be out of my sight until they go!"

He spun around and marched up the beach, white sand spitting out the back of his sandals. In the distance, Paul waved slowly to her. Stunned, Jeanne raised and lowered her arm in answer.

Swinging the red beach towel over her shoulder, Jeanne stood and watched the three generations of the Benelli family gather into two of the three family cars. At the wheel of the second, Franco turned and glared down the beach at the watching figure under the umbrella.

"What happened?" Paul gently asked his father.

"Nothing. Never mind," Franco dismissed his question. The boys fell silent in the back seat as their father nosed the car onto the sand path, through the pine forest and out onto the highway home.

Jeanne turned and sat down on the long, pink and magenta

lounge chair. She stared out at the afternoon choppiness of the Adriatic. A sailboat rocked to shore in the disheveled waves. A darkly tanned, teenage boy was working nearby. One by one, he closed the three rows of umbrellas and covered them with purple, plastic slips. He then began raking the beach, making small mounds of papers and broken shells.

Raking near Jeanne and without lifting his head, he spoke to her.

"Signora, while you were walking with your son, the old man went through your bag."

"What?" her voice croaked. She immediately flashed on the documents and passports.

"*Cosa?*" she asked, startled, and wondering if she had heard correctly.

"The old man went through your bag. Everyone saw."

Without raising his head or changing his measured strokes, he moved on.

The stiff swinging door bruised Jeanne's shoulder as she shakily clamored into the orange telephone booth on the main boulevard of the Marina. Hurriedly she dialed Lia's number and nervously poised the metal phone token over the slot. Outside the booth, Italians in their resort best strolled by with ice cream and children in knee socks and sandals.

"*Pronto?*"

Jeanne released the token.

"Lia? Lia, they're sending the children away! On Saturday. The grandfather, Nuncio, went through my bag and found the passports and documents. He didn't take them but they're watching me."

"*Calma,* Jeanne, *calma.*"

"Lia, were you able to find any flights from Forlì or Bologna tomorrow?"

"O Jeanne, listen. There are no flights. No flights anywhere tomorrow in all of Europe. Skylab is falling."

"What? What are you saying?"

"All airplane flights have been cancelled everywhere. Tomorrow. All day. You Americans! Your Skylab is falling. Skylab is falling."

And so time was gone, evaporated like sandy wet footprints. On Friday afternoon, Jeanne did not get up to say goodbye to her sons.

She felt pinned to the lounge chair with a great heaviness and lit one cigarette off the tip of another.

Side by side, her sons came down to her umbrella to politely say goodbye. They bent over to kiss her cheeks. Tears leaked from under her large dark lenses.

"Be good, kids," she murmured hoarsely. "Have a good time at camp."

5

Jeanne spent a week in the humid, tourist glut of Florence in July.

"What do you mean charging me \$3 for two apricots!" she hollered at the waiter in Italian. "Fruit in season? You mean tourists are in season. Where's the manager!"

Jeanne stalked out of the clogged historical center of Florence. The density of tourists per square meter dwindled with each block she walked. She moved across Piazza San Marco. The wooden door next to the church stood ajar on the timeless serenity of Beato Angelico's Dominican cloister.

She continued along the smooth sienna walls of Via Cavour and climbed the new metal overpass above the frantic traffic of Piazza della Libertà. Young, brown-haired boys in short pants and knee socks darted by her on the narrow walkway, excusing themselves.

Jeanne descended the green metal stairs heavily and continued with an automatic gait through shopping laden women and strolling old men, up the street to Viale Don Minzoni 25 of 15 years earlier. She crossed the same frantic traffic, down quiet condominium streets to Piazza Savonarola where she and Franco so often met. The green benches for lovers, the memory of misty nights, bold kisses, the scratchiness of the shoulder of his green wool coat. As years before, couples dotted the benches around the piazza in the grey afternoon sun. Jeanne sat by herself, stricken and stripped, and not feeling well at all.

Jeanne felt equally ill in an equally humid, exhaust-sick Rome. However, this was tempered with a new feeling. She descended the Spanish Steps in late afternoon. She walked past Caffee Greco, past

the English Lion Book Shop, down Via del Babuino in a slow, purposeful approach to Piazza del Popolo. She threaded her way
through parked cars and motorscooters until her hand rested on
the slick granite of the 13th century B.C. obelisk at the center of
the square. She looked up at the dark tips of the Villa Borghese pines
above the sharply rising hill at the easterly end of the square.

A realization came over her that she had never before stood in
a place that for her commemorated, in part, chapters of women's
history. The previous year she had read news accounts of the
neofascists' machine-gunning of four women broadcasting Radio
Donna in Rome and the subsequent demonstration in this piazza.
She had read how the word had spread by mouth, by telephone,
by balcony. Via del Babuino. Via del Corso. Via Ripetta. Narrow
arteries that converge into the piazza had spontaneously filled with
women.

Fifty thousand came immediately. From where, from
everywhere, from the stoves and shops of Rome. Fifty thousand
filled Piazza del Popolo and have filled it repeatedly and
systematically — for divorce, for abortion, for their own politics,
sexuality, history and voice.

Jeanne knew that throughout her travels in Eastern and Western
Europe and the Middle East, she had no recollection of a church,
temple or building, painting or sculpture with a woman's name af-
fixed. That afternoon she knew that travelling to and com-
memorating a place of battle in women's history was unique in her
life. She savored it accordingly.

That night Jeanne shared a heavy dinner with the loud and
shrewd manager of the penzione and her eight year-old daughter.
Afterwards they strolled to the elongated horseshoe of Piazza
Navona.

Jeanne lurched out of the way of a police car that closed in on
a young man trafficking drugs. She bumped through the conges-
tion of tables and trinkets, hippies and hustlers. Saddened by the
changes, she looked up at Bernini's Fountain of the Four Rivers
and agreed with the oversized statue of the River Nile who, with
Baroque dramaticism, covered his head with a cloth.

That night she packed her blue suitcase. She left Italy the next
day.

6

The Boeing 747 hummed as it cruised towards New York, nine hours into its flight from Rome. The cigarette did not agree with her. Or was it the mushroom sauce on the meat? She moved clamily to the restroom and vomited violently. *Okay,* Jeanne thought. But she couldn't stop.

The stewardess knocked sharply on the door as the RETURN TO YOUR SEAT light began flashing. When the plane landed, the stewardess handed her plastic-lined bags with damp cloths and three lemon wedges as she helped her towards the door.

"*Buona fortuna,*" she said sympathetically to her ailing passenger. "Signora, they just told us it's 100 degrees in Customs."

I'll make it, Jeanne vowed. *Come on,* she urged herself as if whipping a spent horse over the finish line. *One more flight. Just get on the flight to San Francisco at nine.*

Long, multi-national lines spread out from each customs counter but she kicked and shuffled her bag through. Searching for the American Airlines counter, she stumbled to the side of the corridor and used her last sickness bag. *Come on, come on,* she prodded, the thought of New York chilling her. *I've gotta get home. It's killing me coming back without the kids. No, I can make it.*

"Here, would you hang on to this bag... my camera... " She pushed the totebag forward on the American Airlines counter and collapsed.

Jeanne was shuttled by baggage cart and taxi to the small hospital facility at Kennedy Airport. The nurse began an I.V.

"My god, you know you're the third mother we've had this month who's been abroad looking for her kids," the nurse shook her head with compassion. "The last had just come back from Iran. She couldn't find them."

"I'm hypoglycemic," Jeanne mumbled weakly, trying to stem the waves of nausea. "I can't move my legs, nurse. Why, why can't I move my legs?"

The nurse moved out into the hall.

"Doctor, she's not responding to the glucose."

Her condition was critical by the time the police ambulance wheeled Jeanne into the Emergency Room of Queens Hospital,

44

New York. She knew she was dying and she knew they didn't know what to do. *Hypoglycemia. Adrenal failure. It's put me in shock before,* she whispered to them, diagnosing herself.

More glucose solution. EKG. X-rays. *For what,* she wondered. *They're guessing,* she knew. She begged for a phone.

"Sally, Sally, they're giving me stuff and it's not helping. Please come. I don't know if I can make it."

She clung to the iron edge of the table and pulled herself over on her side. She shuffled her body into the fetal position. *I want to live, with or without the kids, I want to live.* She also knew that perhaps, physically, she would not make it.

Three hours later, she was admitted to the Women's Intensive Care Unit. Intensive Care poorman's style, that is. A cavernous 24-bed ward with two nurses and two doctors. She clung to the rail of her bed, I.V. dripping into the vein in the top of her hand. She decided to conserve her strength and finally refused to repeat to one more doctor her medical history. She clung to the thought of Sally, hopefully on her way, as a last thread back to herself.

The next morning at nine, Sally insisted she was Jeanne's sister from San Francisco and walked through the ward. Finally, she stopped at the side of the bed of a white woman with matted curly hair. She could not recognize the bloated face.

"Jeanne, is that you?"

"Sally." She cried into the large hands that reached down and cradled her cheeks.

Over the next few days, Jeanne regained the use of her legs. With Sally's help, she returned to San Francisco. Jeanne did not see her children again for two years.

CHAPTER THIRTEEN

Facing It

Let's face it. Mothers who have lost their children are bitches to live with. Never happy, always complaining, always rearranging things. It's never okay, never good enough, and always ungodly, childlessly quiet. Sadness itself becomes your child.

Slow and hard, that's how the months passed, slow and hard. And while the seasons changed, the state of Jeanne's heart did not. She monitored it, hoping that in the hands of time the feelings would soften and heal. She monitored it, wondering how one lived through this, went on, made the hemorrhaging stop. But she felt no change, only now there was the need to appear normal, to get over it, to let it be, to give up, go on. Now, at work, on the subway, the tears fell backwards into her throat so no one would see.

Through the next two years her relationship with Sally, too, stumbled and crumbled under the endless burden of the mother's sadness and grief. One night upstairs at Sally's house, Jeanne made the mistake of watching the TV movie of Mary Jo Rischer's lesbian custody story in Texas and that night psychically felt herself go over the edge. She roamed the house when everyone was asleep, lashing out at walls and mirrors with belts and hands, choking on air and knowing her sanity had truly slipped from her grasp. It took days but then whatever it is that makes you get up in the morning, put your clothes on right, walk to the bus and give appropriate responses came back to her.

What didn't come to her was what to do. What did come to her was a phone call as a result of a contact she had made at a Family Law Conference. The trails of her search and that of another lesbian mother were to cross, giving Jeanne a friend who truly understood and a source of continued courage. The phone call came from the vicinity of Wheeling, West Virginia, and was prompted by the situation of a ten year-old child.

1

Churches are full on Sunday mornings in Wheeling, West Virginia. On weekdays, hillbilly music drifts out of cars and restaurants along with men dressed in boots and cowboy shirts. It's a town where owning a lesbian bar is, to say the least, an undesirable kind of business. That's why the Mafia, accustomed to dealing with the police, steps in and does it. Only in this case, the police break in, take names and see they are published in the morning newspaper. The single lesbian bar is a private club. A current member sponsors a new member and so on. Hardly anybody in their right mind gives their right name.

Matters in court that concern gay people run basically along the same lines. Thus when a thin religious man appeared in court saying his ex-wife was a lesbian and he was keeping their eight year-old daughter with him for her own good, the court stood judiciously behind him.

Elizabeth was almost ten when a friend picked up the phone, called the number in San Francisco and said there might be some people coming Jeanne's way.

"Liz — that's the child — has been seeing a psychologist and the psychologist is worried, as is her mother. There does not seem to be any chance for resolution through the courts. The father's a real bible-thumper and the court absolutely won't listen to the mother who's a lesbian."

"What's happening with the daughter — Elizabeth?"

"She wants to be with her mother but the father won't let her mention her mother's name, have a picture of her, call her. It's clear she has to pretend her mother, Pat, doesn't exist. So she's one way with her father and another way with her mother. But what started out as an understandable defense mechanism is now slipping out of her control. It's becoming like two personalities and the kid's scared because it's getting so she can't control it. Pat's lover, Joanie, also thinks Liz is near a crack. They may have no choice but to..."

Jeanne pulled at the curls at the back of her head.

"Could they call you if they come your way?"

"Huh? Oh yes, I guess so."

Two months later, Liz came to visit her mother in Wheeling, West Virginia. Pat sat her down, showed her three tickets to San Francisco, and said, "You want to go, babe?"

Liz said yes. Yes, yes, yes, yes, yes. The car was packed and ready to go. Thanks to heels, henna and lipstick, they boarded the night train as three adult women. Three days later they de-boarded the train in a breezy San Francisco. With their belongings on the corner of First and Mission, Pat stepped into a phone booth.

"Jeanne? We're here."

Well, thank heavens Sally was there because Jeanne emotionally certainly wasn't. Soon Sally had found them a small apartment in Twin Peaks and had them settled in. For Jeanne, it took a couple of weeks but then, walking back from the corner store with Pat, sobs broke loose like boulders in her throat. She came to a standstill and leaned her head against the crumbly brick wall. Pat stopped, shook her head slowly and came back beside Jeanne.

"Oh honey, I remember when I used to cry like that."

"But you've d-done it," Jeanne sobbed. "You did it. You got your kid. It's — it's hard for me to be around that, Pat, for me to see that," she confessed, looking up through a grey blur. "I know I've avoided you. I know I was supposed to be the one to help you but the fact is I just can't deal with it. You're together and it tears me up to be around you all."

Pat drew a long cigarette out of her breast pocket. Passersby turned slightly, then discreetly walked on. Jeanne felt like her face was a sea of mucus. Kicking herself for falling apart again, she fumbled in her pockets for tissue.

"Com'on," Pat swung her arm around the taller women's shoulders. "I must admit I thought we'd be dealing with you more. We did come with just your name in our pocket. I guess we did expect... " She drew on her cigarette. "But we're here and we're safe — for the time being, that is. Sally's been a marvel and don't worry about it."

They resumed their climb up the winding street. The peaked roofs and pastel rows of Victorian houses glowed in the evening sun on the hill behind them.

"I'm sorry, Pat," Jeanne cleared her throat hoarsely as they linked arms in the twilight. "I just can't seem to get over this, although I know I'm supposed to."

"Sure, they've cut off your right arm and you're supposed to walk around like everything's normal. I know the feeling. It hurts like hell. Believe me, you're not crazy."

"But why do I keep falling apart? I call the kids, I write them. But it's just not enough. I need at least one of my kids."

Jeanne and Pat's gaze locked momentarily.

"You're not crazy," Pat repeated, stepping on her cigarette. "You're absolutely right."

2

Walking to work, cooking a meal, scattering her two roommates and compulsively cleaning the flat, Jeanne inwardly turned the prism of her experiences over and over. An idea had been germinating ever since she had heard a friend announce that the Department of Social Services in San Francisco apparently would now license a gay home for foster care and that the city's institutional Group Homes were very full of children needing temporary homes.

One day she called her roommates to look at the enclosed back porch of the apartment, an unused space with tall, broad windows that looked out on Mission rooftops and Potrero Hill. It could be made into a child's room, Jeanne suggested. They nodded. The next day, Jeanne called the Department of Social Services and began the process of having their apartment licensed as a foster home.

At the end of the final home visit, the eligibility worker folded her brown vinyl folder and looked at the curly headed woman sitting opposite her on the small sofa of the modest apartment.

"Well, Miss Jullion," she said, "it is department policy not to give children to a parent who has lost a child and may be trying to make up for their own child by becoming a foster parent."

Jeanne looked at the middle-aged woman with her hair pulled arrow-straight into a netted bun on the crown of her head.

"Well, Ms. Jackson, I have lost my children and the way I see it, the many children now in your group homes and institutions have also lost their parents for the time being. It seems to me that one of them might like to be in a home and that we just might understand each other real well."

The foster license came in the mail. But no placement followed. During the licensing process Jeanne had let her lesbianism lie like a stone beneath the water but later learned her name had been recognized and her sexuality noted. The Department of Social Services in San Francisco would license a gay foster home without selective resistance. But would they place a child there?

In early April Jeanne heard twice about announcements being made concerning a lesbian teenager locked up in Juvenile Hall and needing a home. Jeanne's initial response was: A teenager? What's a teenager?

Nonetheless, on April 23rd, the day before her seventeenth birthday, a bee-boppin', basketball-wielding lesbian teenager named Chris officially became Jeanne's foster daughter. Dressed infallibly in Big Bens and tank top, with a life story at age seventeen that read like a textbook on abuse, the short, muscular teenager came up the front stairs with two cardboard boxes of possessions, an acoustic guitar, a hard head, a drinking problem and a heart amazingly still in the right place.

In the *Plexus* May calendar of events, Jeanne noticed the following item:

Support group forming for lesbians with teenage children. Old Wives' Tales Bookstore on Valencia Street. 7 p.m.

It was there that Jeanne met another mother, Carol Morton, and her lover Christina from Switzerland.

3

ZÜG, SWITZERLAND

Christina Yoder grew up in the lakeside town of Züg, south of Zurich. Sinewy and quick, young Christina daily pushed her sailboat off from the wet grass of the lakeside park below her parents' condominium. A blanket draped from the balcony above beckoned her back for meals. After a meal of dark bread and meats, fresh mountain cheese and sausage, the family always gathered in the living room for chocolates from the credenza. Lean and free, Christina grew up the independent and questioning daughter of the esteemed liberal minister of Züg.

When she was twenty, Christina travelled alone through Turkey and Iran, crossing one section by the only means available, three weeks on horseback. She kept a small knife strapped against her leg inside her sock.

After a few years as a journalist for a Swiss paper in Zurich, Christina, feminist and lesbian, moved to San Francisco where she became lovers with Carol, a mother of a thirteen year-old son. Together they joined the support group that took shape out of the large initial meeting that was called at Old Wives' Tales Bookstore and met every three weeks for the next two years.

SAN FRANCISCO
SPRING 1981

Rain poured down in sheets outside a rambling, three-story Victorian on 25th Street known to many travellers as the Women's Inn. Jan Baer, part-owner, manager and mother of three teenaged children, rolled the thick wooden parlor door closed on the March meeting of the mother's group.

"We're going to Europe," Jeanne overheard Carol chatting excitedly. Smiling, Carol brushed back her black hair from her large dark eyes and talked on.

"Really?" Jeanne turned towards blond-haired Christina.

"Yes," she smiled. "Carol and Terry are coming to my house in Züg. He will have his fourteenth birthday there. Then we go to Italy and Greece." A German lilt gave a pleasing sing-song cadence to her speech.

"Com'on, everybody, let's get going," Jan Baer coaxed the ten women in the room. "You know it always takes us three hours just to check in."

"Me, too," Jeanne added as she took a seat on the couch next to Christina and Carol. The two lovers' hands laced fondly together.

"I mean I'll be going to Italy," she clarified. "To see the kids. My body and finances couldn't make the trip last summer. Talk to you later... "

Carol, Christina and Jeanne began periodically going out for coffee and discussing their mutual summer travel plans. They often talked about what it would be like for Jeanne to see her children again.

One evening, Jeanne sat across from them in a small restaurant across the street from Mission Dolores Park. Jeanne folded and refolded her napkin under her cup. Finally, she glanced up across the shiny wood table, convinced she'd be judged clinically insane for what she was about to say.

"You know," she hemmed, clearing her throat, "I realize I haven't seen the kids in two years and I have no idea how they're doing or what they think or want anymore... "

"Yes?" Christina and Carol chorused patiently.

"All I know is how I felt the last time I went there. I mean, I think Paul is pretty settled and doing okay but I don't know about Jesse. And I still miss them so much. All I know," she repeated again, "is how I felt the last time I went there... "

"Yeah?" Christina drawled, her blue eyes sparkling from under disheveled strands of long, blond curls.

"I mean, you know, I can't know 'til I get there. And I'm definitely going to visit them this summer," Jeanne struck her spoon on the table more loudly than she had intended. "Hopefully, I won't croak," she tried to laugh.

"You'll be okay," Carol assured her. "You're stronger now."

"Anyway, I know what I feel. I know that if Jesse wanted to come back and live with me — Paul too — I'd do it," she concluded, looking up at them.

"We know that."

"I just know what happened last time. It was a disaster. It's just too complex a thing to try to put together when you're in the middle of it. And you know what?"

"What?" again in unison.

Jeanne smiled and leaned forward across the table. "Last time there was one thing missing: a driver. I'd need someone to drive us away, across the border, probably to Switzerland."

"Well," drawled Christina, her lips twitching with a smile, "I am a very good driver, you know, in the European way — BRAUM! BRAUM! And I am going to have a very powerful French car when I'm there... "

"I mean, if they want to come back — I have Paul's passport too — I'd just like to know I had a contingency plan. Not like last time. Just in case... "

"Anything we can do, Jeanne," Carol confirmed. "Let's coordinate schedules. We'll be near Zurich."

"Where are the kids, Jeanne?" Christina asked.

"In Ravenna," Jeanne replied, snapping a fresh napkin out of the dispenser. "Look, I'll show you," she said quickly, feeling a warm rush of relief inside at the release of these private concerns. She pulled a red pen from her backpack on the floor.

"Ravenna is here, and here is the beach," she sketched quickly. "Now there's a pine forest that runs along side the beach — real famous, Dante wrote about it and loved it. It's a national treasure now. The Benellis always go to the same concession on the beach called Bagno Trieste, have for years and years. Now, you know, this is all just in case... "

4

Over a year after Jeanne had received the phone call from Pat, Joanie and Liz, bad news came. At the office, Jeanne left early for lunch after Sally's call. She walked up Mission, squinting in the harsh noonday sun. At Second street, she spotted Pat threading her way towards her. Her arm closed immediately around Pat's shoulder. All three had changed names and identities soon after their arrival. Pat was known in San Francisco as Annie, Joanie as Jackie and Liz as Michelle.

"How are you doing?"

"Damn, our one Achilles' heel and the bastard found it," Annie swore. They turned up Second Street. "There's a bar up here that has burgers. That okay for you?"

"Sure," Jeanne nodded.

Seated in the dark interior, Annie ordered a scotch, no food and lit a cigarette. Jeanne ordered and then eyed her friend closely.

"So com'on, tell me," she urged, "Sally just gave me the bottom line."

"The damn social security number, the damn social security number," Annie wagged her light brown head and clenched her jaw. "We knew when we altered the birth certificates and applied for new numbers and then the goddam computer sent Joanie back her old social security number that we were fucked. I mean, it was the Social Security Administration's mistake. They should never issue the same social security number to presumably another person. But we, of course, were in no position to point out their mistake to them, were we?"

"So who called?"

"Our friend from Wheeling. She said she heard he'd traced us to San Francisco through our social security numbers, knows we're working here in the City.

"Goddammit," Annie struck the tabletop with her fist, "just when we both at last got good jobs. I'm making $7.75 an hour and getting good training, dammit."

Annie took a long drink off the tall glass. "And Michelle — you know, Liz — is settled in school with her new best friend. Shit," she waved to the waitress and ordered another.

"Some food?" Jeanne suggested.

"I can't. This is my lunch."

Jeanne reached for another napkin for her dripping hamburger. "So what are you going to do?"

"We gotta get out of here, quick."

Jeanne laid the burger down and they looked at each other in silence.

"Fuck," she exclaimed softly.

"But, Jeanne, I don't want to leave. This is our support system. The school, the jobs, the apartment, our names — all of those have to go. The three of us all know that. But to lose all of our new friends, too... That's the worst." She lifted the glass and closed her eyes on an errant tear. Jeanne slowly pushed her unfinished lunch aside.

"Oh my god. How's J-Jackie doing? My god, how do you all keep your names straight?"

"We've got to. You know, Jackie still hasn't fully recovered from having to leave her whole family back there, without saying a word. Especially her younger brother. But she knows what's gotta be done. We were just all getting good at remembering our new names and birthdates. You know, not turning around at work when someone calls out 'Hey, Pat!' "

"How about Michelle?"

"Oh, the worst will be having to leave her friend, Stacey. Stacey's the only one she's told the real story. But there's no doubt in her mind either. If we gotta go, we gotta go."

"New documents, I.D.'s?"

"Yeah, we've begun... "

"You've meant a lot to me... "

The ice froze against her lip as Annie tilted her glass high. Within the month, they were gone.

5

The airport was garish white with summer light and Chris didn't know what to say. She swung her foster mother's bag down off her broad shoulder and reached up to hug the 37 year-old woman who stood almost a foot taller than she.

"Good luck, moms. I know you've gotta go see your babes."

"Yeah, I do. Take care, Chris. And watch the drinking."

"I'll be good, moms, I'll be good. Don't you worry. You take care of *yourself*."

On board the cramped charter flight to Zurich, the German tourists behind her were miserable. Knees in her back, they pushed her seat forward rudely when she tried to recline, laughing loudly to each other. After the food was cleared away and lights were dimmed, Jeanne inched the seat back and dozed to the drone of the engines.

The train ride from Zurich was splendid. Jeanne leaned out the window incorrigibly. She craned her neck to follow the startling rise of the Swiss mountains. The train sped south into a thunderstorm that was approaching swiftly in the twilight.

"Belle queste case, " Jeanne muttered out loud to a middle-aged

man she presumed was Italian.

"You Americans, you love those old houses, don't you?" he rejoined. He spoke with an earthy accent she guessed was Roman.

"They are so old," Jeanne replied.

"But they're hell to live in and maintain. That's what you Americans don't see."

Jeanne remained willfully enchanted and felt happy to be back.

In Milan, Jeanne rested for two days at the home of Jenny, a young English expatriate who had shared Jeanne's flat in San Francisco for several months the year before.

On the second day, Jeanne and Jenny rode trams to a quiet sector of Milan to consult with a feminist lawyer well versed in international family law. The woman excused herself and called another law office for a further consultation. It confirmed her own opinion.

"They agree. Your husband's family could challenge the custody decision if you try to register the American degree in Ravenna. Furthermore, if you try to leave the country with either or both, they agree that you'll never get from Ravenna across the border. There is stricter control of the borders now. They look for lire leaving the country for less inflationary Swiss banks. They look for the Red Brigades. The government reaches the borders quickly now, by computers. It is all linked, the police, the borders, the airports. It is the world we live in."

"What about by train?"

"You know there they go cabin by cabin, checking passports. You'd probably have the least chance by train. They're accustomed to always looking for someone."

The fast-talking woman looked at the silent American.

"Signora, I must ask you. Do you realize what your situation would be if they stopped you?"

"Yes, yes — " Jeanne waved her hand in front of her face. "I know, I know."

Outside, the white-washed walls of the deserted cobblestoned street seemed to reflect and enhance the silence between Jenny and Jeanne. Without speaking, they walked towards the tram stop.

"I'm sorry, Jeanne," Jenny began in a clipped British accent. Her thin red hair ended squarely over the top of large brown eyes that took in her friend with spunky concern.

"Oh Jenny, I hate lawyers. Lawyers never have good news for me."

6

RAVENNA
JULY 1981

Lia was waiting as the train pulled into Ravenna. In a room at a modest seaside penzione at the Marina, Lia waited as Jeanne changed. Jeanne pulled a bra out of the side compartment of her bag like so much spaghetti. She peeled off her shirt. Fanning her sticky breasts, she looked across the bed at Lia. *I have no straight friends at home,* Jeanne realized. *Do only lesbians do this?* she wondered suddenly. But Lia looked at her shirtless *compagna* with unruffled casualness.

"What heat," Jeanne remarked.

"All week," rejoined Lia, looking out the balcony at the heavy grey air over the sea. "I'll drop you off at Bagno Trieste but I don't think I should come with you. I have to pick up Simone at my mother's anyway."

Jeanne was donning a colorful combination of a tight sleeveless yellow top and bright green painter pants.

"It's better I go alone. How is your son, Lia? Still having garage sales with his toys down in the courtyard?" Jeanne laughed.

"Full of life," Lia exclaimed with a tinge of weariness. "Thank heavens his father does so much with him, more than me! My mother still complains I'm not raising him right."

Jeanne smiled and looked over at her friend. The short, aggressive woman, frequently a national spokeswoman for the *Unione della Donne Italiane* (UDI) in Rome, looked tired and wasn't smiling.

"Listen, Lia, I really appreciate you coming to meet me and reserving this room."

"It's nothing," Lia shrugged. "They know you're coming?"

"Yes. It's Sunday," Jeanne explained, running a pick through her curls at the mirror over the sink. "I said I'd meet them at the beach today."

Jeanne's stomach quaked at the words she just said. She spun around nervously.

"O Lia, I can't believe I'm going to see them today. How do I look?"

"*Sei bella.*" Lia scooped her keys off the high bed. "Come on, let's go."

Jeanne rounded the corner of Bagno Trieste.

"Jesse!"

"Mamma!" Jesse jumped into her arms the minute he saw her. Absent was the stiff hesitation of two years earlier.

"Paul!"

"Ciao, Mamma!" Paul signalled his friends and left his position of goalee in the soccer game in progress on the beach. A tall young adolescent of twelve, he smiled and skipped across the sand towards his mother.

7

The sun reddened the countryside as it sank for the day. From the geranium bordered balcony of Lia and Sauro's apartment, a panorama of fields and vineyards receded in lush rectangular swaths towards the sea. Southeast, far in the distance stood the round silhouette of the Romanesque bell tower of San Appolinare in Classe. Classe, ancient city, port of the Roman fleet, western door of the Byzantine Empire.

Inside, the apartment was dominated by light marble floors, broad white furniture and handsome pine tables and chests that Lia loved to run her hands over. Lia briskly tied the strings of a pressed apron over her flowered dress. Simone, now six years old, rolled over onto the lap of Sauro, his father. Farmworker union organizer and as short in stature as his wife of nine years, Sauro wrapped his hairy arms around his mischievous son and cautioned — "Simon, be quiet. La Jeanne is calling her friend in Switzerland."

"Hello? *Pronto, pronto?* Christina, is that you?" Jeanne rose to her feet. "Christina?"

"Yes, hello. We're here at my parents'. So how is Jesse? How is Paul? What do you think?"

"Oh, they're wonderful. Jesse hasn't left my side for the last ten days. Everytime I sit down, there he is on my lap, picking up my arms and wrapping them around him," Jeanne laughed. "And Paul looks fine. So tall, long legs like me. He's doing pretty well."

"Well," came the familiar drawl, "what do you think?"

"Well," Jeanne replied, "I think you should come."

A somewhat faint voice trickled through the receiver. "O my god. Carol, she says yes," Jeanne heard her say to the side.

"Christina, I think I should in fact ask Jesse. I'm going to talk to Paul as best I can without really coming out and saying it. He seems settled here. And close to his father, very protective of him.

"But he and Jesse do not get along. Jesse was so tight-lipped when I got here. He looks more his old self now. But you know what happened?"

"What?"

"A woman came up to me while I was swimming and said to me — 'Signora, excuse me: It's none of my business and the Benellis would be furious if they knew I said this. I just want to tell you that it brought tears to my eyes when Jesse came and said good morning to me under my umbrella this morning. To see him look like this, so happy. I want you to know, don't think that these children look like this always. It is because you are here.' And then she swam off."

"My goodness."

"I know. It feels right to me, Christina. I need to at least ask him if he wants to come back. Can you come this week?"

"Well... "

Jeanne bent her head and hugged her breasts while there was some discussion between Carol and Christina to the side.

"Well," Christina resumed, "we had some not-so-good news right before we left San Francisco. The Lyon-Martin Clinic called and told Carol she had a five on her pap smear test. That's almost certainly cancer."

"O my god... "

"They told her it couldn't wait two months until we get back. But we caught the plane anyway and this week is the only time she can see the specialist here. I need to be here... "

More talking off line.

"Next week it'll be even harder," Jeanne mumbled outloud as a cold shudder rippled through her. *Please, please.* "It's my last week and they'll be watching closer next week and every day until I leave." She tried to keep her voice even.

"Yes. Listen, Carol says to go ahead."

"But — "

"We'll work it out. Listen, Carol and Terry will wait for us in Jenny's apartment in Milan. Let's see, I can be in Ravenna... on Tuesday."

"Are you sure? I really need you."

"Yes, we're sure. We know this can't wait either."

8

There is no quick and easy way to drive away from Marina di Ravenna. The roads form a natural bottleneck around the town. Jeanne and Sauro poured over maps of Ravenna and northern Italy. Together they drove and timed the various routes, debating advantages of country back roads vs. highways north to Venice or northwest to Milan.

On Tuesday, Christina arrived at Marina di Ravenna. Jeanne slipped into the front seat of the large, white Renault sedan that was parked in the Piazza Rotunda as agreed and Christina pulled away.

"Hi," Jeanne said shortly, stiff with nerves and eyeing passersby.

"Ciao, Jeanne," Christina greeted her in a low voice.

"Out that end of the piazza," Jeanne directed. "Let's stay away from the beach area."

After several turns, Christina dipped the car to a halt beside a low lying tree and turned off the key.

"This is bizarre," Jeanne commented, "I can't believe we're here."

"I know. So how are you?"

"O god, I've never been so nervous in my life, court included. What a lousy choice of things to do," Jeanne swore, continually scanning the street for acquaintances. "If Jesse says he does want to come, I just hope Paul understands. I know just as sure as I'm sitting here, Christina, that Paul would say he wants to live here. But still... " She shook her head. "At this point, I feel more worried about him than Jesse. Yesterday I got a frame for this snapshot of him and me that I'm going to leave for him with a letter. I started crying in the shop. I'm sure the guy thought I was crazy.

"Hey, you know what?" Jeanne slapped Christina's arm. "It sure is good to babble this out in English! Thanks for coming, Christina."

Jeanne noted that her friend looked stiffly nervous herself.

"Well," Christina began, "let's get to work. Show me everything. I have some good maps."

"Let's drive it. You're tired from the trip. Do you feel up to it?"

"Yes, yes. *Molto bene.*" Christina turned on the key.

"Okay then, circle back to the highway that goes through the pine forest along the beach."

"Dante, right?"

"Exactly," Jeanne smiled. "Now the kids are always at the same place — "

"Bagno — don't tell me, Bagno... Trieste." They both laughed.

"You Germans never forget a thing."

"Swiss, my dear, Swiss."

"Listen, I'm getting down. Too many people around here might see us. But listen, Christina, after Bagno Trieste — on the left — look for the next concession, too."

"*Come si chiama?*" Christina asked in Italian. Her German lilt in Italian was amusing.

"Bagno Lucciola," Jeanne answered from under the dash. "We went to the beach the other night — Lia and her husband and two friends of theirs... "

Dinner Sunday night at Lia's house had been a unique experience. The three women — Lia, her friend Gabrielle and Jeanne — sat at the table and talked politics while the men got up, cleared, cooked and brought out the next course.

Conversation after dinner criss-crossed back and forth over the situation at hand. At midnight, all five squeezed into the elevator and then into Vittorio's car.

"It's late. Will we have to wake up the padrone of your hotel?"

"No," replied Jeanne, feeling sleepily stuffed with pasta, fish, peaches, brandy and ice cream. "They close up and go to bed early. So they gave me a key to the side door."

"You know," Gabrielle's husband continued to think out loud, "I think the idea of trying to get your son over to the giant slide they've put up between Bagno Trieste and Bagno Lucciola is the best idea. What do you all say," suggested Vittorio, "why don't we stop and take a look."

"Now?"

"Si, now. What time is it?"

"One o'clock in the morning."

"It will be deserted."

"That's for sure."

"Except maybe for a few lovers — "

They chuckled and agreed to stop.

Vittorio's car danced slightly on the sandy road into the empty concession and came to a slippery stop behind the bath houses. The gentle sea shrugged baby waves onto the sand with a rhythmic hiss in the distance. Their voices dropped instinctively to a whisper as they got out of the car. Just being there at that hour exuded complicity and Jeanne could tell that a small voice inside all of them was insistently asking what they were doing there.

"Look," motioned Vittorio, "this sand dune would protect you. If you come to this path here and your friend waits in the car there on the highway, no one could see you from Bagno Trieste."

"Yes, but *dio buono,* Vittorio, she has to get this far with the child and they watch her," his wife objected with some agitation.

"Then she has to have at least a little time to talk to him, to ask him... " added Lia in *sotto voce.*

"*Dio buono,* I don't know about this," muttered Gabrielle, leaning on Lia's sweatered arm in the dark. "I mean, I'm a mother, too. I know what it must feel like. But to run away. And his brother? What will he feel like if you disappear? I don't know... "

"Gabrielle," Jeanne's voice filled the silence Gabrielle's candor had created, "I don't know 100 percent myself either and I have been thinking about this almost daily for the past three years. But I do think Paul is doing well and I do think Jesse is not, nor, quite frankly, am I. I think Jesse has the right to be asked where he wants to live and to be listened to for once. If he says no, I can live with it much better knowing he's had a choice. If he says yes, then all this must be planned and readied or it will go like last time — nowhere. More pain, more separation, more powerlessness."

Gabrielle leaned back against the red car that had blackened in the moonlight and shook her head slowly, not knowing for sure how she felt. Sauro had walked out around the dunes at the edge of the sweet pine forest towards the giant water slide on the beach.

The group walked out towards him. The towering, two story high, six lane slide stood green and dry in the moonlight, the children's passion by day. The five stood on the edge of the black shadow of what was to be the pretext for walking away from Bagno Trieste.

"So, Christina," concluded Jeanne from the floor of the car, "I think that's where you should park. Do you see it yet?"

"Oh, now I see a little sign, with a bee on it?"

"Exactly. Now, Christina, don't hurry but I'm going to time this again. Go straight at the big intersection up ahead. You see, the roads go in a big circle around the town. Could be blocked real easily if they had the clout to do so. Did I tell you, by the way, that the Chief of Police is a Benelli family friend and lives in the other half of their duplex?"

"No — o," drawled Christina with a tinge of shock.

"I probably suppressed it. Well, don't think about that. Neither will I. Ugh," Jeanne moaned, "I'm going to get up." She crawled awkwardly back up on the plush blue seat.

"Anyway," she continued, "there are basically three ways to go. Let's drive them and you'll see."

As the white Renault pulled back into the piazza rotunda at the Marina, Jeanne could see how strained and tired Christina was.

"It's 3:30, Christina. Rest and I'll come by your hotel at 7:00. We'll have a good dinner."

Jeanne slipped out of the car and left without looking back.

Shops were just beginning to re-open. Beach toys and balloons, sidewalk tables of sandals and shoes. Had the time come to buy clothes for Jesse? The thought threw Jeanne's heart into her throat. She turned and stepped inside a shop.

"Signora, may I help you?"

"Uh — si. Well, I need clothes for a child. An eight year old boy. Uh — shorts and top, underwear, uh — socks. A pair of sandals, too. I'm afraid I don't know your sizes here in Italy. But here is the size of his shoe."

Jeanne pulled out a folded tracing of Jesse's shoe that she had hurriedly drawn in the changing cabin last week. She feigned casualness and the shopowner did likewise, proceeding with no allusion to this slightly unorthodox method of shopping. Jeanne let her

Italian slip into broken phrases to accentuate the fact that she was, after all, a foreigner.

Softly, Jeanne picked up the small clothes being laid across the counter for her inspection. *This time is it for real?* Jeanne purchased everything she needed and, head down, returned directly to her room. She dropped the red crinkly bag onto the floor of the closet and closed the door, cautious of the power of those child's things to haunt and hurt, remembering how it was to look for something at home, open a closet door, run into a toy, his blanket, some tiny reminder that lurches out at you and easily rips through all the progress you'd thought you'd made.

Jeanne blew air out of her lungs like a billows and then opened the closet door again. She reached for the shoulder strap of her suitcase and began packing everything she had brought with her.

At one o'clock in the morning, the large white Renault idled up to the side of the sleeping penzione. Two keys were clutched tightly in Jeanne's hand as she got out.

"So I'll be parked on the highway near Bagno Lucciola from 9:30 on," Christina finalized. "Then we'll just wait, as long as it takes."

"Okay, wait right here. Be right back," Jeanne whispered.

Jeanne went up two flights of stairs and down without stopping.

"Here, quick." Hands trembling, she jammed her suitcase and the red crinkly bag in the back door that had caught in the stubborn branches of a scrawny, low hedge. Jeanne pushed with all her weight, scrapping the back of her hand. Her bag and the child's clothes tumbled onto the floor. Christina dropped the car into gear.

"That's good, that's good," she whispered nervously.

"Okay. Go, go." The car slipped quickly around the corner and disappeared.

Trembling, Jeanne stepped over the hedge. Suddenly, she felt only one key in the palm of her hand. *Oh no, the key fell in the car,* she realized. Quickly, she looked closely in the moonlight at the key she had left. *To the side door. That will get me in.* Trying not to make a sound in the sleeping hotel, she crept up the stairs two at a time, wondering if she had locked her room.

The oblong handle sunk gratefully in her grasp and the light, hollow door swung airily open in her hand. Shaking she quietly closed it behind her. Her hand moved automatically to insert the missing skeleton key. She suddenly became acutely aware of how many single men boarded there and went to bed.

9

Wednesday morning broke clear and tranquil over a warm and calm Adriatic. Daylight fell across Jeanne's bed in slats from the partially raised shutters. She listened for men walking to the toilet and tub down the hall and felt vulnerable inside the unlocked and keyless door.

Naked, Jeanne slid to her feet and opened the closet door. Pants and shirt hung on one hanger, her bikini and towel on a second. A newspaper and one pair of shoes sat on the floor. If all went well, all but the bikini would be left behind under umbrella number 8.

Quickly Jeanne dressed over the bikini and washed her face. She looked in the mirror. Worry had siphoned the color of the last two weeks of sun. She ran an internal check on how she was feeling and knew this had to be done soon. She lowered her head and dampened her curls, then turned and spread the rickety double doors open onto the balcony, the slick sea and the new day ahead.

"*Dio buono!*" the maid exclaimed in surprise as the door flew open in her hand.

Bare feet on the bed, Jeanne looked up from her chair and the letter in her lap.

"*Buon giorno,*" she hastened to say. "The room is fine today. You don't have to clean. Really," Jeanne insisted.

"Are you sure, Signora?"

Perplexed, the maid slowly drew the door closed behind her.

Jeanne cradled the picture of herself and Paul in her lap. She rubbed her forehead and looked down at the words on the unfinished pages. Full of crossed-out lines, she recopied it, slipped it in with the picture, cursed her ex-husband and dropped it in the mail slot of Bagno Trieste.

10

The Adriatic had shrunk back dramatically that morning, drawing curious morning sunbathers out into a broad area of wet sand, peppered with shallow pools and things of the sea. Jeanne watched Jesse and Paul fight their way down to the water's edge. Their father, seeming vaguely at a loss at this sibling bickering, tossed ineffectual reprimands over his shoulder. Behind his back, Paul delivered a swift karate kick to Jesse's stomach.

"Now Paul —, " his father turned around.

Jesse's body seemed stiff and hard as he straightened up.

Franco stood beside Jeanne as she ran her toes over the wet sand and fresh shells. He seemed chatty.

"So, how is your work, Franco," Jeanne squinted into the already warm morning sun.

"Oh, it's a real feudal system," he mocked. "I am the supervisor and they are like children. In fact, they called me this morning. They know what to do for this shipment of machines to Russia but they want me to come in. I'll have to take the boys home at noon today and go to work. And I don't think I can bring them tomorrow either."

"Franco — "

"Well, you have another week or more here, don't you?"

"Yes, but — "

"My mother does not want the responsibility of watching the children while you're here — eh?" His round eyes gave her a sharp look that then faded in the sun. "And my father has work to do."

Franco bent over to extinguish his cigarette in the licking waves of the returning tide. Jeanne glanced over at the slide and Bagno Lucciola. *I wonder if the maid returned to my room, found it empty.* In the silence, Franco rubbed his hands together and then said, "Well, I'm going to play cards."

"Me, too, mamma," Jesse jumped up, dropping a handful of shells.

"How about it, Paul — a game of cards with me and Jesse at the bar?"

"*Va bene.*"

Paul smiled and made a quick move on his brother at the small white table under the eave of the concession.

"You're cheating!" yelled Jesse. "I'm not playing anymore!"

In an instant, Jesse threw his cards across the table and stomped out of sight around the corner of the concession.

Startled by this outburst and his abrupt disappearance, Jeanne looked across the table at Paul who was laughing.

"Ah, he does that all the time."

"Com'on, Paul," his friends called to him, "let's play soccer."

"Paul," Jeanne took ahold of his arm as they both stood up, "no matter what happens, would you promise me to remember one thing?"

"Sure, mamma. What is it?"

"Just remember that I love you."

Paul smiled with amusement at this unexpected statement. He tilted his bushy head and looked up at the intent face of his American mother.

"Are you happy here?" she asked. "You seem happy."

"Oh yes."

"Well, go play. But remember that I love you, no matter what. I guess that's the best we can do... " He looked at her again, quizzically. "By the way," she called out as he began to sprint across the sand, "where does Jesse go when he gets mad?"

"Bagno Lucciola."

11

Christina jumped as Jeanne and Jesse rounded the corner of the path at a dead run. She sprang the back door open with one hand and started the motor with the other. Jesse slid in onto the plush back seat.

"Jesse, I think you had better get down," Jeanne said, "just until we get out of Ravenna."

"Christina, take whatever route you want. I don't think we were seen," Jeanne said tersely over her shoulder from the floor of the back seat. The car was already moving at high speed.

Jesse rested his head on the blue cushion of the back seat.

"Why, why, doesn't my father understand that I want to go back with you?" He rolled his head on the cushion and then looked over at his mother.

"I don't know, Jesse, I don't know," Jeanne replied, watching his face anxiously. She refolded her long legs under her on the floor. "What your father needs is a good swift kick in the behind, if you ask me," she blurted.

Jesse laughed at this in spite of himself.

"Yeah, a good swift kick in the behind," he echoed nervously.

Jeanne felt the car bend right at high velocity. It meant that Christina was taking the on-ramp to the highway that runs along the deepest canal and away from town. They spun out past entrances to the Autostrada del Sole, avoiding the policed freeway, and sped past the last freeway entrance. The wide divided road shrunk suddenly to a simple two-lane country road. The engine groaned as Christina bore down through the fertile countryside and ancient towns. They sped to the northwest, bearing for the anonymity of Milan.

"We can sit up now, Jesse," Jeanne coaxed the little boy huddled down in the car beside her. "And here are some clothes."

"Thanks, mamma. But why, why won't he just let me go?" he strained to understand. Tears rolled down his salty cheeks. He brushed them aside.

"Jesse, I don't know. It's terrible to have to leave like this, decide like this. Let's just go as far as Milan. We'll sleep on it and see how we feel in the morning, okay? You know you can always come back."

The vibration of the car jiggled a new box of Lego blocks out from under the front seat. Jesse perked up and started towards them. Then he turned sharply away and fell asleep.

Jeanne exhaled slowly and covered her face with her hands. After a minute she slowly climbed into the front seat beside Christina. Their eyes met somberly.

"Oh Christina."

"Tell me what happened."

"He got mad at a game of cards and went exactly where he was supposed to be," Jeanne recounted in a low voice, staring out at the fields that were skimming by.

"What did you say to him?"

"I told him that I loved him and that he was supposed to have come back and that if he wanted to he still could."

"What did he say?"

"It was interesting," Jeanne wagged her head stiffly. "I think they may have even talked about it at home. Because he said immediately that he couldn't come to America because he didn't speak American and he had to go to his school. I told him he'd re-learn

English in a few months and could go to school there. Then he said yes, but we were walking slowly. It was so much. How could I hurry him any more than was already happening?''

"Did he understand why you had to leave without saying goodbye?"

"Yes, perfectly. He knows his father will just say no, no, no if he asks. Then as we were walking, he said he really wasn't happy there and really wanted to come back. And that's when we took off."

"But Paul, oh my god, Paul." Her head leaned forward into her hand and then snapped back up. "They know by now, don't you think?"

"Oh yes, by now... "

"Paul." Tears bit at her eyes. "I tried to talk to him. Now maybe it'll be clear to him. Clear — pah! I wonder if they gave him the package, the picture, the letter — "

Jeanne's voice trailed off and she too fell into a sudden sleep that lasted to the humid and choked outskirts of Milan.

12

Carol and Terry exploded joyfully down the stairs of Jenny's apartment house when the bell rang, but it was wooden and subdued individuals that they found moving slowly into the lobby below.

Christina rolled her blue eyes and said, "We're pretty wiped out."

"Com'on, com'on up. Terry, help with their bag."

Jesse seemed so Italian, so refined, as Jeanne spent her first hours with him inside a home for several years.

"Why don't you take a nice hot bath," she suggested weakly.

He emerged a half hour later, a little shy, a little man, his towel trimly tucked in around his waist.

After he went to bed, Jeanne chanced a call back to friends at Bagno Trieste.

"You had been gone about a half hour. Franco was playing cards per usual and it was the grandmother who came up from the beach and said that she hadn't seen Jesse or Jeanne in a while. They started looking and then they realized you'd gone.''

"And Paul? Please tell me about Paul?''

"Well, he's okay — '' The answer came with a perceptible halt. "We went and got the package you left for him right away. He read your letter and cried a little bit. And then they left for home.''

"*O dio mio.*''

"*Si.*''

"So have they done anything to trace us?''

"Well, Franco called the emergency number from the phone at the bar. But it's Nuncio that you have to watch out for. He's trying to get you. He told the police that you didn't pay your bill at the penzione — you did pay it, didn't you, Jeanne?''

"*Si, si, certo.*''

"My money is going fast,'' she remembered joking with the obese owner of the penzione. "I'd like to pay now. You'd better get your money while you can.''

"They are trying to get the police to stop you. I also understand that he's called a judge in Rome. Connections, you know. Listen, Jeanne, may I ask, where are you?''

Jeanne hesitated. "In — in Milan.''

"You should keep going. Don't stop. They're trying to alert the border to stop you. Don't stop now. Leave Italy as soon as possible.''

"I can't. Neither of us can. This is as far as we can go today. It's too much, too much for any of us. We'll make it.''

Jeanne translated the news for Carol, Christina and Jenny's friend, Anita. She looked at Christina, curled in Carol's arms on the bed.

"I can't go any further tonight,'' Jeanne repeated, feeling light-headed.

"Now, don't worry,'' affirmed Anita. "Today is Wednesday. You and Jesse rest. Friday half of Milan will be leaving for the weekend. When the traffic is horrible, we lose ourselves in the middle of it and go across the border. I'll follow you in my car. With that many cars, they can't possibly stop and check them all. I'll follow you in my car.''

The phone on the bed rang. It was Sally from Oregon.

"How are you?''

"It was horrible. The most horrible thing I've ever been through, court included. But we're here, Sally, — and that's plural.''

Rosetta buns, cold patties of butter, orange marmalade and scalded milk. After breakfast, Jeanne scooted Jesse onto her knee.

"I'm going to America," he reasserted.

"Glad to hear it. Now, it's best to go out of Italy tomorrow. So today let's all visit Milano, okay?"

Thick, uncertain weather clung to Milan on Friday as well. In the small kitchen, Anita and Carol laughed hilariously through a broken conversation, tossing the Italian-English dictionary back and forth across the white table. Terry and Jesse played with blue, rubbery Smurf figures. The 5:00 news came on the radio.

"*Attenzione!*" shouted Anita, jumping over to the dial. "Listen!"

The announcer's voice intoned the Friday report.

"All roads north to Switzerland are extremely congested. Traffic is at a total standstill in many places. It is strongly advised that you do not attempt to leave Milano for Switzerland this evening."

"Yahoo! Traffic jams! Let's go."

Baggage and all, they poured into the street below — Jeanne and Jesse with Christina, Carol and Terry to Anita's red Citroen. Not far outside the confines of Milan, traffic came to a complete halt. Only two cars were delighted with this state of affairs.

But nerves twisted Jeanne's muscles even tighter.

"Jeanne," said Christina, grabbing her wrist, "relax! Look normal," she cautioned, glancing through the windshield at the approaching guard stations. She gave her a nudge to shake her brittleness. It was like rocking a cage.

"Okay, okay," Jeanne agreed hollowly. She turned and looked at Jesse in the back seat. He smiled back obliviously.

"Should I explain to him, Christina, about the border?"

"No, no," Christina assured her in her sing-song German lilt. "It's going to be okay. He doesn't need to know."

Jeanne appreciated the opinion and refocused her attention on the string of guard cubicles that lay across the widened border crossing. Fluorescent lights bleached out the green uniforms of the Swiss border guards. Under her breath, Jeanne methodically chanted the Italian partisan anthem.

Avanti, popolo
Alla riscosa
Bandiera rossa
Triumfera'

Christina's light blue eyes scanned the gates ahead. Her thin, blond hair fell in disheveled strands over her shoulders. Committing the large Renault to the final bottleneck, she suddenly pulled the steering wheel sharply to the right, accelerated, then braked in behind a cream colored Jaguar.

The guard walked over to that gate. He bent and looked into the Jaguar. Then, glancing back at the endless line of cars, he waved it through with a sharp sweep of his arm. Christina kept the nose of the Renault close to the tail of the Jaguar and stopped at the yellow line. Keeping her window up, Christina smiled and held her Swiss passport up to the window. Another sharp sweep of his arm and they bounded over the line. Jeanne's hand locked over Christina's sinewy arm.

"I know, I know! Now, the other car."

They looked back. Terry's head was leaning forward between his mother and Anita. After a brief pause, they too were waved through. Anita shifted gears and the red Citroen lurched into Swiss territory as well.

With a gush of relief, Christina accelerated into the parking lot. The Citroen rocked to a stop behind them. Doors flew open. Jeanne kissed the ground. Jesse jumped towards her. She caught him in her arms and held him tight, at last.

EPILOGUE

My son has been with me three years now as I dot the final i's. From the border we went to Christina's home in Züg. Two days later we took a night train across France to England and flew to Seattle where my family now lives.

The first few weeks and months were spent mostly in the country. Jesse did not feel safe, a feeling that became more acute when we briefly returned to the city, and I wasn't sure what to expect. Jesse wanted to change his name and would put marbles in his cheeks trying to disguise his face. A safer solution was found. He asked that his blond curly hair, his most striking feature, be cut and dyed. Thus a few days later, he sat on a stool on the beautician's swivel chair and closely watched the transformation. As he stepped out onto the sidewalk looking much like The Fonz, he looked up at me and smiled with relief. You're really something, I told him.

We returned to the country for a few months, giving his English a chance to come back. I don't know why, but it was a much slower process to regain his English than I had ever thought. As Jesse walked down a dry creek bed with giant blackberry bushes laced in a natural arbor overhead, he gathered handfuls of wild berries and exclaimed in Italian, "Well, this is paradise!"

But it is not paradise, it has been hard. After three months, he started school under his own name. His English was marginal, his accent thick, and he was teased accordingly. He has had difficulty in making close friends, a process that is at last taking root now as he approaches Junior High School. He still vehemently cusses the Judge for taking him away to begin with.

Our disappearance from the beach was a great blow to his brother, Paul. During the first year, we called and talked to him at length the first Sunday of every month. Now we write and talk occasionally by phone and he knows we love him and miss him. He looks adolescent and happy in the pictures we receive and is studying computers, "like you, mom."

Franco remarried at forty and Paul is very close to his father's new wife. He goes sailing on the Adriatic every chance he gets in the sailboat Grandpa Nuncio bought him. Packages arrive regularly for Jesse from his Italian grandparents and I am told that Paul is even taller than I am now. How can that be? So much time has passed.

Someday we are going to sit down and have a very long talk.

Resources

Lesbian Rights Project
1370 Mission Street, 4th Floor
San Francisco, California 94103
(415) 621-0674
Legal representation, briefs and nationwide referrals.

Lesbian Mothers' National Defense Fund
P.O. Box 21567
Seattle, Washington 98111
(206) 325-2643
Financial assistance, expert-witness and legal referrals.

Custody Action for Lesbian Mothers (CALM)
Rosalie Davies
225 Haverford Avenue
Narbeth, Pennsylvania 19072
(215) 667-7508
Legal representation; legal and expert witness referrals.

Lesbian Mother Defense Fund
P.O. Box 38, Station "E"
Toronto, Canada M644E1
(416) 645-6822
Financial aid and support for Canadian and U.S. mothers.

Lesbian Mothers Defense Fund
P.O. Box 11009
Dunedin, New Zealand
Financial aid and legal referrals.

Boston Gay and Lesbian Advocates and Defenders (GLAD)
P.O. Box 218
Boston, Massachusetts 02112
(617) 426-1350
Publishes the Glad National Lawyers Directory *with annotations on lawyers experienced in gay custody litigation.*

Lambda Legal Defense and Education Fund
132 W. 43rd Street
New York, New York, 10036
(212) 944-9488
Support and legal referrals for the New York area.

Texas Human Rights Foundation
1519 Maryland
Houston, Texas 77006
(713) 526-9139
Support and legal referrals.

Contact your local American Civil Liberties Union (ACLU) chapter.

Books

Lesbian Mother Litigation Manual, Donna J. Hitchens. 1982. Includes bibliography for lesbian mothers and gay fathers. Available through the Lesbian Rights Project.

Mothers on Trial: Women and Child Custody, Phyllis Chessler. Fall 1985. Comprehensive historical analysis with case histories.

Lesbian Mothers and Their Children: An Annotated Bibliography of Legal and Psychological Materials, 2nd Edition; D. Hitchens and A. Thomas, Eds. June 1982. Available through the Lesbian Rights Project.

Considering Parenthood: A Workbook for Lesbians, Cheri Pies, Spinsters Ink 1985. The distillation of the author's six years work with lesbians considering the options of parenting.

Womanspirit: A Guide to Women's Wisdom, Hallie Iglehart. Harper & Row, 1983. For spiritual resources and endurance. Tape ($10).

Books From Cleis Press

LONG WAY HOME
Jeanne Jullion
ISBN: 0-939416-05-0
8.95

WITH THE POWER OF EACH BREATH:
A DISABLED WOMEN'S ANTHOLOGY
ed. Debra Connors, Susan Browne, Nanci Stern
ISBN: 0-939416-06-9
9.95

THE ABSENCE OF THE DEAD
IS THEIR WAY OF APPEARING
Mary Winfrey Trautmann
ISBN: 0-939416-04-2
8.95

WOMAN-CENTERED PREGNANCY
AND BIRTH
Ginny Cassidy-Brinn, R.N., Francie Hornstein,
Carol Downer & the Federation of Feminist
Women's Health Centers
ISBN: 0-939416-03-4
11.95

VOICES IN THE NIGHT:
WOMEN SPEAKING ABOUT INCEST
ed. Toni A.H. McNaron & Yarrow Morgan
ISBN: 0-939416-02-6
7.95

FIGHT BACK! FEMINIST RESISTANCE
TO MALE VIOLENCE
ed. Frederique Delacoste & Felice Newman
ISBN: 9-939416-01-8
13.95

ON WOMEN ARTISTS: POEMS 1975-1980
Alexandra Grilikhes
ISBN: 0-939416-00-X
4.95